INHABITING UNITY

D0711784

INHABITING UNITY

*Theological Perspectives on the Proposed
Lutheran-Episcopal Concordat*

Edited by

Ephraim Radner and R. R. Reno

WILLIAM B. EERDMANS PUBLISHING COMPANY
GRAND RAPIDS, MICHIGAN

© 1995 Wm. B. Eerdmans Publishing Co.
255 Jefferson Ave. S.E., Grand Rapids, Michigan 49503

Printed in the United States of America

00 99 98 97 96 95   7 6 5 4 3 2 1

ISBN 0-8028-0815-8

Contents

CONTENTS

Acknowledgments

Our work in coordinating and collecting these essays was greatly aided by the financial support of the Dean of the Graduate School of Creighton University. That support allowed us to rely heavily on the excellent staff of the Theology Department of Creighton University, especially Mrs. Diane Kriley and Dr. Mary Kuhlman. We thank also George Lindbeck for reading and commenting on a number of essays in draft form. Finally, we are grateful that Wm. B. Eerdmans Publishing Co. has so willingly and ably supported this effort to serve the church.

Introduction

EPHRAIM RADNER AND R. R. RENO

This volume of essays seeks to provide "unashamed" support for the proposed Concordat between the Evangelical Lutheran Church in America and the Episcopal Church, USA. The character of shame and shamelessness is crucial here, for it ties our writing and its object to the core of our vocation in Christ. As editors and contributors we are without shame in our unequivocal hope that the Concordat will be affirmed by the appropriate national legislative bodies of the two churches. Even more, we are unabashed in our desire for the full communion in the gospel that the Concordat will make possible. Yet, for all this enthusiasm, and perhaps because of the seriousness of this enthusiasm, our unashamed backing of the proposal does not translate into uncritical support. Indeed, those who read these essays may find our critical questioning of the Concordat, its prospects, and most of all the two churches' capacity to receive its fruit of full communion, so rigorous and at times so pessimistic that this unabashed support will seem less than reassuring. Still, such rigorous questioning is necessary if we are to be truly unashamed of the Concordat and willing to speak honestly and directly about and on behalf of its prospects, however painful or discomfitting they may prove to the future of our two denominations. We strive, then, to stand before the harvest of the Concordat much as did Paul before the power of the gospel of which he was not ashamed (Rom. 1:16), even though, like Paul's gospel, the full communion made possible by the Concordat might well prove to be a future of "suffering" (2 Tim. 1:8ff.) for Lutherans and Episcopalians.

1

Our unashamed support of the Concordat rests on the essential connection between the prospects of this proposal for both denominations and the promise of the gospel. For the whole notion of and the very hope for Christian communion is founded on the promise of Christ's gospel, a promise that deeply penetrates rather than hovers over our lives (cf. the entire argument about the church in Ephesians, summed up in 3:6). As such, the promise of Christian communion, a promise so intimate with the promise of new life in Christ, must be sought after and seen within the life of the world. These essays find their distinctive purpose in our desire to keep this definite and realized form of the gospel ever prominent in both its opportunity and challenge. Indeed, across the many different foci of the essays, this thread remains common: to take the promise of unity seriously as a *particular* form and destiny.

This commitment, however, is hard won. We often approach Christian unity as a "hope" or even as a "prayer" that we utter after Jesus' example (John 17:21). Such an approach is proper in itself, but we often hope and pray with hearts that search only for a future fulfillment. As mere promise, Christian unity can become for us something we must always await. As we lean toward the future, we consider less and less the possibility that Christian unity might come to us, take hold of us, grab us by our collars, and shake us in the present. And so this longed-for unity becomes ever more invested in the purity of the unrealized "end of time," a point of only vaguely imagined beauty when "our divisions cease" as the lion and the lamb lie down together. Thus, when a proposal such as the Concordat confonts us, it appears small, weak, and ugly, its stipulations and requirements either too vague or too specific, but altogether unsuitable for the exalted aspiration of Christian unity that we have constructed. And all around we are beset with doubts and questions. Why should our churches, churches grounded in the integrity of their own traditions, risk their inheritances for a document only a canon lawyer could love? Why accommodate the awkward and seemingly partial demands of acknowledging and joining ministries? Why allow ourselves to be rattled by the mandates of the Concordat when, in view of the larger promise of the gospel, the constricted and halting possibilities of full communion between the ELCA and the ECUSA seem to fade into inconsequence? Why embark upon a course of ecclesiastical change that undoubtedly will not measure up to the transforma-

2

tions to be wrought by God in eternity? Born of a sense of the fullness of the promise of unity in Christ, these doubts and questions tempt us to dismiss the concrete unity offered by agreements such as the Concordat.

The essays here firmly oppose such dismissal. We believe that hope and prayer for the future fullness of Christian unity must be joined with a willingness to embrace its concrete form in the present. The promise of Christian unity is the promise of the gospel of Jesus Christ, and we are not ashamed of this gospel and its promises. Moreover, this gospel does not hover before us, blurred and diffused, as an unrealized future. In the gospel of Christ, all of God's promises are particularized, sharpened, and concentrated. The good news is proclaimed in the flesh of the Incarnate Lord, that particular first-century Palestinian Jew, Jesus of Nazareth, "in whom all of God's promises find their 'Yes'" (2 Cor. 1:20). In him, all of God's promises to humanity and to his people are not only proclaimed, but those promises are fashioned into particular forms that we can grasp and live with, and they are realized in specific actions, events, and endeavors, in discrete successes and failures within human history. In short, within the gospel of Christ, God's promises are particularized in forms that call, demand, constrain, and thereby transform. This is what Paul teaches when he "glories" in the limiting shape of the cross, in the particular pattern of Jesus' death imposed by the promise of the gospel on the particular form of his own existence. Because of this, and only because of this, can Paul hope to apprehend God's "new creation" (Gal. 6:14f.). His hope reaches not toward a diffuse future, but forward from the vividly particularized shape of discipleship to which God has called him in the present.

The promise of Christian unity is likewise informed by this particularization of the gospel's promise. No unity awaits apart from the particular acts, adjustments, and submissions found in the church's simple effort to live in communion. These often constraining efforts, such as inhabiting the unity of the Concordat, stand as the very means by which the church is conformed to the particular shape of Christ's own life. To "have the same mind and the same love," to be "in full accord and of one mind" as a single body of Christ, is to "have this mind among yourselves which is yours in Christ Jesus, who, though he was in the form of God, did not count equality with God a thing to be grasped, but emptied himself, taking the form of a slave" (Phil.

3

2:2-7). If the prospect of Christian communion is, in fact, shaped by the pattern of Christ, then we need not worry about the meanness of a proposal like the Concordat's; rather, we should pray for the courage to accept its constraints as the particularized power of Christ's promise, a promise that, because of the One whom we believe, will surely transform us, through such particularities, into his image.

For this reason, whatever critical spirit, whatever urgency and even foreboding that might characterize our unashamed support for the Concordat, our essays are written in hope and prayer for the courage to inhabit the particularized form taken by the promise of unity in Christ. We should not daydream away the particularizing power of the promise. Nor should we try to ward off the demands of unity given under the sign of the cross. For example, some critics of the Concordat view it as a threat to the diversity of American denominationalism. The pluralism of worship styles, theological traditions, and spiritual outlooks, they argue, embodies the "many gifts" and "many members" of the gospel's own vision of the church. On this basis the Concordat must be rejected as an attempt to efface the differences between Lutherans and Episcopalians. In the rhetoric of the present, the Concordat promotes oppressive notions of "uniformity" and "singularity" rather than liberating values such as "difference" and "otherness." Or — and this train of thought is yet another form of flight from the concrete promise of life in Christ — others argue that the Concordat ought simply to be ignored, since the proposal is "merely" about church polity, and not about Jesus or the Spirit or the kingdom. Here, the language of objection may be far more biblical than that used by the defenders of pluralism, but the results are the same: the gospel is left to float above the life of the church as a platitudinous abstraction instead of reaching into the Christian community's most intimate inner workings with particular and inescapable demands.

The basic premise of *Inhabiting Unity* is that such negative arguments are really an escape from the particularizing power of the gospel's promise, and thus they represent a defense of the present order as untransformable. This reaction to the Concordat may even betray the rampant spiritualism of contemporary gnosticism by detaching the language of the faith from the tangible and worldly power of the gospel. Against such a tendency this volume of essays stands as an implacable opponent. Our collective motivation for this

4

project is more pungent than the broad desire for unity that has so effectively sustained the ecumenical movement in this century: We seek the transforming presence of the gospel in its concrete forms, and we come to the Concordat with the conviction that this proposal is a particular demand that the gospel puts on us *even now.* The unity we must inhabit is an intergral part of the Lord's way within the world, a way whose liberating "difference" lies in the transformed possibility of a new life in Christ *now,* not in a complacent "appreciation" of the fragmented state of Christ's church in America.

But has God in fact given us, in the Concordat, a moment to be seized? Essays in this volume argue in the affirmative. Some church members, we realize, worry that *this* proposal at *this* time is wanting. Granted, complacent appreciation of differences is not the future into which we are called in Christ, but the prospects of the Concordat, some say, lack integrity, the integrity of Christ's very form. Specifically, some Episcopalians view the temporary suspension of the Ordinal requiring episcopal ordination, a suspension required in order to recognize the full authenticity of the Lutheran ordained ministry, as making mockery of Anglican convictions. Similarly, some Lutherans regard the requirement of joint Episcopal consecration of future Lutheran bishops as a betrayal of the Reformation insight into the freedom of the gospel. Both sides desire communion, but neither regards the other as a suitable or willing partner in the present. A great deal hangs on the ability of our essays to convince the reader that the Concordat does in fact propose a form of Christian unity that is genuinely of Christ, that has integrity. And yet the reader should not expect various gestures toward "mediation." The writers of these essays are committed to the truth of the gospel, not to some *tertium quid* between Anglicanism and Lutheranism. To us, this truth has the power to draw both denominations into a transformed future in which our Lutheran and Anglican "identities" may be as abused as the Lord whom we follow.

Other reasons for deferring or rejecting the particular promise of the Concordat in the present emerge on related grounds. Perhaps the Episcopal Church is itself too decadent to act as a faithful and fruitful partner to the ELCA, as the clever and widely reported comment about "ecclesiastical necrophilia" has suggested. Or, more plausibly, both denominations might be in such a state of decline that linkage will only further their doctrinal relativism, evangelical dissipation, and moral decline. Or perhaps, and this thought is as widespread as unspoken, the Concordat is a good idea in theory, but not suited to a current situation in which financial uncertainties and strains in clergy deployment have demoralized the leadership of the two churches. Or again, the whole question might be better delayed until greater denominational consensus is achieved. In each of these cases, critics of the Concordat show themselves to be well aware of the particulars of the present situation. In each case the critics recognize the specific conditions affecting our churches and are alive to the pressures and fears, the burdens and hurdles that surround the Concordat.

Yet, in each case, the criticisms discount the power of the gospel's promise, a power to work within the very particulars that seem so likely to impede or sabotage Christian unity. They forget that the lever of the gospel is a cross, a particular and quite unpromising instrument for the triumph of grace. To be sure, at moments in the church's life the warning or plea, "Not yet!" is properly heard as from God's own lips. However, we cannot proclaim such moments only because we fear our own weakness or the weakness of our brothers and sisters in Christ. Our discernment of the concrete form of the future into which we are called depends solely upon our ability to find the form of Christ in our lives and the life of the church. Our essays do not discount the weaknesses of our present situation. Indeed, not a few of the authors worry that our weaknesses are overwhelming. In spite of this awareness and these worries, the consensus that guides this collection is that the Concordat draws us into a fuller life in Christ, regardless of our apparent inability to inhabit that future. For the volume's contributors, the promise of the gospel is properly particularized in the Concordat, and our weaknesses should not hinder us from clinging to that promise. Our hope in this promise, in fact, is that our very limitations will be transfigured as the form of our salvation.

*   *   *

Our collective search for the particularizing power of the promise of gospel unity in the proposed Concordat takes three basic forms: integrity, challenge, and opportunity. The first five essays attempt to show that the concrete promise of the Concordat is consonant with, even a fitting form of, the gospel promise. The full communion made possible by the Concordat, argue these five essays, affirms rather than

6

compromises the apostolic integrity of both Anglican and Lutheran traditions; because of this, the Concordat ought to be adopted. The essays in the second section highlight the challenge posed by the Concordat. Precisely because all three authors in this section affirm that the unity made possible by the Concordat is a growth in the gospel for both Lutherans and Episcopalians, they press themselves and their readers to see the strenuous future that the agreement forces upon both denominations. Inhabiting the gospel involves finding oneself and one's community ever more Christ-formed, and this prospect entails inhabiting the ever-fuller challenges of proclamation, communal discipline, and cruciform ecclesial existence. The book concludes with meditations on the opportunity for renewal and new growth offered by the Concordat. Assuming that Christian union is a decisive and potentially transformative event in the life of the church, these four essays suggest specific avenues of development that the Concordat offers within its promise of unity.

Integrity

The Concordat faces a major theological objection from the Anglican side. Worries concentrate upon the Concordat's proposal that the Episcopal Church immediately recognize the full authenticity of ELCA ordained ministry. This recognition seems to imply that the historic episcopate is not a necessary condition for apostolic ministry, an implication that therefore jettisons the historic episcopate as an Anglican "fundamental." Bishop S. W. Sykes meets this concern directly in the first essay of the volume. His contribution, "The Apostolate of Bishop and People as Sign of the Kingdom of God," shows how a proper understanding of the sign-character of God's activity in history allows Anglicans to recognize that faithfulness to the apostolic calling of the whole church can be preserved by means other than the sign of historic episcopal succession. Thus, the historic episcopate may be justly cherished and, in ecumenical agreements, its practice enhanced and expanded — for its sign-character serves the gospel — without turning its presence and use into the decisive "test" of apostolic continuity. Further, this understanding of the sign-character of the gospel invites Lutherans to recognize the value of the episcopal

7

sign, and to embrace it as a deepening of their already apostolic ministry of word and sacrament.

Sykes concludes his essay with a theme that echoes throughout the volume and dominates the next three essays. He observes that there is an urgent need to prevent the separation of pnuematology from Christology. The pneumatic trajectory of the gospel in our lives and in the life of the church should not be separated from that particular first-century Palestinian Jew, Jesus of Nazareth. The need to avoid such a separation drives Wolfhart Pannenberg, Michael Root, Bruce Marshall, and R. R. Reno in their discussions of the problem of "conditions" for full communion. All four seek to overcome the worry that the Concordat requires Lutherans to forsake their Reformation insight into the freedom of the gospel. The arguments in each essay converge on the same basic insight: God's freedom in Christ is precisely the freedom to inhabit a *particular* destiny in the man Jesus, and through Christ, to bind himself and his church to a *particular* destiny. As such, that promise which we know to be part of the destiny of the church, the promise of Christian unity, will confront us in a particular, and in that sense conditional, form.

Bruce Marshall's essay, "The Lutheran-Episcopal Concordat: What Does It Say? Why Does It Matter?" provides a close reading of the Concordat's purpose and implications for Lutheranism. The key issue at stake, he observes, is the question of the apostolicity of the church, which takes concrete and controversial form with respect to the historical episcopate. Since the historic episcopate is neither a necessary nor a sufficient condition for apostolic church life, Marshall reads the Concordat as proposing a course of action which treats the historic episcopate as an effective and fitting sign of the apostolicity of the church, especially the apostolic unity of the gospel. Having clarified the crux of the Concordat, Marshall argues that this proposed agreement is a prudent and sensible course of action that expresses Lutheranism's enduring commitment to the apostolic unity of the church, and is entirely in accord with Lutheran confessional documents. The latter argument is especially important in view of the Dissenting Report issued by a minority of Lutheran participants in the ecumenical dialogue that produced the proposed Concordat. This Dissenting Report claims that the Concordat establishes conditions for full communion that violate the Lutheran confessional commitment to the sufficiency of word and sacrament for the apostolic unity of the church. By requiring the ELCA to adopt the historic episcopate over time, the Dissenting Report detects a condition for unity beyond word and sacrament. Hence, their rejection of the Concordat.

In order to demonstrate the confessional integrity of the Concordat, Marshall shows that the logic of the Dissenting Report entails the contradiction of affirming that the Augsburg Confession both urges Lutherans to seek Christian unity on the basis of agreement in word and sacrament and prohibits Lutherans from accepting any particular or concrete form of Christian unity, because any and all agreements or proposals for unity would involve something more than the agreement already present in word and sacrament. Marshall assumes that the Augsburg Confession is not a contradictory document, and thus reaches the conclusion that if a tradition or sign serves the gospel rather than opposes it, then an evangelical desire for unity dictates an embrace of that tradition or sign. As Marshall shows, the Concordat assumes no other understanding of the historic episcopate than that it serves the gospel as an effective public witness to the continuity and unity of the gospel. Thus, Marshall commends the adoption of the historic episcopacy, precisely as servant of the gospel, as proposed in the Concordat.

The next two essays take direct aim at the Dissenting Report, expanding and reinforcing Marshall's argument. Michael Root's essay, "Conditions of Communion: Bishops, the Concordat, and the Augsburg Confession," surveys the historical context of the Augsburg Confession. Root shows that the Reformers were willing to accept the jurisdiction of Roman authorities in Germany, provided that jurisdiction did not require a repudiation of the gospel as Lutherans understood it. In this sense, the Augsburg Confession was crafted with the recognition that quite concrete and potentially unfriendly "conditions" were compatible with the truth of the gospel. This willingness to accept conditions for reunification with the church in Rome, argues Root, stems from the distinction between conditions for unity in Christ and conditions of communion among separated churches. For unity in Christ, the Augsburg Confession is clear: agreement in word and sacrament is sufficient. However, when Luther considered the gospel imperative of visible unity, he was willing to submit to quite rigorous conditions for communion with Rome. For Root, the lesson for modern Lutherans is clear. Lutheran confessional faithfulness is entirely compatible with accepting conditons for communion with other churches. Thus, when considering the Concordat, Lutherans need to ask *not* whether it establishes conditions for communion, for clearly it does; it binds the ELCA to a future incorporation into the historic episcopate. Instead, Root directs attention toward the question that he believes animated the Reformers: Do the proposed conditions for communion serve or hinder the word and sacrament that constitute the true unity of the church in Christ?

In "Gospel and Church: The Proposed Concordat between Lutheran and Episcopal Churches in the USA," Wolfhart Pannenberg provides a close consideration of the objection raised in the Dissenting Report. As Pannenberg glosses the objection, the Dissenting Report rejects the concrete form of episcopal ordained ministry as in any way necessary or essential for the unity of the church. To assess such a rejection, Pannenberg turns to the historical question of the relation of the episcopal ministry to other ministries in early Christianity. Amid complexities of development, Pannenberg identified two clear episcopal functions. First, the ministry of bishop developed in order to secure the unity of the church with its apostolic origins. Second, the episcopal presidence at the eucharist signified the unity of the congregation in the faith of the one gospel. In both respects, Pannenberg discerns a development in the ministry of the gospel that is so intimately bound up with the authority and effectiveness of gospel that one can hardly separate the two. The subsequent calcification of both "the gospel" and "the historic episcopate" into separable and hypostesized theological concepts should not, he argues, obscure the *de facto* link between the episcopal function and the authority of the gospel, a link latent to greater and lesser extents through the history of Reformation church life. As such, Pannenberg rejects the Dissenting Report. Pannenberg observes that the episcopal function, far from being an unnecessary condition for the unity of the church, is essential to that unity. Thus, the Concordat is not simply a permissible option for Lutherans, but rather is a matter of theological urgency.

R. R. Reno's essay, "The Evangelical Significance of the Historic Episcopate," concludes this section on the integrity of the Concordat with a discussion of the role of "conditions" in God's redemptive work in Christ. This line of analysis supports in a broad way Pannenberg's specific affirmation of the contingent, historical development of the episcopal office as a form of the continuity and unity of the gospel. Reno argues that the gospel glories in conditions. Indeed, the gospel is the good news that God assumes the human condition

10

in the man Jesus of Nazareth. Reno argues that from this primary conditioning of God in Christ flow two kinds of conditons for human beings. First, we are called to preach the gospel fully and widely. Second, we are called to live not for ourselves but for others in worship and service. In this way, Reno argues, God saves us "conditionally," that is, as members of his body, the church. Reno's approach to "conditions," then, parallels Root and Marshall's, and directly supports Pannenberg's. The decisive question is not whether the Concordat imposes conditions. Instead, both Lutherans and Anglicans need to discern whether the conditions of the Concordat are evangelical, are of the gospel. Reno concludes by arguing that the evangelical significance of the Concordat is that it requires new patterns of ecclesiastical governance that call both churches to live more fully in the tangible, public, and durable demands of the gospel.

Challenge

Where Reno's essay ends looking beyond the Concordat itself to its challenging call to inhabit more concretely the promises of Christ, the essays contributed by George Sumner, Philip Turner, and Ephraim Radner spotlight the painful transformations that the Concordat might require. The Concordat is but a partial fulfillment of the promise of Christian unity, yet it is a genuine movement toward God's ultimate purpose in Christ. As such, it cannot but draw both churches toward divine judgment as well as mercy. This section strikes a note uncommon in ecumenical discussions. Instead of concentrating on the positive fruits of unity, the contibutors direct our attention to the hard work ahead for both churches, work that may well require us to set our faces against the ways of the world that we have unwittingly incorporated into the heart of our missionary (Sumner) and disciplinary (Turner) practices, and have allowed to dominate our hopes for the future (Radner). All three authors in this section ask us to face the judgment of the fuller gospel.

George Sumner and Philip Turner address the weakness, if not the outright corruption, of contemporary church practices, especially Episcopalian ones. Sumner's essay, "Episcopalians, Lutherans, and Full Communion for Mission," describes the separation of proclamation from mission in the life of the churches. This separation is not alien to the ecumenical dialogue leading up to the Concordat. Sumner analyzes *Implications of the Gospel,* the document that expresses the consensus between Lutherans and Episcopalians, as typical of a tendency to substitute abstractions like the "radical newness" of "the future" for the quite particular and concrete proclamation of Christ crucified. Echoing Reno's understanding of full and wide proclamation as a conditon of the gospel, Sumner interprets the separation of proclamation from mission as part of a larger failure to inhabit more fully our destiny in Christ. Since the Concordat's rationale and purpose is to draw the ECUSA and ELCA more deeply, through full communion, into a life in Christ, Sumner finds reason to hope that Episcopalians and Lutherans will be both driven and empowered to reclaim the proclamatory mission of the church.

Where Sumner views the Concordat as a challenge to recover proclamation in mission, Philip Turner's essay, "Episcopal Oversight and Ecclesiastical Discipline," turns to the question of the proper function of authority in the common life of the church. Turner surveys three instances in recent decades when the Episcopal House of Bishops proved unable to exercise authority, uncovering an ever-more pervasive pattern of both willfulness on the part of bishops who claim the mantle of prophet, and cowardice and lassitude on the part of the gathered House of Bishops. These failures reveal a decline in the moral traditions that support and guide the exercise of authority and the expression of dissent, a decline that threatens to efface any recognizably apostolic continuity in the doctrine and practice of the Episcopal Church, rendering the historic episcopate an empty sign. Moreover, Turner suggests in conclusion that the confessional documents of the Lutheran tradition, which the Concordat makes common property of both Lutherans and Episcopalians, may not provide sufficient ballast to guarantee apostolic doctrine. The same evasions of the apostolic tradition that have dominated the Episcopal House of Bishops may undermine the Lutheran confessions. Thus, both Lutherans and Episcopalians face a future in which the apostolic consensus that makes the Concordat possible may evaporate at the very moment in which full communion becomes a possibility.

Sumner's judgment against separation of proclamation from mission and Turner's negative assessment of episcopal practice in recent decades are both taken up into Ephraim Radner's reading of

12

the Concordat within the context of scriptural prophecy. Reading the Old Testament's history of Israel's division, exile, and reintegrated return as a figure for our destiny in Christ, Radner suggests that the challenges associated with the Concordat are prefigured in the life of Israel as hammer blows that will reshape the church. This involves three elements. The first element is the actual disappearance of denomination. Second, full communion will be a step toward the formation of a postdenominational remnant based upon renewed unity in remembrance of the source of Christian identity. Third, the figure of Israel shows a future of "constricted penitence" for the church. In light of scriptural prophecy, Radner argues, events such as the Concordat, and the full communion that it might make possible, will reveal the foolishness of promoting Anglican and Lutheran "identity," and will, in judgment, drive some (but by no means all or even most) Episcopalians and Lutherans toward a penitent pilgrimage into the figure of Christ prophesied in the fate of Israel and awaiting us in the future of the church.

Opportunity

To the extent that the Concordat participates in the promise of the gospel, we should expect to find blessing as well as judgment. The final section of *Inhabiting Unity* provides some possible avenues for viewing the fruits of the full communion proposed in the Concordat. Those fruits find expression in both theology and practice. J. A. DiNoia and Christopher Seitz identify features of church practice that might find renewal in the Concordat. Kenneth Appold and David Yeago treat the Concordat as an event in the life of the church that has the potential to reorient the theological reflection of both churches.

Writing as a Roman Catholic observer, DiNoia ventures some observations about the theological justification and historical conditions that give rise to *magisterium,* the mechanism of doctrinal and disciplinary unity within the church. *Magisterium* serves the church by cultivating in its members the dispositions appropriate to the "reception" of God's offer of fellowship with Christ. These teaching activities are primarily oriented toward the presentation of the fundamental truths of Christianity. However, DiNoia observes, the teaching office of the Roman Catholic Church has also developed a secondary orientation toward an official articulation of definitive or authoritative doctrines. This orientation arose, he suggests, from the distinctive pressures of modernity that threatened to corrupt the primary cultivation of receptivity for fellowship with Christ. When DiNoia considers the Concordat, he argues that the primary form of magisterial activity will be necessary if the proposed full communion is to have any shared substance. Further, given the erosion of liberal Protestant culture and the sudden isolation of former mainline Protestant churches, DiNoia speculates that something like the secondary or "governing" magisterial function may be the most judicious pastoral response to the challenges of the common life in faith proposed by the Concordat. Here, DiNoia sees an opportunity to develop new structures and traditions to meet the challenge so convincingly and troublingly exposed in Turner's essay.

In "The Lectionary as Theological Construction" Christopher Seitz addresses, on a concrete and practical level, Sumner's call for revitalized proclamation. Seitz considers the changes in church polity mandated by the Concordat an apt opportunity for the two denominations to reexamine the formal ways in which the church presents the gospel. In particular, he examines the Sunday lectionary, generally shared by both ELCA and ECUSA, in terms of its public scriptural witness, and suggests that a new life in communion offers freedom for both churches to refashion the lectionary into a more faithfully evangelical tool of proclamation. How we hear the scriptural texts invariably shapes what we think of as "the gospel," and Seitz argues that the current, three-reading structure obscures the relationship between the Old and New Testaments. He proposes, instead, a two-reading structure in which the reciprocal relations between the two testaments, relations that are at the heart of the gospel itself, can be heard more forcefully. Thus contemporary mainline Protestantism might begin the recovery of reading the Old Testament in such a way that allows the text to "preach Christ," instead of relegating the Old Testament passages to the arid desert of historical-critical readings of ancient Israelite religion. One might thus view the Concordat as a mandate to scrutinize and reform the church's structured liturgical witness to the gospel.

Kenneth Appold's essay, "On the Union of Churches and the Efficacy of the Gospel," treats the Concordat as an opportunity to

14

recover the christological source of Christian unity from the eschatological vacuum created by ill-considered ecumenical documents such
as (ironically) *Implications of the Gospel,* which helped lay the ground-
work for the Concordat. Appold speaks from the standpoint of traditional Lutheran theological commitments when he argues that a
proper understanding of the gospel views the good news not as a
prediction of some still undefined future event, but rather as a *fait
accompli* of redemptive love historically realized. This *fait accompli* of
the gospel directs the common life of the church to find its center
and purpose in the already and really present Christ. Appold restates
the theme of conditions that dominates the first section of essays on
the Concordat's "integrity": the gospel becomes "effective" in the
condition of Christ. On this basis, Appold judges the Concordat an
embodied reminder that the promises of the gospel, in this case the
promise of unity in Christ, are not merely proleptic. They also have
the present power of fulfillment. Thus, by engaging a line of thinking
in traditional Lutheran theology about "evangelical promise," Appold
shows how the gospel's efficacy can be furthered by the opportunity
given in the Concordat.

With David Yeago's essay, "Theological Renewal in Communion: What Anglicans and Lutherans Can Learn from One Another,"
the book returns to Sykes' observation that we have too much separated pneumatology from Christology, too much separated the concrete form of our life of faithfulness from the even more concrete
form (because it is sealed in the death and confirmed in the physical
resurrection) of Jesus of Nazareth. In the terms of dogmatic theology,
this could well be the key to the volume's desire to unashamedly
champion the Concordat so that our two small churches might inhabit
more fully the particular and worldly forms of God's promise of unity
in Christ. Yeago's essay envisions the fuller theological vision that
might follow in the train of the Concordat's proposals. Taking his
cues from the Concordat's mandate that ordinands of each church
study the authoritative documents of the other partner, Yeago meditates on the providential complimentarity of the theological ethos of
the two traditions. He describes Anglicanism as invested in a "concrete
pneumatology" that focuses on the particularities of ecclesial and
faithful life. In Lutheranism, Yeago finds a characteristic "radical
Christology." Both traditions, however, are vulnerable to a debilitating
one-sideness. Anglicanism can lose the radical newness of the offer

of grace in Christ, while Lutheranism can become untethered from the real, lived possibilities of that grace. And in their characteristic failures, both theological traditions lose their capacity to give expression to the church's communal quest for apostolic identity. Yet together, Yeago speculates, these respective pneumatological and christological emphases might provide the fruitful resources for discerning and articulating on behalf of this troubled age the concrete and graspable way into the radical newness of life in Christ that God has promised to the world.

*　　*　　*

Precisely in an age like our own, troubled by the competition of multiplied demands upon our energies, we are tempted to hope and pray for an expanding freedom of life among proliferating possibilities, an unconstrained experience of God that must nonetheless necessarily lapse into the ethereal. This volume supports a proposal in the life of the church that stands opposed to such hopes and prayers. The Concordat is a document that seeks to concentrate rather than expand, that binds us to a determinate course of action rather than leave us to a future series of unending and unrealized possibilities. Though the document is studiedly equivocal on a number of important theological questions about the role and status of the episcopal office in historic succession, the function of formal confessions such as the Augsburg Confession, and other issues, the Concordat does not and cannot evade the necessity of offering a concrete proposal. If adopted, the Concordat will discipline the ELCA and ECUSA to take the steps necessary for full communion. It is this concrete proposal and this discipline that will offend the gnosticizing sensibilities of our world, a world that claims so much of what we call our church. To a great extent, the passion and vigor that the contributors bring to this collection of essays stems from a shared desire to inhabit the concrete and disciplining form of Christ. The Concordat may fail to win approval, and even if approved, its mandates may be eviscerated and evaded by the lack of virtue so pointedly described by Philip Turner. Yet even if this is so, these essays will, we hope, testify to the faith that God's promises in Christ are tangible, concrete, and real, and that as members of his body, the baptized *can* and *must* live within the fulfillment of those promises, in particular, the promise of a common love.

16

PART 1

INTEGRITY

The Apostolate of Bishop and People as a Sign of the Kingdom of God

S. W. SYKES

The Church as Visible Sign

A great deal of Western European theology since the Reformation, and especially since the European Enlightenment, has been developed on the assumption of a fundamental dichotomy between "Catholic" and "Protestant" principles. Friedrich Schleiermacher, the so-called father of modern theology, neatly encapsulated the alternative movement of faith as either through the church to Christ (the Catholic principle), or through Christ to the church (the Protestant principle).[1] Contemporary ecumenism still produces a similar discussion about the existence of "fundamental disagreements."[2]

Both the Orthodox and Anglicans are generally treated as marginal to this discussion. Anglicans, in particular, may feel themselves uncomfortable with the terms of the alternative. What, for example, do they make of the question whether the church is fundamentally and essentially visible in character? This is the question refined by centuries of Roman Catholic apologetic with a view to embarrassing Protestants. The Catholic tradition gives an unequivocally affirmative answer, and points to the Roman Catholic Church as its exemplification. Protestants, on the other hand, are supposed to believe that the

1. Friedrich Schleiermacher, *The Christian Faith* (2d German ed., par. 24; ET, Edinburgh V. 128), pp. 103f.
2. See esp. A. Birmelé and H. Meyer, eds., *Grundkonsens — Grunddifferenz* (Frankfurt: Verlag Otto Lembech, 1992).

true church is invisible, because its extent is known only to God who alone can interpret a believer's faith. "Church" occurs as and when God's promises and the summons to faith are offered in word and sacrament. In terms of their structures, then, many churches can enjoy harmonious but autonomous membership in the One Church. Little justice though such an account does to more recent exposition of the ecclesiology of Luther or Calvin, such is popularly supposed to be the opinion of Protestantism. As a consequence, it is polemically dismissed as individualistic.

So much of the doctrine of the church in Western tradition has been argued out through the distorting lens of late medieval canon law, both in affirmation and negation, that one must often refer to the Eastern tradition for the sake of balance and new insight. Under the subheading "The 'Iconic' Character of the Ecclesial Institutions," John Zizioulas argues for the importance of eschatology to all interpretations of the institutional character of the church, including tradition, apostolic succession, scriptural foundation, or actual historical needs. The Holy Spirit points beyond history, and as a result institutions become sacramental, losing their self-sufficiency, and existing *epicletically* (i.e., they depend for their efficacy on prayer, the prayer of the community).

> It is not in history that the ecclesial institutions find their certainty (their validity) but in constant dependence on the Holy Spirit. This is what makes them "sacramental," which in the language of Orthodox theology may be called "iconic."[3]

To return to the blunt question of whether the church is essentially visible or invisible, it turns out to be no mere evasion to say that it is both, and to insist (in Orthodox language) on the iconic character of its historical institutions and forms. We can go further. The dichotomy between visible and invisible is precisely one of those dualities or oppositions that are full of ambiguity, and that appear to require their own opposites. The church's visibility is the necessary appearance in history of its beyond-historical character, to which it points. While it is not complete or perfect in its historicality, neither is its historical being inessential or lacking in instrumental power. The

3. J. D. Zizioulas, *Being in Communion* (New York: St. Vladimir's Press, 1985), p. 138.

visible structures are never self-sufficient, but always and only effective in the context of prayer and by the action of the invisible Spirit, who both governs and gives life to the church and is therefore its Lord.

We may well prefer the category "sign" to that of sacrament or icon in our discussion of the status of the church as visible and invisible because it is a biblical way of speaking of Jesus' own ministry, especially in the fourth Gospel. As C. H. Dodd has pointed out, the writer of the fourth Gospel saw no reason why a narrative should not be at the same time factually true and symbolic of a deeper truth.

> Whilst in the first intention the feeding of the multitude signifies the timeless truth that Christ, the eternal Logos, gives life to men, and the healing of the blind that He is the Bearer of light, yet in the development of the argument we discover that Christ's work of giving life and light is accomplished, in reality and actuality, by the historical act of His death and resurrection. In that sense, every *semeion* [sign] in the narrative points forward to the great climax.[4]

This conclusion is fully consistent with recent work on the sectarian background of the fourth Gospel's sacramentalism.[5] Being baptized represented the threshold between the world and the community for John, as the believer publicly confesses allegiance to Christ as Son of God come down from heaven. The eucharist reinforces the boundary this creates between believer and nonbeliever, and at the same time builds up solidarity between those who faithfully abide in Jesus. The "sacraments" of baptism and eucharist count as signs precisely because they are both efficacious on their own terms *and* point to the passion of Christ and to the resurrection. Together with Jesus' miraculous deeds (which continue in Paul's experience — see 2 Cor. 12:12; 1 Cor. 2:4; Rom. 15:19), these signs are part of the reality of divine sovereignty in history (see Luke 11:20). They are thus likewise eschatological and inseparably linked to the presence and activity of the Spirit. The church fundamentally belongs to this sign-character of God's activity in human history.

4. C. H. Dodd, *The Interpretation of the Fourth Gospel* (Cambridge: Cambridge University Press, 1953), p. 142.

5. E.g., in David Rensberger, *Overcoming the World* (London: SPCK, , 1988).

The Concept of Sign, Philosophically Considered

It is very difficult indeed to define a word like "sign," which has a wide range of meanings in ordinary language. One way to deal with the difficulty is to legislate strictly, and to say, "When I use the word 'sign' what I mean is this [give particular meaning]." A theory of signs would be bound to attempt a degree of precision, since the whole point of a theory is to introduce clarity into a confusing and complex subject. Yet the problem of clarity is that the people who use the word "sign" in ordinary speech do not know the theory, and as a consequence may use the word improperly. On the other hand, theory has to be sensitive to ordinary usage if it is not to be simply an arbitrary imposition upon language.

One of the most general and helpful definitions was offered by the American philosopher C. S. Peirce. "A sign," he said, ". . . is something that stands to somebody for something in some respect or another."[6] Very many things fall within that definition: a word in language, uttered or written; a sound like a sigh or a groan; a gesture or other body language; a physical state, like blushing or a high temperature; any action that might signify an attitude — all these come directly from human beings. But many more examples of signs are found within nature or in physical objects: smoke may be a sign of fire; a sound from a machine may indicate that it is functioning; an object can be designated as a symbol for a political or religious group, or in dreams can be interpreted to represent an event, an attitude, or a person.

Augustine discussed the rules for interpreting the Scriptures, and included various distinctions between signs: the words, which are signs, can be known, unknown, or ambiguous to the interpreter; they can also be, in themselves, either literal or figurative. The word "ox" literally signifies an animal; figuratively it may stand for an evangelist, as in 1 Corinthians 9:9 (citing Deut. 24:4), "You shall not muzzle an ox while it is treading out the grain."[7] Here the concentration is upon words, but elsewhere Augustine interprets the sacraments as signs of a sacred thing (*Letters* 138.1). But this was part of a still broader understanding of *sacramenta* that included the Lord's prayer, the Ni-

6. C. S. Peirce, *Collected Papers,* vol. 2 (Cambridge: Cambridge University Press, n.d.), par. 228.

7. Augustine *De Doctrina Christiana,* 2.10, 3.29.

cene Creed, the Easter liturgy and the sign of the cross, the baptismal font and its water, the ashes of penitence, and the oil of anointing.[8] Each one of these has the inherent ability to "bring some further idea to mind" (*Against Faustus* 2.1); it stands to somebody, in this case an instructed Christian, for something else, in this case, a further idea.

Augustine's broad approach to the word "sign" is consistent with what has recently developed as "semiotics," the study of the ways in which nonlinguistic phenomena can generate meaning. If speech and writing are the chief ways in which cultural meanings can be formed or expressed, so also are material objects and aspects of behavior. Dress (not the least ecclesiastical dress) may be intended to have a meaning, and it frequently conveys a quite precise meaning. So may pictures, visual signs, modes of eating, and forms of building or architecture. Sociologists and anthropologists have recently become very fascinated with the analysis of "semiotic systems," that is, nonverbal cultural meanings. The site of a church placed on high ground, for example, may not simply be a precaution against flooding or invasion; it may stand for the transcendence of God in God's all-seeing knowledge of humankind.

A word must be said about the term "symbol," since that is very commonly used in an unclarified relation to "sign." Peirce's definition of "symbol" was "a sign which is constituted a sign merely or mainly by the fact that it is used and understood as such."[9] Here the stress is laid upon the conventions established within a given community; typical examples include the use of the cross in Christianity and gestures such as genuflection, crossing oneself, or kneeling. Anyone not belonging to that community would need verbal interpretations of such symbols. But it is a matter of considerable importance to note that the verbal interpretation of the cross, for example (that it stands for the fact that Jesus Christ died for the sins of humankind and rose again), does not abolish or make redundant the world of "sign." The explanation of the symbol involves new signs (what, e.g., does it mean to "die for the sins of humankind"?), which themselves require interpretation (e.g., the "meaning" of the cross may need to be interpreted by Christians living in grace and freedom).

It helps to see the word "symbol" as one way of specifying a

8. J. Martos, *Doors to the Sacred* (New York: Doubleday, 1992), p. 59.
9. Peirce, *Collected Papers,* vol. 2, par. 307.

kind of sign, and that signs and their interpretation are ineradicable from understanding human culture, including the religions. I offer the propositions that follow as an indication of the kind of position that I believe to be defensible:[10]

1. Human beings are sign- and symbol-using animals, employing words, objects, gestures, images, and so forth to create sense and order in the world.
2. Human experience is inescapably precarious and ambiguous, and not capable of reduction to certain, clear verities or structures.
3. As a consequence of this, all of the signs and symbols that are used to construct meaning are themselves penetrated by, and tend to reinforce, this ambiguity. This does not imply that these symbols are chaotic and meaningless; rather it implies that their interpretation needs to be carried out with care and attention, not just to conceptual content, but also to emotional overtone. The concept of sign and symbol needs to be humanly and culturally rich if it is to function with any success within the analysis of culture.

The Sign of the Bishop and the People of God

Toward Full Communion, the theological preface to the proposed Concordat, recalls some words of mine from an international Anglican-Lutheran consultation:

> The frustrating character of the historic disagreement between Anglicans and Lutherans — its sheer folly — can be formulated thus. Anglicans say to Lutherans, "If you have no objection in principle to episcopal government, then your refusal to adopt it can only be obstinacy." Lutherans say to Anglicans, "Of course we can adopt it, provided you Anglicans say it is not necessary for us to do so." To which Anglicans reply, "We haven't got any official theology which says that it, the episcopate, is of the essence of the Church, but we

10. They are defended in Bernice Martin, *A Sociology of Contemporary Cultural Change* (Oxford: Blackwell, 1981), pp. 25-52.

couldn't possibly, dogmatically, say that it wasn't." This conversation is not merely frustrating, it is dumb.[11]

Those who framed the Concordat believe that they have found a way through this thicket by paying attention to the idea that episcopal succession should be viewed "as a sign, though not a guarantee, of the continuity and unity of the Church." Here they are drawing on the Lima text on *Baptism, Eucharist and Ministry* from the Faith and Order Commission of the World Council of Churches (*Ministry,* para. 38); we can be grateful that this wider ecumenical statement has proved to be a doorway through which many of the helpful insights of the Eastern churches have been able to enter and penetrate the developing ecclesiological discussions of Western Christians.

A welcome, from the Lutheran side, to this understanding of the historic episcopate as a sign (or meaningful symbol) is summarized in a passage from George Lindbeck, found in *Toward Full Communion:*

> What the Reformers objected to was the idea that succession con-
> stitutes a guarantee or criterion of apostolic faithfulness, but once
> one thinks in terms of the sign value of continuity in office, this
> difficulty vanishes. Signs and symbols express and strengthen the
> reality they signify, but the sign can be present without the reality,
> and the reality without the sign (as, for example, is illustrated by
> the relation of the flag and patriotism). Thus it is apostolicity in
> faith and life that makes the episcopal sign fruitful, not the other
> way around, but this ought not to be turned into an excuse for
> neglecting the sign.[12]

But, before we too glibly contemplate the positive value of the historic episcopate as a sign, a word must be said first about the potentially negative connotations of the episcopate. First, it is paradoxical to assert that all share equally in the gifts of the Holy Spirit, but that only

---

11. Originally from my *Papers of the Consultation: Background for the Niagara Report* (Geneva: World Council of Churches, 1987), p. 16, and cited on p. 12 of *Toward Full Communion.*

12. From George A. Lindbeck, "Episcopacy and the Unification of the Churches: Two Approaches," in *Promoting Unity,* ed. H. George Anderson and James R. Crumley, Jr. (Minneapolis: Augsburg, 1989), pp. 53-54, and cited on p. 14 of *Toward Full Communion.*

some receive the gift of leadership. On the face of it there is a contradiction between equality and hierarchy. Second, there is a specific problem about power within the church, and the apparent conformity of church structure to the structures of domination existing in secular society (in seeming contradiction to the explicit teaching of Jesus, Mark 10:35-45 and parallels). Third, the sociocultural trappings of episcopacy (the assigning of social, financial, residential, and processional privileges to the bishop) carries the unwelcome connotation of authoritarianism in cultures that have experienced all too much of that vice. In all these ways a bishop is an ambiguous symbol, much as church buildings, art, vestments, and vessels, however intended to glorify the Creator, likewise carry the aura of the world of wealth.

Even given this fact, however, the quest for the unambiguous symbol itself presents unexpected difficulties. In particular the embodiment of humility seems to elude human intentions. Similarly the facts about the human exercise of power are such as to frustrate all attempts to eliminate inequality in the church. There is a serious argument in favor of accepting the ambivalence of the episcopate, which at least openly identifies the bearer of great responsibilities and inescapably presents the bishop with the challenge of personal humility and corporate service.

In the ecumenical discussions between Lutherans and Anglicans, most especially in the *Porvoo Common Statement* between Nordic-Baltic Lutherans and Great Britain–Irish Anglicans, the method pursued has been to unravel the precise "sign" of historic succession (that of bishops being ordained by bishops in intended continuity from the apostles themselves) within the context of the apostolicity of the whole church: visually it may be represented as a series of Chinese boxes, as on the facing page.

Much has gone wrong in the post-Reformation disputes about historic episcopal succession precisely because of the isolation of the historic succession of bishops from its rich context within the theology of the church. Thus, for example, if historic episcopal succession is included as one of a list of "essentials" or "fundamentals," then its absence jeopardizes the very presence of the church. Anglicans have long had the difficulty of not wanting to *deny* that churches lacking in the historic episcopal succession are genuine churches, while at the same time wanting to *affirm* that the transmission of the episcopate in historic succession has an effect.

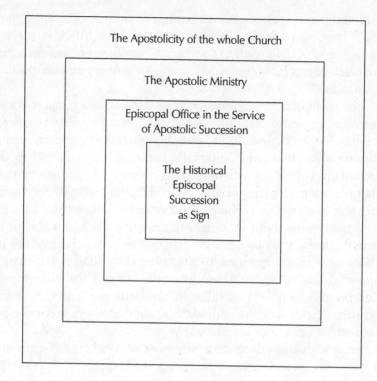

The Apostolicity of the whole Church

The Apostolic Ministry

Episcopal Office in the Service
of Apostolic Succession

The Historical
Episcopal
Succession
as Sign

The concept of "sign" (or "symbol") helps all parties to this complex and long-running dispute. First, it insists that the church as a whole is apostolic, and that every member receives his or her gift for participating in and contributing to the communication of the gospel in words and deeds. In this sense everything spoken or done by Christians in the name of the church is part of a great symbol system, signifying God's kingdom, helping to bring it about, and offering a foretaste of its enjoyment.

Within the apostolic church, the ordained apostolic ministry has particular God-given tasks, one of which is that of coordination of all of God's gifts. This is the ministry of oversight, and it is exercised personally, collegially, and communally (as the Lima text on *Ministry* says in the widely accepted paragraphs 26 and 29)

Thus episcopal office serves the apostolic succession of the whole church. At the consecration of a bishop the biblical sign of laying on of hands with prayer is used. This practice is rich in significance, and has four effects: it witnesses to the church's trust in God's faithfulness and in Christ's promised presence; it expresses the church's intention to be faithful to God's initiative and gift; it signifies the acceptance by other churches of the new bishop; and it transmits ministerial office and authority.[13]

The point of retaining the sign of consecration *in historic succession* now is made clear: to communicate the fact that the church cares for continuity in the whole of its life and mission. It is a visible expression of our trust in what has traditionally been called God's gift to the church of *indefectibility* (which is, of course, sharply to be distinguished from any notion of its *infallibility*). By embracing a sign of continuity we are able to affirm in a visible way that we are in solidarity with the church of the past, both in its faithfulness and truth, but also in its human weakness and potential for getting things wrong. A visible sign of continuity gives expression to the belief (also sharply contrasting with the claims of some relatively modern sects) that despite our frailties, God is faithful to his calling of us. He has never had to restart the church "from scratch," although he continually calls it to reformation and renewal in the light of the gospel.

Because of this inherent requirement of constant self-examination and renewal, and because the sign of the historic succession is by nature a culturally construed symbol, it needs the corrective and interpretation provided by a public declaration of the historic faith of the church and a biblical exposition of the ministry to which the bishop is called.

This theological argument enables Anglicans to affirm that faithfulness to the apostolic calling of the whole church can be preserved by means other than the sign of historic succession. It enables Lutherans to affirm that there is genuine significance in embracing the sign, without the fear that it thereby denies or underrates its past apostolic continuity. The Concordat does not use the word "validity," which belongs to the older theological tradition of lists of canonically re-

---

13. These four effects were spelled out in these terms in the *Porvoo Common Statement* of 1993, a document arising from discussions between the Anglican churches of the U.K. and Ireland and the Lutheran churches of the Nordic and Baltic states. The *Porvoo Common Statement* went on to say, "Thus, in the act of consecration a bishop receives the sign of divine approval and a permanent commission to lead his particular church in the common faith and apostolic life of all the churches" (par. 48).

quired "essentials" that guarantee the "grace" unobtainable without them. It denies that the use of the sign guarantees the fidelity of a church as a whole, or of any particular bishop, although concrete provision is envisioned in the terms of the Concordat for a process that is intended continually to recall the episcopate to dependence on the Spirit for the service of the gospel:

> The Episcopal Church hereby endorses the Lutheran affirmation that the historic catholic episcopate under the Word of God must always serve the gospel, and that the ultimate authority under which bishops preach and teach is the gospel itself. In testimony and implementation thereof, the Episcopal Church agrees to establish and welcome, either by itself or jointly with the Evangelical Lutheran Church in America, structures for collegial and periodic review of its episcopal ministry as well as that of the Evangelical Lutheran Church in America, with a view to evaluation, adaptation, improvement, and continual reform in the service of the gospel. (Par. 6)

The significance of the theological work lying behind the Concordat is that, in effect, Anglicans are invited not to view the current Lutheran episcopate in America negatively, in the light of lapses in the past from historic continuity, but to recognize in the contemporary Evangelical Lutheran Church in America the signs of a church living and working within the apostolic tradition. In a way this "recognition" is an exercise in discerning family likeness. Through their mutually agreed-upon portrait of apostolicity, the Anglican and Lutheran churches involved in this process are able to recognize each other as brother-and-sister churches, living by grace in the same family. Historic succession, strictly preserved by Anglicans, fits within that mutuality, and the Lutheran partner to the Concordat is invited to say that it is free to recognize the value of the sign and to embrace it without denying its own apostolic continuity.

The Inseparability of Bishop and People

If the church's visibility is the necessary appearance in history of its beyond-historical character, the question arises, Of what is the bishop the sign? John Zizioulas's argument on this point deserves attention. In sum, Zizioulas says that there is an urgent theological requirement to prevent the separation of Christology and pneumatology in relation to the doctrine of the church. In Western theologies too frequently Christology has been taken as the guarantee of the transmission in history of gifts and powers originally bestowed by Christ on his church; whereas the Spirit, by reaction, has been taken to be the guarantor of a nonhistorical, disembodied or interior faith, justified or realized in eternity. Thus structural-sacramental ways of thinking have been separated from the spiritual-fideistic, to the detriment of both. To unite the perspectives of Christology and pneumatology is to create a synthesis of the historical and eschatological approaches to the church and its life. Thus one must understand the event of Christ as constituted pneumatologically. Christ is eschatological humanity, not as an individual but as the church. To see the church as founded on the apostles in an eschatological sense gives the church its existential significance as a sign of the redeemed creation.

The church constantly receives from the Spirit her eschatological meaning.

> The tension therefore between history and Kingdom is not one of ontological dualism. The way we can describe it is as longing for a *change of form,* for transfiguration. In the expression of St. Paul, we are anxious to exchange the present form for the eschatological one (2 Thess. 2:7-9, 2 Cor. 4:7) . . . because the presence and activity of the Antichrist in history makes the present form of the Church fragile and a cause of suffering.[14]

As a result, there is nothing in the life of the church that does not participate in the ambiguities and tension of both the historical reality and the eschatological meaning.

Zizioulas, therefore, criticizes those developments in Western theology that have tended to isolate the bishop from the rest of the church. On the contrary, both are mutually dependent. The task of the bishop is to call the scattered people of God together into unity, to the sacrament of unity and of eschatological truth. Without the community the eschatological perspective disappears. All we are left

---

14. Zizioulas, *Being in Communion,* p. 186.

with is juridical guarantees for a particular isolated individual, who happens to be historically linked to the apostles by a chain of ordination.

Zizioulas's argument is focused, naturally, upon the sacrament of the eucharist, and upon the community of God as the eucharistic community. There are particular reasons, however, why one should emphasize baptismal incorporation into Christ as the foundation of the church, and constitutive of its eschatological meaning, without in any way minimizing the importance of, or its interconnection with, the eucharistic feast. The task of the bishop, in its most simple terms, is to ensure that men and women are ordained and sent to lead the mission of the church and to celebrate the sacrament of baptism by water, in the name of the Holy Trinity, thereby perpetuating the faith-community in history as a sign of the eschatological kingdom. In this way we can also see the inseparability of bishop from the rest of the people of God, specifically in the church's mission and apostolate.

In thinking of mission, we look forward. The Concordat is, as its conclusion makes clear, a forward-looking proposal, with mission as the dynamic that drives and commends it. Reconciled churches, whether in North America or elsewhere, will of course have many further tasks to carry out together beyond that of achieving full communion between themselves. But a start has been made, and the theological basis of it is, in my view, rich in potential.

The Lutheran-Episcopal Concordat: What Does It Say, and Why Does It Matter?

BRUCE D. MARSHALL

A Revolutionary Proposal

The "Concordat of Agreement" between the Episcopal Church and the Evangelical Lutheran Church in America makes a revolutionary proposal: two Christian churches, representatives of worldwide confessional families which have never been in communion with one another since each was forged in the European religious ferment of the sixteenth century, will enter into a relationship of full communion. Prior to the ecumenical dialogue of which the Concordat is the final and decisive step, Lutherans and Episcopalians in the United States never shared the Lord's Supper; they were never able to receive from one another the one eucharistic bread that makes Christ's followers one body in him. Doctrinally, the eucharistic disunity of Lutherans and Episcopalians stems, especially since the nineteenth century, from the historic inability of the two churches to recognize as authentic each other's ministry of the gospel through Word and sacrament. And while the two churches have never formally anathematized or condemned one another's teaching, neither have they formally even recognized one another as churches. The Concordat proposes to reverse radically this history of disunity. The ELCA and the Episcopal Church would formally recognize one another as true churches of Jesus Christ, and would come to have a common ministry. The two churches would thereby come to full eucharistic fellowship, sharing the one bread by which, precisely through sharing it, "we who are many are one body" in Christ (1 Cor. 10:16-17; cf. 11:17-22).

32

The austere legal language of the Concordat naturally obscures the revolutionary character of what it proposes. As all who have read it know, this is a document only a canon lawyer could love. Consideration of the Concordat by the two churches therefore requires careful attention to what the document actually says, and on what grounds. On this there has been, at least in Lutheran circles, considerable misunderstanding. In the following remarks I will try to identify the chief proposals actually contained in the Concordat, and distinguish them from other ideas neither contained nor advocated in that text. I will have an eye particularly, but not exclusively, on Lutheran concerns. My chief aim is to show why Lutherans — precisely in order to be faithful to their own Lutheran identity — ought to support the Concordat. I will conclude with some brief reflections on why members of the two churches, indeed Christians everywhere, ought to care about this proposal for full eucharistic fellowship between two shrinking American denominations.

Focus of the Concordat

Even a cursory reading of the Concordat and its primary supporting document, "Toward Full Communion," reveals that these texts are almost wholly preoccupied with the nature and function of the ordained ministry, and in particular that of bishops.[1] This intense focus on ministry and ministers, and especially on the historic episcopate, may seem odd, even perverse. Few subjects are more remote from the concern of most Christians, clergy almost as much as laity, than the responsibilities and prerogatives of bishops, and whether this or that bishop stands in the historic succession. The Concordat's preoccupation with bishops may lead laity and clergy of both churches to worry that it makes bishops and ordained ministers generally more important than the gospel, and urges Episcopalians and Lutherans to unite not around the gospel and that mission to the world which the gospel enjoins, but instead around a clerical elite.

1. References to "Concordat of Agreement" (Conc) and "Toward Full Communion" (TFC) will be made parenthetically in the text by paragraph number (§). These documents are found in *"Toward Full Communion" and "Concordat of Agreement," Lutheran Episcopal Dialogue, Series 3,* ed. William A. Norgren and William G. Rusch (Minneapolis: Augsburg; Cincinnati: Forward Movement, 1991).

While understandable, this reaction to the Concordat's focus on ministry and episcopacy stems, I think, from a misapprehension. The Concordat proposes that by entering into full communion, the ELCA and the Episcopal Church would each recognize in the teaching and practice of the other "the essentials of the one catholic and apostolic faith" (Conc, §2). "Toward Full Communion" roots this proposal in a "theological consensus on the gospel," spelled out in the doctrinal agreements on Scripture, worship, justification, baptism, eucharistic presence, and the church articulated in previous rounds of Lutheran-Episcopal dialogue (cf. TFC, §§16-17). To characterize the ecumenical goal of full communion as a common life in "the apostolic faith" helps to highlight the fact, acknowledged by Lutherans and Episcopalians alike (e.g., in their confession of the Nicene Creed), that the faith on which we hope to agree — the gospel itself — comes to us from Christ's apostles. For Lutherans and Episcopalians to share the apostolic faith therefore means not only for them to believe together what the apostles believed (although it certainly means that), but also to receive together from the apostles the faith that we hold in common with them. Sharing the apostolic faith thus means not only that we Lutherans and Episcopalians become contemporaries in the common life of one community, but that we belong to the same historically and spatially extended community as did the apostles themselves — a community where receiving the gospel from Christ's apostles and believing it with them is a necessary condition for membership.

This raises an obvious and important question: How can Lutherans or Episcopalians be sure that we, or each other, belong to the same community as did the apostles — that is, to the church, the community that receives the gospel from them and believes it with them? Talk of sharing the apostolic faith raises, in a word, the question of the church's apostolicity, the nature of that apostolicity and the criteria for discerning it. The Concordat and "Toward Full Communion" rightly perceive that the question of the church's apostolicity, in particular the issues of apostolic succession and the historic episcopate, poses the most difficult obstacle to full communion between the ELCA and the Episcopal Church. Thus the Concordat focuses on ministry and episcopacy: not because it is the most important topic for Episcopalians and Lutherans to agree upon, but because it is the most difficult one. Its attention to ministry and episcopacy signals not clericalism, but practicality; the Concordat simply tries to scratch where the itch is.

The Concordat and the Historic Episcopate

The Concordat not only proposes that the churches can agree on the historic episcopate, but can, armed with this agreement, come to share a common episcopal and pastoral ministry. We need to examine with some care what the Concordat says on this score, and why. The proposed doctrinal and practical solution to the traditional disagreement over the historic episcopate is more complex than it might seem at first glance, and implicates the more basic issue of the apostolicity of the church — the issue of how we can be, and know that we are, in the same community with Christ's apostles, from whom we receive the gospel, and with whom we believe it.

Apostolicity and the Ministry of Oversight

In order to show how Lutherans and Episcopalians can overcome their long-standing impasse on the historic episcopate, the Concordat (together with "Toward Full Communion") begins by making two doctrinal or conceptual moves, each of which turns on noticing a pertinent distinction. First and most basically, the Concordat distinguishes between the apostolicity of the church and the ministry of bishops. Apostolicity is fundamentally an attribute of the church as a whole, which the present proposal, drawing on the language of earlier Lutheran-Episcopal dialogues, defines as "the Church's continuity with Christ and the apostles in its movement through history" (TFC, §20). Another term for "movement through history" or time is "succession," so the concept of apostolicity includes the concept of succession; "apostolic succession" is at bottom simply apostolicity itself, with a stress on continuity across time. Like apostolicity, therefore, "apostolic succession" is fundamentally an attribute of the whole church. The church lives in continuity with Christ's apostles and the community they founded in a rich variety of ways, each of which has its own irreducible role in creating and strengthening that continuity: faithfulness to apostolic teaching, preaching, and witness, sharing in the apostolic practices of baptism, eucharist, and prayer, caring for and building up the church's common life (especially though not solely through the divinely established office of the pastoral ministry), service to the world, and so forth (cf. TFC, §20).

35

Also among the means by which the church lives in continuity with the apostles is the ministry of bishops. But this is only one among many aspects of the church's apostolicity or apostolic succession. The ministry of bishops — and in particular of their own succession, the "historic episcopate" — cannot be equated with the apostolicity of the church, but must always be understood in the wider context, and in the service, of that apostolicity which belongs to the church as a whole. In this regard the supporting documents to the Concordat are quite blunt: "apostolic succession is not to be understood 'primarily in terms of historic episcopate'" (TFC, §20).

The Ministry of Oversight and the Historic Episcopate

In order to bring out the distinctive contribution of bishops to the church's apostolicity, the Concordat trades on a second distinction, that between the ministry of oversight and the historic episcopate. Lutherans and Episcopalians both recognize the need for a distinctive kind of oversight or supervision in the church, by which provision is made and responsibility taken to ensure pure preaching of the gospel and right administration of the sacraments in a group of local congregations. Following now widespread ecumenical practice, the Concordat denotes this distinctive ministerial function of oversight by the Greek term *episkope,* and notes that both churches already agree upon its necessity (Conc, §3; cf. TFC, §22). Since it is a function, an activity, *episkope* can in principle be carried out in different ways. While most of the world's Christians (Roman Catholics, Orthodox, and Anglicans) maintain the historic episcopate as the institutional means for carrying out the ministry of *episkope,* the Concordat explicitly maintains that this ministry can be exercised authentically without the historic episcopate, and is so exercised in Lutheran churches past and present (Conc, §4; cf. TFC, §§19, 22, 25).[2]

If an authentic ministry of oversight already exists in the ELCA, despite the absence there of the historic episcopate, why should Lutherans be concerned about sharing in the historic episcopate (aside,

---

2. On the ecumenical background of this distinction between *episkope* and episcopate see esp. the Faith and Order document, *Baptism, Eucharist and Ministry* (Geneva: World Council of Churches, 1983) (e.g., BEM, M, §§34-38; 52-53).

for the moment, from the contribution this would make to church unity by enabling full communion with the Episcopalians)? Or, for that matter, why should Episcopalians, who are prepared to recognize the authenticity of this ministry of *episkope,* be concerned whether Lutherans acquire bishops in historic succession? In answer to these questions the Concordat presupposes a broad ecumenical consensus that has developed over the last generation, and to which its own supporting documents have contributed, regarding the distinctive contribution of the ministry of *episkope,* and of the historic episcopate as the traditional form of that ministry, to the unity of the church across both space and time.

As I have already observed, the special responsibility of the ministry of *episkope* is to provide for the pure preaching of the gospel and the right administration of the sacraments in a group of local congregations. *Episkope* unifies local churches in the gospel by providing for and overseeing (correcting, if necessary) the gospel ministry of word and sacrament in those congregations. As Lutherans and Episcopalians agree, this ministry is itself a divinely instituted office in the church (cf. TFC, §22).[3]

Given this responsibility for unity in the gospel, what is the best way to carry out the ministry of *episkope* — or as we might equally well call it, the ministry of unity? In principle at least, *episkope* could be exercised by a committee, whether clergy, laity, or both (such as the Reformed consistories or presbyteries, or the ELCA Division for Ministry, or for that matter the ELCA Churchwide Assembly), or by a layperson who also has local secular authority (as the Lutheran churches in Germany were generally run, from early in the Reformation, by the territorial princes; cf. TFC, §34). But *episkope* is best exercised, so the emerging ecumenical consensus proposes, by individual persons set aside for the task. Like the ministry of word and sacrament itself, oversight of that ministry is at heart a profoundly personal task that cannot be carried out in a fully

---

3. For the Lutheran assent to this, see the Augsburg Confession (CA), German version (G) 5.1: "God instituted the office of the ministry, that is, provided the gospel and the sacraments." Text in *Die Bekenntnisschriften der evangelisch-lutherischen Kirche* (BSELK), 8th ed. (Göttingen: Vandenhoeck & Ruprecht, 1979), p. 58; English translation in *The Book of Concord: The Confessions of the Evangelical Lutheran Church,* ed. Theodore G. Tappert (Philadelphia: Fortress, 1959), p. 31 (Tappert). I have sometimes modified Tappert's translations.

adequate way simply by seeing whether certain rules are being followed (as a committee, or even a computer, could do). Rather, it requires the nuanced good judgment of particular cases that only the experience of skilled practitioners can provide.[4] This also indicates why persons charged with the ministry of oversight should themselves be ordained ministers of word and sacrament; they need the formation of judgment concerning what they will oversee which only practice of it can bring. Finally, the ecumenical consensus argues, bishops should not only be ordained but ordaining, since in ordaining to the ministry of the gospel the personal task of overseeing that ministry finds its most decisive exercise.

Thus the Concordat presupposes the now dominant ecumenical view that the ministry of *episkope* is best exercised by individuals who are both ordained and ordaining — that is, by bishops — though it can if necessary be carried out in other ways. This has a crucial implication regarding the church's spatial unity. Christians confess that the church of Jesus Christ is one, that the local congregation belongs to a single trans-local and ultimately universal community. This community is not hidden, but is public and visible; its unity must therefore also be public and visible. When the local ministry of oversight is carried out by bishops (rather than, say, by committees), the public communion of these bishops in word, sacrament, and service (their collegiality, as it is traditionally called), serves as a uniquely clear and decisive witness to the genuinely trans-local and ultimately universal unity of Christ's church.[5]

But the church is unified across time as well as space. Christians in Northfield confess that they belong to the same community as did the apostles, not only that they belong to the same community as do Christians in Nome. We confess, moreover, that we and the apostles together belong to the same community that will acclaim the Lord Jesus when he returns in glory. As we have seen, the church's unity

4. Of course discerning whether rules (e.g., doctrinal ones) are being followed itself requires experienced judgment, which militates further against *episkope* by committee.

5. The term "trans-local unity" is borrowed from George A. Lindbeck's summary of the ecumenical consensus on episcopacy in "Episcopacy and the Unification of the Churches: Two Approaches," in *Promoting Unity: Themes in Lutheran-Catholic Dialogue,* ed. H. George Anderson and James R. Crumley, Jr. (Minneapolis: Augsburg, 1989), pp. 51-65; here, p. 52.

across time is its apostolicity. It is precisely here, in promoting and manifesting the church's apostolicity, that the historic episcopate has a distinctive role to play. From a very early point in the church's life (already by the second century), the succession of local bishops, signaled in particular by the laying on of hands in episcopal consecration, has proven an effective sign — a uniquely clear and decisive witness — to the genuinely trans-temporal unity of Christ's church. The succession of bishops is an effective sign of the whole church's apostolicity, not an arbitrary sign. This is in part because the bishops, with their responsibility for oversight, have a special charge to teach the apostolic faith, to hand it on in its fullness to succeeding generations. Just as the exercise of *episkope* by bishops in communion with one another rather than by committees best serves the trans-local unity of the church, so the ordered and public succession of these bishops is that exercise of *episkope* which best serves the apostolicity of the church, its trans-temporal unity.

If the public temporal succession of bishops functions as a sign of that apostolicity which is to characterize the church in all aspects of its life, then the effectiveness of the sign obviously depends on the presence of what it signifies. In other words, the historic episcopate does not by itself guarantee the church's apostolic succession, its continuity with the faith and teaching of the apostles; still less does the historic episcopate by itself constitute the church's apostolic succession. Moreover, apostolic succession can be maintained where episcopal succession is not. As we have seen, the Concordat, together with the wider ecumenical consensus on episcopacy, makes both of these points bluntly (Conc, §4; cf. TFC, §§19, 20, 22, 25). Nonetheless, churches without the historic episcopate have a very good reason to accept it and to share in it: The succession of bishops is an especially effective sign of the whole church's continuity with Christ and his apostles, a sign which enjoys very ancient lineage in the church. And the fact that most of the world's Christians share the historic episcopate gives another, at least equally important, reason for adopting it: Such action by traditionally nonepiscopal churches will contribute significantly to the unity of the presently divided church. Thus in our own day adoption of the historic episcopate will contribute to the spatial as well as temporal unity of the church.

The Historic Episcopate and the Lutheran Confessions

The Lutheran Confessions are quite clear about the desirability of the historic episcopate for the sake of the church's unity and continuity, as the Concordat and its supporting literature observe. "We have given frequent testimony," the Apology of the Augsburg Confession avers, "that we have the deepest desire [nos summa voluntate cupere] to maintain the Church polity and various ranks of the ecclesiastical hierarchy" — that is, the threefold ministry and the historic episcopate.[6] The Augsburg Confession and the Apology assert, moreover, that the authority of bishops in the church (though not their "temporal authority"), both their "power of order" to oversee the ministry of Word and sacrament and their "power of jurisdiction" to exercise church discipline (namely, to excommunicate), belongs to them by divine right; that is, these powers are assigned to them by the gospel itself.[7] "Churches are bound necessarily and by divine law to be obedient to the bishops according to the text, 'He who hears you hears me.'"[8] All these things are said, it is important to note, not about officeholders the Lutherans themselves might appoint and to whom they might give the title "bishop," but about actual bishops, the only bishops there were at the time — those who not only stood in the historic succession, but were loyal to Rome.

Here as elsewhere the Lutheran Confessions seem clearly to regard the traditional ordering and succession of ministry as an important feature of the church's life that ought to be retained (TFC's remark that they "endorse the historic episcopate in principle" [§42] seems more than a little understated); the question is not whether the historic episcopate is useful or desirable, but whether the bishops of the time will exercise episkope in a fashion that serves rather than opposes the gospel. Even this crucial point often gets put rather mildly: "It is not our intention that the bishops [that is, the Western Catholic — and so Roman — bishops] give up their power to govern, but we ask for this one thing, that they allow the Gospel to be taught purely

---

6. Apology 14.1 (BSELK, p. 296; Tappert, p. 214; cited in TFC, §44). All of the confessional texts on bishops are cited at length in TFC, §§43-47.

7. CA (G) 28.21; Apology 28.12-14 (BSELK, pp. 123f., 399f.; Tappert, pp. 84, 283; cited in TFC, §§43-44).

8. CA, Latin version (L) 28.22 (BSELK, p. 124; Tappert, p. 84).

and that they relax some few observances which cannot be kept without sin."[9] Should particular bishops prove persistent enemies of the gospel, the Confessions reserve the right not to obey them,[10] and should they be unwilling to ordain priests for churches that have undertaken the evangelical reform, those churches "retain the right to ordain for themselves" (i.e., for their pastors to ordain new pastors).[11] On this score the Confessions appeal to the authority of St. Jerome, who held that the distinction of bishops from presbyters is of human rather than divine right, a claim not disputed in the Western church of the day (not even by the Council of Trent).[12]

The Lutheran Confessions thus suggest, as the Concordat also maintains, that the church's apostolicity, its faith in the gospel from and with the apostles, is fundamentally an attribute of the church as a whole, and is not simply to be identified with the succession of bishops. At the same time, ordination outside the historic episcopate is an "emergency" act, brought on by unhappy circumstance; the clear preference ("deepest desire") of the Confessions is for the "canonical polity" of the Western church, including the historic episcopate.[13] The condition that needs to be met in order for Lutherans to act on this preference, the Confessions suggest, is that bishops in historic succession serve the gospel rather than oppose it. The Concordat itself

9. CA (L) 28.77 (BSELK, p. 132; Tappert, p. 94; cited in TFC, §43).

10. The right of churches to resist bishops who become enemies of the gospel is not a Lutheran innovation. On ancient precedents for it, acknowledged in the West at least through Thomas Aquinas, see Walter Kasper, "Die apostolische Sukzession als ökumenisches Problem," in *Lehrverurteilungen — kirchentrennend? III: Materialien zur Lehre von den Sakramenten und vom kirchlichen Amt,* ed. Wolfhart Pannenberg (Freiburg: Herder; Göttingen: Vandenhoeck & Ruprecht, 1990), pp. 329-49; here: pp. 337f.

11. Treatise on the Power and Primacy of the Pope, 66; cf. 72, 65 (the latter on pastoral ordination) (BSELK, p. 491; Tappert, p. 331; cited in TFC, §46).

12. See "Treatise," 62f. (BSELK, pp. 489f.; Tappert, pp. 330f.); Smalcald Articles (AS) II.4.9; III.10.3 (BSELK, pp. 430, 458; Tappert, pp. 300, 314). Trent nowhere asserts that the distinction of bishops from presbyters is by divine right, though Canon 6 on the Sacrament of Order (Session 23) could be read as attempting an end run around Jerome: "If anyone says that in the catholic Church there is not a hierarchy, established by divine appointment, which consists of bishops, presbyters, and ministers, let him be anathema" (*Decrees of the Ecumenical Councils,* ed. Norman P. Tanner, S.J. [London: Sheed & Ward; Washington: Georgetown University Press, 1990], p. 744). See also the discussion, drawn from the U.S. Lutheran-Roman Catholic Dialogue, in TFC, §45.

13. Apology 14.1, 2, 5 (BSELK, pp. 296f.; Tappert, pp. 214f.).

stipulates emphatically that this traditional Lutheran concern about the historic episcopate is correct and normative: "The Episcopal Church hereby endorses the Lutheran affirmation that the historic catholic episcopate under the Word of God must always serve the gospel, and that the ultimate authority under which bishops preach and teach is the gospel itself" (Conc, §6). And the Concordat proposes, of course, that Lutherans and Episcopalians agree on the gospel to which the episcopate is subject.

This new ecumenical way of understanding *episkope* and the historic episcopate, together with the Lutheran Confessions' preference for the episcopate, suggests that these traditionally divisive issues now pose no doctrinal barrier to full communion between the ELCA and the Episcopal Church. But the presence of the historic episcopate in the Episcopal Church and its absence in the ELCA still poses a difficult practical problem. As with all efforts to reconcile the ministries of historically episcopal and nonepiscopal churches, the problem is how to handle the question of who receives what from whom without drawing invidious distinctions between the ministries that are to be joined. As members of the Anglican Communion, Episcopalians are bound by tradition and communal consensus (perhaps most clearly stated in the Chicago-Lambeth Quadrilateral of 1886–1888) to enter into communion with other Christian groups only in a way that includes the historic episcopate (cf. TFC, §§7, 63-64).[14] They are further bound by Anglican canon law and the Anglican ordinal (in particular the preface, dating from 1662; cf. BCP [1979], p. 510) to allow only those persons to function as priests and bishops in Episcopal churches who are themselves episcopally ordained (cf. TFC, §55). For their part, Lutherans are naturally reluctant to accept any suggestion that their own existing ministries of Word and sacrament are in any way deficient because they take place without benefit of ordination by bishops in historic succession.

Against the background of the doctrinal convergence just outlined on *episkope* and the historic episcopate, the Concordat proposes a very carefully worked out solution to this practical problem. A full discussion of the details of the legal arrangement is not necessary here, though these details are essential to the success of the proposal. The decisive point is the Concordat's provision for immediate full mutual

14. For the full text of the Quadrilateral, see the Book of Common Prayer (1979), pp. 876-78 (BCP).

recognition and interchangeability of existing diaconal and pastoral ministries between the ELCA and the Episcopal Church, and future joint ordination of, and cooperation in oversight by, Lutheran and Episcopal bishops (Conc §§3-5, 9-10, 14).

On the one hand, the Episcopal Church must recognize the unconditional authenticity of the current episcopal and other pastoral ministries of the ELCA, despite the absence there of the historic episcopate. This recognition, entailing that Lutheran pastors could henceforth function as priests in Episcopal churches, requires of the Episcopal Church temporary suspension of its canonical requirement that all ministers be ordained by bishops in historic succession, until such time as bishops of both churches are all incorporated into the historic episcopate (Conc, §5, 14; TFC, §78).[15] No concession of equal moment, it may be observed, is required of the ELCA.

On the other hand, the provisions of the Concordat require the ELCA to recognize the unconditional authenticity of the current episcopal and other pastoral ministries of the Episcopal Church, and to accept the incorporation, through joint ordination (Conc, §3) of future ELCA bishops into the historic episcopate. Following their confessional mandate, Lutherans would here accept the historic episcopate for the sake of unity in the gospel, as "a sign, though not a guarantee," of the church's fidelity to the gospel across time and space. However, inclusion in the historic episcopate would not confer upon Lutheran ministries any authenticity or authority they do not already have (TFC §§25, 49, 78).

Lutheran Objections to the Concordat

What should Lutherans make of this proposal, particularly in light of what the Lutheran Confessions have to say about the church, its unity

---

15. The status of *current* ELCA bishops is more complex. On the terms of the Concordat, their ministry of *episkope* would be recognized as fully authentic, but unlike their jointly ordained successors they themselves would not be recognized as bishops in the historic succession, and so (again unlike their successors) would not be able to perform those functions in the Episcopal Church reserved for bishops in the historic succession (viz., ordination and confirmation). This does, of course, fully grant all claims regarding the ministry of its bishops which the ELCA actually makes for them.

and apostolicity, and the historic episcopate? The easiest way to pursue this is to consider two objections that people in the ELCA have raised, and will no doubt continue to raise, to the Concordat. While these objections come from points along the theological and church-political spectrum in the ELCA that are in important respects opposites, the objectors share the conviction that accepting the Concordat would deal a fatal blow to the Lutheran identity of the ELCA. Both would vigorously repudiate, in other words, my suggestion that the Episcopalians have offered the most significant concession in the Concordat.

The first objection goes like this. The Lutheran Confessions famously maintain that the proclamation of the gospel and the administration of the sacraments are necessary, but also sufficient, conditions for the unity of the church.[16] They further maintain that when traditions and practices which are not necessary for the church's unity (matters which are, to use the terminology of the Formula of Concord, *adiaphora*) are treated as though they *were* necessary for it, then we must refuse to accept them or to engage in them.[17] The Concordat makes the historic episcopate necessary for the unity of the church, in the sense that there will be no shared administration and reception of the gospel and its sacraments (pivotally, of the eucharist) with Episcopalians unless Lutherans adopt the episcopate. This manifestly adds a necessary condition for church fellowship beyond those which Lutherans are confessionally bound to regard as sufficient. Thus Lutherans are confessionally bound to reject the proposed condition, and with it the proposed fellowship.

This objection has considerable power to suggest to contemporary American Lutherans that in accepting the Concordat they would be giving up something indispensable to their own confessional identity. It is basically the objection made by two Lutheran members of the dialogue team in the "Dissenting Report" appended to the Concordat, in which they explained why they did not vote in favor of the final text (Conc, pp. 111-12). We need to ask, however, whether

16. CA 7 (G): "It is sufficient for the true unity of the Christian Church that the gospel be preached in conformity with a pure understanding of it and that the sacraments be administered in accordance with the divine Word" (BSELK, p. 61; Tappert, p. 32).

17. For the confessional discussion of *adiaphora*, see Formula of Concord, Epitome and Solid Declaration, 10 (BSELK, pp. 814-16, 1053-63; Tappert, pp. 492-94, 610-16).

or not this objection arises from either an adequate reading of the Concordat or a plausible interpretation of the Lutheran Confessions.

First, would the full communion between Lutherans and Episcopalians proposed by the Concordat — in particular full eucharistic fellowship and a common ministry of word and sacrament — in fact require, as a condition for its existence, that Lutherans adopt the historic episcopate? To this decisive question the answer is obviously No. The Episcopal Church offers in the Concordat immediate full recognition of the present episcopal and pastoral ministries of the ELCA, and full interchangeability of present ELCA pastors with Episcopal priests in the ministry of word and sacrament, even though the former have not been ordained by bishops in historic succession (Conc, §§ 4-5). This means that the conditions for the unity of the church identified in CA 7, namely the full sharing of word and sacrament, administered by a common ministry of word and sacrament, would be realized the moment the Concordat was officially accepted by both churches, before any ELCA bishops actually entered the historic succession (and long before they all did). On the basis of this already existing unity in word and sacrament — and not in order to bring it about — the ELCA would then begin actually to adopt the historic episcopate as an effective sign, though not a guarantee, of this unity in word and sacrament, through joint consecration. The actual entrance of ELCA bishops into the historic episcopate would be made freely and for the sake of unity, not out of necessity or coercion, in accordance with the permission granted for it in the Lutheran Confessions. On the scenario developed in the Concordat, Lutheran adoption of the historic episcopate would thus be a consequence of, rather than a condition for, unity in word and sacrament.

If Lutheran adoption of the historic episcopate is not a practical condition for unity in word and sacrament, still less is it a doctrinal condition. The Concordat and its supporting documents nowhere suggest that Lutherans need, either as a condition for or as a consequence of full communion with the Episcopal Church, doctrinally or confessionally to regard the historic episcopate that they would be adopting as necessary for the unity of the church. On the contrary, it everywhere supposes that they will not (e.g., TFC, §22). Episcopalians and Anglicans more generally have long differed on the interpretation and significance of the historic episcopate; the Concordat effectively includes the Lutheran confessional view — that the episcopate is clearly desirable but not strictly necessary for the unity of the church — within the limits of allowable doctrinal diversity on this topic.

Second, by making actual Lutheran adoption of the historic episcopate a consequence of unity rather than a condition for it, the Concordat seems to meet the Lutheran objection that we are considering. But the objection could be restated. True, actual adoption of the historic episcopate by the ELCA, and the entry of its bishops into the historic succession, would follow unity in word and sacrament. But Lutherans would still have to *agree* to adopt the episcopate in order to bring such unity about. And this means that the Concordat requires what Lutherans are confessionally bound to regard as unacceptable conditions for church unity. We need to look at the merits of this restated objection. Is there anything wrong — anything confessionally amiss — with Lutherans accepting whatever conditions may be necessary to bring about the unity of the church in the gospel?

Defenders of the objection obviously think so. Their interpretation of the Lutheran Confessions suggests that Lutherans are permitted, in cases where unity with other Christians is absent, to agree on the gospel and the sacraments in order to bring unity about. But if other Christians are concerned that we agree on anything else for the sake of our unity in the gospel and the sacraments — whether the historic episcopate, Mary and the saints, papal primacy, the veneration of icons, or whatever — it seems we must in principle refuse. Take the case of the episcopate. The Episcopal Church has sought communion in the gospel and the sacraments with us, and has asked that we *agree* to adopt (not actually adopt) the historic episcopate in order to bring this unity about. Presumably *any* adoption of the historic episcopate by Lutherans would, at least for obvious practical reasons, have to be preceded in time by an agreement to adopt it with those from whom we would adopt it. But according to the present objection, the very fact that agreement to adopt the historic episcopate would have to precede, in time, the unity in gospel and sacraments for the sake of which the agreement was undertaken makes the historic episcopate a "condition" or "necessity" for unity, and so makes such agreement confessionally intolerable. Given this interpretation of the Confessions, it seems impossible that Lutherans, once having foregone the historic episcopate, could ever take it back. Or more precisely, they could agree to adopt it only if no unity in gospel and sacraments actually resulted, or were intended to result. Only so, it seems, can they avoid making agreement to adopt the historic episcopate an illicit "condition" for unity.

Surely something has gone seriously wrong. According to this reading of the Confessions on church unity and *adiaphora,* Lutherans cannot accept the historic episcopate for the sake of unity — indeed, especially not for the sake of unity. The proviso that the episcopate must always serve the gospel is clearly no help, since agreement for the sake of unity on any disputed matter besides the gospel and the sacraments has been ruled out in principle by this reading. But the Confessions themselves urge that Lutherans retain the historic episcopate for the sake of unity, on the sole condition that it serve the gospel.[18] Luther makes a particularly instructive remark on this point in the Smalcald Articles: "If the bishops were true bishops and were concerned about the Church and the gospel, they might be permitted (for the sake of love and unity, but not of necessity) to ordain and confirm us and our preachers."[19] Here, once again, is the standard confessional proposal: We will accept bishops in historic succession for the sake of unity, provided that they serve the gospel (Luther in 1537 thought it highly unlikely that they would, but the present objection concedes this point). This must not be done "of necessity." But obviously it must be possible for Lutherans to rejoin the historic succession without violating this stricture against "necessity," otherwise it would be contradictory to permit (as Luther has just done) the episcopate at all.

So what *sort* of necessity is here being excluded? Surely it cannot be the necessity of agreeing on disputed points, including the theory and practice of the historic episcopate, in order to restore unity; this is just what the Lutherans repeatedly tried to do throughout the 1530s, most notably at Augsburg in 1530. Nor can the problem be reestablishing unity, precisely in territories where the historic episcopate had been given up by Lutherans, with those who think the traditional "canonical polity" is necessary for unity; Rome, and the Roman bishops with whom Luther here permits reunion, obviously think it is

---

18. On "sole" here, see, e.g., Apology 14.5: "We want to say once again that we will willingly retain the ecclesiastical and canonical polity, if only *[si modo]* the bishops stop raging against our churches" (BSELK, p. 297; Tappert, p. 215).

19. AS 3.10.1 (BSELK, p. 457; Tappert, p. 314).

necessary. Rather, the "necessity" Luther excludes seems to be necessity for salvation. Lutherans will accept the historic episcopate precisely for the sake of unity in the gospel, but not as though the saving efficacy of the gospel ministry of word and sacrament in their churches depended on it. By its recognition of the full authenticity of present ELCA ministries of word and sacrament, even without the historic episcopate, the Concordat agrees with Luther in excluding precisely this sort of necessity for unity.[20]

What then of the principle that the gospel and the sacraments are sufficient for the unity of the church? Precisely *because* the gospel and the sacraments constitute the reality and unity of the church, Lutherans ought to be, because of their confessional commitments, willing to seek agreement on *whatever* serves, promotes, or advances the unity of the church in the gospel. The Confessions urge Lutherans to seek agreement, out of love for the gospel and the gospel's God, on whatever matters — whatever conditions or necessities — serve the gospel and the church's unity in it. Far from requiring Lutherans to refuse prior agreements — prior conditions — on *any* matter that would lead to unity in the gospel, the Confessions impose only one requirement on such agreements and conditions: that they serve the gospel, and the church's unity in it. Read in the context of the Confessions as a whole, CA 7 does not prohibit Lutherans from seeking the sort of agreement proposed by the Concordat, but requires that they do. Such, at least, is the sort of interpretation that is consistent with the Confessions's insistence both that the gospel and the sacraments suffice for unity and that the historic episcopate, once foregone, may still be accepted for the sake of unity. By interpreting the sufficiency of gospel and sacraments in a way that logically excludes the confessional permission to accept the historic episcopate, the objection offers a plausible account of neither; wherever possible, one should avoid interpretation that yields radical incoherence in the interpreted text.[21]

20. For a detailed analysis of the historical setting and original meaning of the Lutheran confessional texts bearing on conditions for church unity, see Michael Root's essay in this volume.

21. Curiously, Lutherans who make the objection that we have been considering (e.g., in the "Dissenting Report" to the Concordat) often concede that CA 7 unity exists with another group of Christians (e.g., Episcopalians) — and then go on to insist that we cannot accept the "conditions" that group requires of us for the sake of church unity (e.g., the historic episcopate). This compounds the incoherence. If

The second objection to the Concordat can be stated and answered more briefly. If the first comes on the whole from the self-described "radical Lutheran" wing of the ELCA, the second tends to come from the self-described "evangelical catholic" wing — though, it should be stressed, many evangelical catholics support the Concordat. The objection, crudely put, is that we Lutherans cannot enter full communion in the apostolic faith with Episcopalians because they no longer hold it. The problem is not the historic episcopate, still less the general idea of bishops; it is Episcopal bishops — like John Spong, whose name is regularly trotted out when this objection comes up. The problem, more generally, is the deep complicity of the Episcopal Church in the broad sellout of "mainline American Protestantism" to "neopagan" culture. As a result the apostolic faith has been overwhelmed in the Episcopal Church by ideologies radically opposed to it.

The short answer to this objection is for Lutherans to recall Luther's interpretation of the eighth commandment — *alles zum Besten kehren,* put the best construction on everything — and hope that our Episcopal sisters and brothers apply it to us more readily than the objectors seem willing to apply it to them. But a further issue needs attention here. Evangelical catholics (rightly, it seems to me) set considerable theological store by tradition — the unity and continuity of the apostolic faith in the church over time, and its faithful transmission to each succeeding generation — and also by worship, above all eucharistic worship. Being Lutherans, however, they tend not to connect the two. In particular, they tend to regard doctrine and theology as the primary bearers of tradition in the church, and the apostolic faith as transmitted primarily by the teaching of doctrine and theology. But surely this is wrong. Worship, not doctrine, is the primary (though of course not sole) means by which the apostolic faith is learned and held by any present generation of Christians, and passed on to the next.

CA 7 unity already exists, obviously no conditions can be required for attaining it (since the notion of X attaining, and therefore of conditions for X attaining, what X has already attained, is incoherent). We may therefore embrace the historic episcopate, or whatever, without raising the issue of "conditions," licit or illicit, at all. If CA 7 unity does not obtain (as in the present case it does not, since that unity includes eucharistic fellowship), then the issue becomes, as just outlined, whether the proposed condition serves unity in the gospel.

Here the Episcopalians have a big advantage: the Book of Common Prayer. The point is not simply that Cranmer's liturgy, for its clarity about the gospel, scriptural resonance, penetration of the trinitarian and christological heart of the faith, and sheer glorious beauty, is better than just about anything we Lutherans, or the rest of the Western church, have been able to come up with. The point is that the Episcopalians use it. Indeed, the BCP is so basic to Anglican identity throughout the world that Episcopal canon law proceeds on the assumption that it will always be used in Episcopal dioceses for eucharistic liturgy and the divine office, and stipulates, for example, that Episcopal priests can be disciplined for failure to use it in these contexts.[22] At the moment, ELCA Lutherans have no liturgical law (in this they differ from most of world Lutheranism). Though the Lutheran Book of Worship is of course widely used, pastors and congregations of the ELCA can worship week by week in whatever manner, and by whatever means, they see fit. Thus when it comes to transmission of the apostolic faith at the most basic level, the Episcopal Church seems rather better off, in the present situation, than the ELCA. For this reason, among others, it seems to me that evangelical catholic Lutherans ought to embrace, not repudiate, the Concordat.

Eucharistic Unity

Why does all this matter? In a word, because unity matters. The unity that matters, that is worth the effort it will take to see the Concordat through to full implementation, is certainly not structural merger, which no one wants, nor is it the formation of a common ministry, which, while important, is only the means to an end. The end for the

---

22. BCP (1979) itself clearly states the assumption: "The Holy Eucharist, the principle act of Christian worship on the Lord's Day and other major Feasts, and Daily Morning and Evening Prayer, *as set forth in this Book,* are the regular services appointed for public worship in this Church" (p. 13, my emphasis); see also the Constitution of the Episcopal Church, Article X. The sanction against liturgical freelancing by the clergy reads: "A Bishop, Presbyter, or Deacon of this Church shall be liable to presentment and trial for the following offenses: (7) . . . habitual neglect of Public Worship, and of the Holy Communion, *according to the order and use of this Church*" (Canons of the Episcopal Church, Title IV, Canon 1, sec. 1; my emphasis).

sake of which all this matters is, as I suggested at the outset, eucharistic fellowship: sharing the one bread that, by being shared, makes us one body in Christ. By publicly sharing the bread and cup that are Christ's body and blood we show forth to the world the Lord's death, as Paul says, until he comes (1 Cor. 11:26). By showing the world the Lord's death in our eucharistic unity, we show the world nothing less than the final depths of the love that is the life of the triune God. We may think it too great a thing that our eating and drinking together should do this. But the unity among his followers for which Jesus prays, and that the promised Spirit comes to create, is nothing less than the unity Jesus himself has with the Father in eternity and in time. "As you, Father, are in me and I am in you, may they also be one in us" (John 17:21). As Jesus goes on to pray, the credibility of the gospel in the world, the credibility of the church's proclamation that the death of Jesus enacts the triune God's infinite love for the world depends on our unity, on our showing that death to the world by eating and drinking together. "May they also be one in us, so that the world may believe that you have sent me" (v. 21).[23]

We of the ELCA and the Episcopal Church cannot by ourselves solve the problem of the church's eucharistic disunity. But we can do our part. We can come to share the one bread across a doctrinal and practical divide to the formation of a common ministry that the modern ecumenical movement has only very rarely been able to cross. In so doing we will strike a blow for the gospel, one in which all Christians — and perhaps even the world — can take heart. And that is a good enough reason for the Concordat to matter to us.

---

23. For a more developed account of the intimate link between eucharistic fellowship and the truth of the church's proclamation, see Bruce D. Marshall, "The Disunity of the Church and the Credibility of the Gospel," *Theology Today* 50, no. 1 (1993): 78-89.

Conditions of Communion: Bishops, the Concordat, and the Augsburg Confession

MICHAEL ROOT

Does the proposed "Concordat of Agreement"[1] make Lutheran acceptance of episcopal succession a "condition of communion"? Disagreement over this question led a minority of the Lutheran participants in the dialogue to dissent from the proposal and has been the center of an acrimonious Lutheran debate since the Concordat's publication. Episcopalians are left on the sidelines of an argument whose technicalities and vehemence they find puzzling.

Both sides in the Lutheran debate have shared two presuppositions: that the meaning of the question they have been debating is unequivocal and that the Concordat can be acceptable to Lutherans only if episcopal succession is in no sense a condition of communion for either of its participants. Both of these assumptions are in fact false. Episcopal succession can be a condition of communion in different ways, not all of which conflict with what should be Lutheran ecumenical principles. In fact, the way in which episcopal succession is a condition of communion in the Concordat should be fully acceptable to Lutherans since it not only does not violate the Lutheran Confessions but in fact embodies the Confessions' own ecumenical outlook. The bulk of this essay will be devoted to demonstrating this assertion. I will not address the wider question of whether adopting

1. William A. Norgren and William G. Rusch, eds., *"Toward Full Communion" and "Concordat of Agreement," Lutheran-Episcopal Dialogue, Series 3* (Minneapolis: Augsburg; Cincinnati: Forward Movement, 1991). References to the Concordat will be by paragraph number and will be given within the text.

episcopal succession is a good or bad idea, but only the narrow issue of conditionality. First, something must be briefly said about the way episcopal succession is and is not a condition of communion in the Concordat.[2]

Episcopal Succession as a Condition of Communion in the Concordat

There is no simple Yes or No answer to the question, Does the Concordat make episcopal succession a condition of communion? In one sense it does and in another it does not. These senses need to be distinguished.

On the one hand, the Concordat does not make the actual presence of ordained ministries in episcopal succession a condition of communion.[3] Crucial here is the provision that ELCA pastors and

2. For a fuller discussion of the internal logic of the Concordat, see Bruce Marshall's essay in this volume. I thank Marshall also for helpful comments on a draft of my essay. My own analysis of the logic of the Concordat, along the same lines as Marshall's, can be found in "The Proposal for Lutheran-Episcopal Fellowship: Unity and the Gospel," *Lutheran Forum* 25, no. 2 (May 1991): 22-25, and in "Anglican-Lutheran Relations: Their Broader Ecumenical Significance," in *One in Christ* 30 (1994): 22-33.

3. Discussion has been confused by some unclear language in section E of the Concordat, "Full Communion." The impression is given that full communion is achieved only after all bishops in the ELCA are in episcopal succession. Several comments need to be made. First, the drafters of the Concordat have noted that the language here is misleading (see Walter Bouman, "Concordat: Thumbs Up," *dialog* 32 [1993]: 219f.). If there is a precise moment at which full communion comes to exist, that moment is at the beginning of the process.

Second, it is nevertheless the case that until all ELCA bishops are in episcopal succession, ELCA bishops will not be invited to perform certain functions that the Episcopal Church reserves to bishops, such as confirmation. In this sense, full communion during this period will have certain anomalies. Even at the end of the process envisaged by the Concordat, however, anomalies will exist, such as the status of clergy who transfer into the ELCA from a non-episcopal church. Short of a full reunion of divided Christendom, every reasonable plan for communion among churches will have anomalies.

Third, my argument in this essay holds whether full communion is achieved at the beginning of the process or only after all bishops are in succession. Even after

Episcopal Church priests will be fully interchangeable immediately upon the Concordat's acceptance. Interchangeability will not await the long process of generational change during which the ordained ministries of the ELCA in fact enter episcopal succession, nor is any rite foreseen that might be interpreted as reordination or supplemental ordination. Since the churches will be in communion prior to the ministries in the ELCA actually being in episcopal succession, ordination in episcopal succession obviously is not itself a condition of communion in the Concordat.

On the other hand, the Concordat is obviously built on a variety of conditions. If "conditionality" means "X will occur, if and only if Y also obtains," then the Concordat is clearly conditional on, for example, the mutual recognition of "the essentials of the one catholic and apostolic faith" (§2). In this sense, the communion the Concordat would establish, while not conditional upon the actual presence of ministries in episcopal succession in the ELCA, undoubtedly is conditional upon the commitment of the ELCA to enter into episcopal succession in the future. As the Concordat itself states, the Episcopal Church will recognize the "full authenticity" of the ordained ministry within the ELCA "*in light of* the agreement that the threefold ministry of bishops, presbyters, and deacons in historic succession will be the future pattern of the one ordained ministry of Word and Sacrament in both churches" (§4, emphasis added). No one with much familiarity with the Anglican churches and their commitment to episcopacy can be surprised at this form of conditionality.

Lutheran supporters of the Concordat have, nevertheless, tended to shy away from a clear admission of this form of conditionality in the text. The "Assenting Report" of the Lutheran majority within the dialogue, written in criticism of the "Dissenting Report," actually

---

all ELCA bishops are in succession, many ELCA clergy will not be, namely, all those ordained earlier by bishops not in succession. The dissent emphasizes the confusing language of section E, but in fact this language is irrelevant to the issue. If, as the dissent argues, episcopal succession cannot in any sense be a condition of communion, then the Concordat would be unacceptable even if this confusion were clarified. If, as I will argue, the decisive issue is whether the Episcopal Church is willing to accept the ministry of ELCA clergy who have been ordained outside episcopal succession, then the confusion in section E is again irrelevant. The misleading language of section E points to a potentially confusing idiosyncrasy of the Concordat's proposal but finally is unimportant to its general character.

denies such conditionality, ignoring the logical connectives within the Concordat itself.[4] Behind this reluctance, I believe, lies the false assumption, already noted, that if episcopal succession is in any way a condition of communion for either partner in the dialogue, then the proposal is unacceptable. It is this assumption that needs the scrutiny of those who see in the Concordat a sign of ecumenical hope in our churches.

Satis Est and the Unity of the Church

At the root of the Lutheran debate over conditionality and episcopal succession lies a dispute over the right understanding of what is said about the church and its unity in the Augsburg Confession (hereafter, CA) of 1530, the most authoritative Reformation statement of Lutheran doctrine. The seventh article of the CA reads:

> Our churches also teach that one holy church is to continue forever. The church is the assembly of saints in which the Gospel is taught purely and the sacraments are administered rightly. For the true unity of the church it is enough [*satis est*] to agree concerning the teaching of the gospel and the administration of the sacraments. It is not necessary that human traditions or rites and ceremonies, instituted by men, should be alike everywhere. It is as Paul says, "One faith, one baptism, one God and Father of all," etc. (Eph. 4:5, 6).[5]

4. The Assenting Report states:

The initiative of the Episcopal members of the dialogue has been to recognize the existing pastoral ministry of the ELCA as authentic. . . . That initiative has made it *possible,* not necessary, for us to propose simultaneously and in concert with our Episcopal colleagues the joint consecration of *future* bishops resulting in the future participation of ELCA bishops in the historic episcopal succession. (P. 113)

This statement perhaps reflects the order of events within the dialogue process, but it simply ignores the clear logical structure of the Concordat, in which the recognition is made in light of the ELCA's commitment to enter episcopal succession.

5. Translation of Latin version of CA in Theodore G. Tappert, ed., *The Book of Concord: The Confessions of the Evangelical Lutheran Church* (Philadelphia: Fortress, 1959), p. 32. Hereafter referred to simply as Tappert.

This article forms the background for the minority dissent from the Concordat:

> We believe that Scripture and the Augsburg Confession clearly teach that the Word of God rightly preached and rightly administered in the sacraments of Baptism and the Lord's Supper constitutes the sole and sufficient basis for the true unity of the Christian church. . . . In this *Concordat,* however, the historic episcopate is made to be a necessity for church fellowship and thus essential to the unity of the church.[6]

The dissent reads CA 7 as exclusive in a double sense: If agreement exists on that which is essential to the true unity of the church, then any claim that something else may in any sense be necessary for concrete fellowship is excluded. Any proposal that does not exclude such claims is itself excluded.

If one is working from the CA as an authoritative document (as Lutherans do), then the dissent has a certain surface plausibility. Read in isolation, CA 7 can seem to imply such an exclusive interpretation, in which case the Concordat does seem unacceptable. If one reads CA 7 in its textual and historical context, however, the dissent and the exclusive reading of CA 7 on which it rests prove self-contradictory: The reading of CA 7 that justifies a rejection of the Concordat would also require a rejection of the Augsburg Confession itself.[7]

---

6. Concordat, p. 111. In the omitted ellipsis, the dissent emphasizes the confusion created by section E (see n.3 above). See that note for an explanation of why this confusion is irrelevant both to the dissent and to my argument here.

7. I am assuming that one should not read CA 7 in isolation from either its historical context or from its textual context within the totality of the CA. Gerhard Forde, "The Meaning of Satis Est," *Lutheran Forum* 26, no. 4 (Nov. 1992): 14-18, offers a reading of CA 7 in which the historical and textual context is simply ignored. Rather, the context in which he interprets it is his own neo-Lutheran theological system. In "Theological Impasse and Ecclesial Future," *Lutheran Forum* 26, no. 4 (Nov. 1992): 36-45, David Yeago has shown how shaky are the Reformation bases of this system, especially in relation to ecclesiology.

The Augsburg Confession as Reconciliation Proposal

The last twenty years have seen an intense historical examination of the CA and the events that surrounded it.[8] One result of that examination has been a recognition of the confession's genre. It was not written simply as a statement of faith, but as a concrete proposal for a reconciliation between the Lutheran estates within the Holy Roman Empire and the Catholic authorities, represented most powerfully by the emperor himself. The question was, Under what conditions (if any) would the Lutheran estates again be willing to come under some form of jurisdiction of the Catholic bishops? The answer is most clear if one reads the confession in the order in which it was constructed, that is, backwards, from Article 28 to Article 1. Article 28 (titled in German, "The Power of Bishops") outlines the sort of episcopal jurisdiction to which the Lutherans were willing to submit: a spiritual jurisdiction in the service of the gospel. Articles 22-27 outline those reforms which the Lutherans would insist on maintaining within their territories even under such jurisdiction (the sacrament in both kinds; married priests; an evangelical, nonsacrificial mass; private confession reformed so that it comforted rather than oppressed consciences; the end of mandatory rules about such matters as fasting; the abolition of monastic vows and a works-oriented monasticism). Articles 1 through 21, Part 1 of the CA, outline the faith as it is taught in the Lutheran estates. The intention of the articles that make up Part 1 is explicitly stated:

> Since this teaching [in Part 1] is grounded clearly on the Holy Scriptures and is not contrary or opposed to that of the universal Christian church, or even of the Roman church (in so far as the latter's teaching is reflected in the writings of the Fathers), we think that our opponents cannot disagree with us in the articles set forth

---

8. An entry into the most important results of this study can be found in Wilhelm Maurer, *Historical Commentary on the Augsburg Confession*, trans. H. George Anderson (Philadelphia: Fortress, 1986), and in *Confessio Augustana und Confutatio: Der Augsburger Reichstag 1530 und die Einheit der Kirche*, Reformationsgeschichtliche Studien und Texte, 118, ed. Erwin Iserloh (Münster: Aschendorff, 1980). I have sought to summarize some of this work in "The Augsburg Confession as Ecumenical Proposal: Episcopacy, Luther, and Wilhelm Maurer," *dialog* 28 (1989): 223-32. This last article provides support for what is said in this paragraph.

above. Therefore, those who presume to reject, avoid, and separate from our churches as if our teaching were heretical, act in an unkind and hasty fashion, contrary to all Christian unity and love, and do so without any solid basis of divine command or Scripture.

Within the CA read as a whole, Article 7 with its statement on the true unity of the church plays a specific role.[9] In eliminating what they considered human traditions opposed to the gospel and as a result falling out of communion with the Catholic bishops, had the Lutheran estates in fact left the unity of the one church? Article 7 provides, in capsule form, the argument that they had not. It argues that there is but one church, which will continue forever. This church is simply the assembly of saints among whom the gospel is truly preached and the sacraments rightly administered.[10] Since true preaching and sacraments constitute the means by which people are made saints and bound together into the church, preaching and sacraments are the essential and sufficient elements of that unity which makes the church one. As long as the Lutheran estates are rightly preaching the Word and celebrating the sacraments, they have not left the unity of the one church. Whatever changes they

9. The interpretation of CA 7 presented here is developed in greater detail with full primary and secondary textual support in "*Satis est:* What Do We Do when Other Churches Don't Agree?" *dialog* 30 (1991): 314-24. Citations of other literature will here be kept to a minimum; those interested in the full interpretive argument should see that essay.

10. Article 5 of CA asserts that "the ministry of teaching the Gospel and administering the sacraments" was divinely instituted. That the divinely instituted office of ministry is not mentioned in Article 7 is not insignificant and points to the subordination of that ministry to its tasks in relation to Word and sacraments. Nevertheless, if we assume that the CA is internally consistent, a right preaching of the Word and administration of the sacraments cannot be understood apart from the office of ministry. Particularly useful on the relation between articles 5 and 7 of the CA are Edmund Schlink, *Theology of the Lutheran Confessions* (Philadelphia: Fortress, 1961), p. 202; Bernhard Lohse, "Die Einheit der Kirche nach der Confessio Augustana," in *Evangelium — Sakramente — Amt und die Einheit der Kirche: Die ökumenische Tragweite der Confessio Augustana,* Dialog der Kirchen, vol. 2, ed. Karl Lehmann and Edmund Schlink (Freiburg: Herder; Göttingen: Vandenhoeck & Ruprecht, 1982), p. 72; and Harding Meyer and Heinz Schütte, "The Concept of the Church in the Augsburg Confession," in *Confessing One Faith: A Joint Commentary on the Augsburg Confession by Lutheran and Catholic Theologians,* ed. George Wolfgang Forell and James F. McCue (Minneapolis: Augsburg, 1982), pp. 186f.

had introduced among "ceremonies instituted by men" did not break that unity, because uniformity in such ceremonies is not necessary to true unity.

Episcopal succession in general was not a theme at Augsburg. The issue was more narrowly the status and authority of the Catholic bishops. The Reformers held that submission to the jurisdiction of such bishops, especially when they oppressed the gospel and coercively upheld unevangelical practices, was neither sufficient nor necessary to the true unity of the church.

Decisive for the logic of what the CA says on the unity of the church is an assumption that was self-evident to all sides at the time: that to have left the unity of the church was to have left the church entirely; it was to be no church at all and thus outside the pale of salvation. The *true* unity of the church, of which CA 7 speaks, is that unity which "is to continue forever" because it is that unity with other Christians which is inseparable from being one with Christ. Melanchthon makes this meaning of "true unity" clear in the *Apology* to the CA, written the following year and accepted by Lutherans as a normative interpretation of the CA:

> We are talking of the true, that is, spiritual unity, without which there can be no faith in the heart nor righteousness in the heart before God. For this unity, we say, a similarity of human rites . . . is not necessary. The righteousness of faith is not a righteousness tied to certain traditions.[11]

"True unity" is that unity which is inseparable from inclusion in the body of Christ and thus from salvation and justification. Preaching and sacraments, the means of grace by which God works faith and righteousness in sinners, mediate this unity because they mediate justification. If a human tradition, something other than the divinely instituted means of grace (and thus a work), were to be necessary to unity, it would also be necessary to salvation and thus to justification. For Melanchthon, then, what was at stake here was precisely what was necessary for salvation:

11. *Apology*, 7.31; Tappert, p. 174. I have slightly altered Tappert's translation to make clear that "spiritual" is a gloss on "true." The Latin reads: *"Nos de vera, hoc est, spirituali unitate loquimur."*

With a very thankful spirit we cherish the useful and ancient ordinances, especially when they contain a discipline that serves to educate and instruct the people and the inexperienced. Now, . . . another issue is involved. The question is whether the observance of human traditions is an act of worship necessary for righteousness before God. This must be settled in this controversy, and only then can we decide whether it is necessary for the true unity of the church that human traditions be alike everywhere.[12]

What is at stake in Article 7 is so important because it is not a matter of unity as something separable from the existence of the church as the assembly of the saints, that is, of the justified. To concede that something other than the gospel audible in the Word and visible in the sacraments was necessary to this true unity would also be to concede that something other than the gospel was necessary to justification. On this point, Lutherans judged they could not compromise.

True Unity and Life in Communion

If this interpretation of CA 7 is correct, what does it imply about life in communion and its possible conditions? At Augsburg, the argument centered precisely on the shape of life in communion. The true unity of the church is itself a visible communion in the proclamation of the one gospel and the celebration of the same sacraments (and, in a subordinate sense, in the ministry that serves them). The Lutherans did not argue, however, that this true unity or communion represented the end point, the totality of life in Christian community. *Because* we are one in faith and the sacraments, they said, we must seek a common life of love, both around pulpit and altar and also in the wider Christian life.[13]

12. *Apology,* 7.33f; Tappert, pp. 174f.
13. George Lindbeck has rightly noted:

When this [the Confession's historical context] is remembered . . . , it becomes evident that Article VII assumes that there is a necessary connection, though not an identity, between what it calls "the true unity of the church" and full communion understood as an ecclesiastical fellowship with some degree of common governance. When true unity is present, the breaking or absence of outward communion is wrong. Everyone agreed to this in the

This mandated movement from true unity to wide-ranging communion can be seen in the way that both Luther and Melanchthon sometimes refer to love as that which binds together the church. In his Large Catechism, Luther says that the church "possesses a variety of gifts, yet is united in love without sect or schism."[14] In the Smalcald Articles, he says that "the church cannot be better governed and maintained than by having all of us live under one head, Christ, and by having all the bishops equal in office . . . and diligently joined together in unity of doctrine, faith, sacraments, prayer, works of love, etc."[15] Paul Althaus summarizes Luther on this communion in love that should grow out of common participation in Christ: "The marvelous transaction, the 'joyful exchange,' the 'sharing of goods' between Christ and men also means that there is a complete exchange, an unconditional sharing of life, of goods, and of troubles by this people among themselves. The body lives *one* life."[16] When the Augsburg Confession was paraphrased in 1536 for the sake of a possible alliance between Henry VIII of England and the Lutheran princes, the *satis est* clause was expanded to include a reference to love:

> It is sufficient for the maintenance of true unity that there be unity in the right teaching of the Gospel and in the correct use of the sacraments and that people live in love with one another in accordance with [the] Gospel, as St. Paul says: "One faith, one baptism, etc."[17]

---

sixteenth century. ("The Meaning of Satis Est, or Tilting in the Ecumenical Wars," *Lutheran Forum* 26, no. 4 [Nov. 1992]: 21f.)

On the general relation between the true unity referred to in CA 7 and a more extensive communion, see "The Relation between *Satis Est* and Full Communion: An Opinion from the Institute for Ecumenical Research, Strasbourg," in *A Commentary on "Ecumenism: The Vision of the ELCA,"* ed. William G. Rusch (Minneapolis: Augsburg, 1990), pp. 105-15.

14. Luther, *Large Catechism,* II:51; Tappert, p. 417.

15. Smalcald Articles, II.4.9; Tappert, p. 300.

16. Paul Althaus, *The Theology of Martin Luther* (Philadelphia: Fortress, 1966), p. 305.

17. Slightly altered from the English translation in N. S. Tjernagel, *Henry VIII and the Lutherans: A Study in Anglo-Lutheran Relations from 1521 to 1547* (St. Louis: Concordia, 1965), p. 273. The original text in Latin and German is in *Die Wittenberger Artikel von 1536,* ed. Georg Mentz (Darmstadt: Wissenschaftliche Buchgesellschaft, 1968).

There is no indication that this paraphrase was understood to say anything different than the original text. It was drafted by Melanchthon but issued under Luther's name and with his cooperation.

The Reformers understood the unity referred to in CA 7 *foundationally* rather than *exclusively*. The true unity referred to in CA 7 is both gift and call, to use recent ecumenical jargon. Its gift, the gift of Christ in whom we are united with our brothers and sisters, itself calls us to a broader realization of that unity in a living communion. This pursuit of communion is no more an *adiaphoron,* something one can take or leave as one wishes, than is love of neighbor.

Implicit in everything the Lutherans did at Augsburg was a distinction between that which had not been lost and could not be lost as long as the Word is rightly preached and the sacraments rightly administered, namely, the true unity of the church in Jesus Christ, and that which was crumbling and in danger of being broken, namely, that wider communion with the Western church and its historic leadership. True unity demanded that this wider communion be sought. As the Preface to the CA states, "we on our part shall not omit doing anything, in so far as God and conscience allow, that may serve the cause of Christian unity."[18] Yet, as this statement shows, a limit existed. Unless convinced by Scripture or right reason, the Lutherans were not willing either implicitly or explicitly to recant their essential commitments to what they understood to be the gospel of justification and its implications. To abandon the proclamation of the gospel described in Part 1 of the Confession would have been an explicit recantation; to abandon the reforms described in Articles 22-27 would have been an implicit recantation.

Within this limit, however, the Lutherans were willing to go much farther than anything represented by the Concordat. It occurred to no one at the time that something like the modern denominational order, friendly tolerance with occasional cooperation, could represent an adequate model of a reconciled Western church. For the sake of communion (among other things), the Lutherans were willing to resubmit to the jurisdiction of the Catholic bishops if such submission did not involve implicit or explicit recantation. They did not demand that the Catholic authorities agree with or adopt the practice and theology laid out in the CA. They asked only for the freedom to continue these

18. Augsburg Confession, §13; Tappert, p. 26.

reforms in their own lands. Most notable for our concerns here, they did not insist that the Catholics agree with them on episcopacy. For the Catholic authorities, the jurisdiction of the bishops was a "condition of communion." The Lutherans at Augsburg did not demand that the Catholics abandon in either word or deed episcopal authority as a condition of communion, if such jurisdiction were made compatible with the gospel. The Lutherans were not conceding their contention that it was not necessary, but they were not insisting that the Catholics abandon the argument that it was. For the sake of the wider communion that must follow from true unity, they were willing to accept what for the Catholics were conditions of communion.

If one follows the reasoning of the dissent, then the Lutherans were acting contrary to right Reformation principles. But the Augsburg proposal was not a function of Melanchthon's alleged tendency to compromise, nor was it a momentary aberration. The essentials of the Augsburg proposal were worked out in cooperation with Luther prior to the Diet.[19] Luther himself states the proposal (admittedly, in a highly aggressive fashion) in his *Exhortation to All Clergy Assembled at Augsburg,* written just prior to the Diet.[20]

Nor was the proposal abandoned by the Lutherans after the failure of the negotiations at Augsburg. Melanchthon repeats it in the *Apology.*[21] When Count Palatine and the Archbishop of Mainz sought to reopen discussions in the spring of 1531, the Wittenbergers essentially repeated the Augsburg offer to resubmit to a form of Catholic episcopal jurisdiction that would permit the proclamation of the gospel.[22] The same offer is found in Luther's Smalcald

---

19. On Luther's relation to the development of the CA, see Wilhelm Maurer, "Erwägungen und Verhandlungen über die geistliche Jurisdiktion der Bischöfe vor und während des augsburger Reichstags von 1530," in *Die Kirche und ihr Recht: Gesammelte Aufsätze zum evangelischen Kirchenrecht,* ed. Gerhard Müller and Gottfried Seebass (Tübingen: J. C. B. Mohr [Paul Siebeck], 1976), pp. 213ff.

20. English translation in *Luther's Works,* vol. 34, *Career of the Reformer* (Philadelphia: Fortress, 1960), 4:49ff.

21. *Apology,* 14; Tappert, pp. 214f.

22. On these developments, see Martin Brecht, *Martin Luther: Shaping and Defining the Reformation 1521-1532,* trans. James L. Schaaf (Minneapolis: Fortress, 1990), pp. 421ff. In a memorandum of May 1531, the Wittenberg theologians, including Luther, repeated the Augsburg proposal: "If now the bishops are willing to permit the pure teaching of the gospel and our priests, then our priests should submit and be obedient to them as bishops (not as wolves)" (*WA* Br., 6:113; my translation).

Articles[23] of 1537 and it was again made at the dialogue between the Lutherans and the Catholic authorities at Regensburg in 1541.[24] The Lutherans ceased to press the proposal only after the collapse of the final reconciliation attempt at Regensburg and, even more, after the Smalcald War and the Council of Trent dramatically altered the background conditions against which discussions could be carried forward.[25] The willingness to submit to "conditions of communion" that did not involve recantation of the gospel was the consistent Lutheran policy as long as reconciliation appeared a live possibility.[26]

In the CA, then, the Lutherans were insisting that they had not left the true unity of the church, and had not abandoned anything essential to the identity of the church in their reforms. This true unity, however, drives Christians to seek wider communion and reconciliation. In the pursuit of reconciliation, the Lutherans were willing to accept what were "conditions of communion" on the part of the Catholic authorities as long as such conditions did not either implicitly or explicitly imply a recantation of the gospel as the Lutherans understood it.

23. Smalcald Articles, III.10; Tappert, p. 314.

24. See Georg Kretschmar, "Der Reichstag von Regensburg 1541 und seine Folgen im protestantischen Lager. Verpaßte Gelegenheit oder Stunde der Wahrheit?" in *Das Regensburger Religionsgespräch im Jahr 1541: Rückblick und aktuelle ökumenische Perspektiven* (Regensburg: Verlag Friedrich Pustet, 1992), p. 59. Kretschmar notes that while the structure of the offer remained unchanged, by 1541 the Lutherans were demanding a much clearer commitment to the gospel from the bishops than they were at Augsburg in 1530.

25. On the changes in the 1540s that essentially closed off the discussions, see ibid., pp. 72f. and also Kretschmar, "The Diet of Regensburg and the 1541 Variata of the Augsburg Confession," in Carter Lindberg, ed., *Piety, Politics, and Ethics: Reformation Studies in Honor of G. W. Forell*, vol 3 of *Sixteenth Century Essays and Studies* (Kirksville, Mo.: Sixteenth Century Journal Publishers, 1984), p. 102.

26. Robert Goeser, one of the two signatories of the dissent from the Concordat, has denied the argument here in a series of articles: "The Historic Episcopate and the Lutheran Confessions," *Lutheran Quarterly* 1 (1987): 214-32; "Word, Ministry, and Episcopacy according to the Confessions," *Lutheran Quarterly* 4 (1990): 45-59; "Word of God, Church, and Ministry," *dialog* 29 (1990): 195-202. I have briefly addressed Goeser's arguments in "A Reply to Robert Goeser," *dialog* 30 (1991): 63-66. Besides having evidential problems, Goeser's interpretation forces him to conclude either that the Reformers were unconsciously contradicting their own deepest principles in making the reconciliation offer at Augsburg or that they were dissembling, making an offer for appearance' sake that they had no intention of carrying through. As I noted in my reply, Goeser comes close to saying both of these things at various points.

Conditions of Communion and the Concordat

Care must be taken in any move from the Augsburg Confession to the Concordat. On the one hand, the stakes are much lower in the Concordat than they were at Augsburg. The Concordat is of considerable ecumenical significance, but it will not restore the broken unity of Western Christendom, which the Augsburg discussions might have averted.

On the other hand, the ecumenical problems surrounding episcopacy and ordained ministry have become more difficult. In 1530, the Lutheran estates had not yet begun to ordain their own clergy in significant numbers. Thus, a question that did not need to be discussed at Augsburg was whether the Catholics would recognize Lutheran ordinations. The move by the Lutherans over the following years to ordain their own clergy changed this situation. In ordaining clergy, a body is making a strong ecclesial claim. Even if that body grants that ordination in isolation from the fellowship of the universal church is undesirable and to a degree irregular, by ordaining it is exercising an important task of oversight that only the church can exercise. If Lutherans have in fact not left the true unity of the church and if they ordain, then such ordinations must be adequate for a true sacramental ministry. Conversely, if another church insists that such persons be reordained or supplementally ordained as a condition of receiving their ministry, such an insistence suggests a belief that these Lutherans have in fact left the true unity of the church.

This last comment points the way back from the sixteenth century to the Concordat. We can now see the importance of the distinction noted at the beginning of this essay between the senses in which the Concordat does and does not make episcopal succession conditional. The important question here is whether the Concordat involves conditions that would imply that the ELCA needed to recant any commitments it understands to be central to the Reformation understanding of the gospel. The ELCA (and the Episcopal Church and every church body) has things to repent. The ELCA certainly can (I would say should) grant that in lacking the episcopacy in succession, it has lacked something at least desirable and of not inconsiderable significance. It would be quite something else for the ELCA to grant that it had left the true unity of the church referred to in CA 7. Such an admission would call into question the Reformation understanding

65

of what constitutes the life of the church. If the Concordat involved a reordination or supplemental ordination of ELCA clergy, that might seem to imply that the ELCA in fact had left that true unity. Thus, it is of the utmost importance that the Concordat in fact calls for no such reordination or supplemental ordination. The recognition and mutual interchangeability of clergy from the outset of the new relationship means that each church is recognizing the other as genuinely church, capable of ordaining to the ministry of Word and sacrament, an action that only the church can perform.

The decisive conditionality in relation to episcopacy and episcopal succession thus turns on whether the actual ordination of all ELCA clergy in episcopal succession is made a precondition of receiving their ministry. The breakthrough in the Concordat is its elimination of this problem.

But what about the second form of conditionality, that which in fact is present in the Concordat? The Episcopal Church (and probably every other Anglican church in the world) is unwilling to enter full communion without a commitment from the other church to enter episcopal succession. The ELCA's commitment to enter episcopal succession is thus a condition of communion. Should this conditionality form a barrier to Lutheran acceptance of the Concordat?

We need to focus this question carefully. It does not concern whether episcopal succession is a good or bad thing in general, whether entering episcopal succession would be good for the ELCA, or whether such an action would further the ecumenical movement as a whole. The question is simply, Does the fact that the acceptance of episcopal succession is a condition of communion for the Episcopal Church mean that the ELCA must reject the Concordat?

I have already shown that the Augsburg Confession centrally involved the acceptance of even more far-reaching conditions of communion. The dissent's argument that Lutheran principles embodied in CA 7 require the rejection of the Concordat is thus historically dubious. An analysis of the argument offered in the dissent further weakens its case. The dissent states: "In this *Concordat* . . . the historic episcopate is made to be a necessity for church fellowship *and thus* essential to the unity of the church" (emphasis added). The dissent assumes the validity of the deduction: If something is a condition of communion, it is *thus* a condition for the (true) unity of the church referred to in CA 7. Crucial for the Concordat is that it allows a distinction to be drawn between what the dissent equates: What is necessary for the true unity of the one church and the conditions that any particular church may contextually stipulate as needed for full communion.

All agree that true unity drives us toward deeper communion; true unity without deeper communion is a self-contradiction. Yet a church body may have contextual, historical, or even theological grounds for specifying certain conditions of communion beyond that which is strictly necessary to the true unity of the church. Such grounds would certainly need to be exceedingly weighty, but they are imaginable. Lutherans may maintain that they put no conditions on communion beyond those necessary for true unity, but historically some Lutheran churches have, as a condition of communion, insisted upon formal subscription to the Augsburg Confession — which certainly is not a strict necessity for true unity.[27] For a variety of reasons, Anglicans have made the common participation in the historic episcopate a condition of full communion. (The Chicago Quadrilateral of the Episcopal Church also specifies the Nicene Creed as "essential to the restoration of unity," although the creed in itself is certainly not essential to the true unity strictly conceived.)[28]

The great merit of the Concordat is that it clarifies the nature of this commitment to episcopacy in the context of ELCA-Episcopal Church relations. The Anglican action called for by the Concordat is plausible only on the basis of some distinction between, on the one hand, what is necessary for true unity and, on the other, what constitute conditions of communion.[29] By accepting the ministry of ELCA

27. A Lutheran-Anglican example: In 1718 the bishops of the Church of Sweden rejected an inquiry from the Anglican bishop of London about closer relations between the Churches of Sweden and England. They judged the Church of England to be Reformed; a number of the Swedish bishops insisted that explicit subscription to the CA must be a condition of communion. See Carl Henrik Lyttkens, *The Growth of Swedish-Anglican Intercommunion between 1833 and 1922,* Bibliotheca Theologiae Practicae, vol. 24 (Lund: Gleerups Förlag, 1970), pp. 149f.

28. If conditionality beyond agreement in gospel and sacraments is in itself sufficient grounds for the rejection of an ecumenical proposal, then insistence upon any particular verbal form is most likely also objectionable. Thus, Lutherans should also object to the second article of the Quadrilateral (which relates to the creed) as well as to the fourth (which relates to episcopacy).

29. Such a distinction has been justified in Anglican theology on various

clergy ordained outside of episcopal succession, the Episcopal Church would then be implicitly saying that the presence of episcopal succession is not necessary for the "true unity" referred to in CA 7 (otherwise, the ELCA would not be a church and could not ordain).[30] Nevertheless, the Concordat does not ask the Episcopal Church to abandon its commitment to episcopal succession. Within the terms of the Concordat, the Episcopal Church can continue to hold a commitment to episcopal succession as a condition of communion, but in such a way that need not call into question the Lutheran commitment to what constitutes the true unity of the church.

Within the Concordat, Lutherans are not called on to agree in either word or deed with an Anglican understanding of episcopacy as a condition of communion. The ELCA will remain free to seek communion with both episcopal and nonepiscopal churches. That ELCA-ordained ministries will come into episcopal succession should not inhibit such relations. Communion among the member churches of the Lutheran World Federation (LWF) is not hindered by differences among them in relation to episcopal succession. Within the Concordat, the ELCA will be able to witness to the desirability of episcopal succession by adopting it, while also witnessing to its nonnecessity by remaining in fellowship with the nonepiscopal churches of the LWF (and perhaps also with the Reformed churches involved in *A Common Calling*).

---

grounds. The distinction between the *esse* and the *plene esse* of the church might justify such a distinction. The Lambeth Appeal of 1920 justified the need for the historic episcopate not on the basis of its necessity to the being of the church, but rather on its promise as the form of ordained ministry capable of winning the widest possible recognition. In this case the distinction is drawn precisely in the hope of the ecumenical reconciliation with the greatest number in the long run.

30. This implication could be avoided if the Episcopal Church understood its action as one of "economy," or if the Episcopal Church were to interpret the commitment of the ELCA to enter episcopal succession as itself remedying any defect in ELCA orders. It must here suffice to say that neither interpretation has much basis in the Concordat. As far as I can see, the possibility of private interpretations along such lines is almost impossible to eliminate, but such private interpretations remain simply private.

Red Herrings and the Ecumenical Spirit
of the Reformation

In this essay I have focused almost exclusively on the issue of conditionality in relation to the Concordat, and as such have sought to aid in a certain ground-clearing operation. This issue is, for the most part, a red herring. Lutheran argumentative energies can be much more usefully invested in the question of whether the adoption of episcopal succession and the creation of a new relation with the Episcopal Church is a good idea. The majority who endorsed the Concordat did not look upon episcopal succession as an onerous condition imposed by the Anglicans but as something positively desirable, both for the sake of the ELCA and for the sake of the broader cause of reconciliation. The dissent clearly disagrees with this judgment, without saying so explicitly.[31] A focus on this question would produce a far more substantial and informative debate.

Within the question of conditionality, however, lurks a broader issue. Is Lutheranism so committed to the essential arbitrariness of church order that it must make a similar commitment to such arbitrariness a condition of communion? The logic of the dissent naturally leads to such a result. According to this logic, if another church makes any matter of church order a condition of communion, then Lutherans must reject such fellowship, whether the matter of church order involved is good, bad, or indifferent. In effect, the dissent makes the nonconditionality of all matters beyond gospel and sacraments narrowly defined itself a condition of communion. To accept the logic of the dissent is to limit Lutheran ecumenical involvement to those churches which agree that church order is arbitrary. A common theme of a certain sort of Lutheran self-celebration has been the "ecumenical freedom" that CA 7 allegedly makes possible. In the dissent one can see how this freedom can become highly limiting. Only with those who agree with CA 7 (read in a certain way) could we have communion.

31. The dissent states: "We believe that Christian ecumenism best serves the apostolic mission of the church when it provides for the speaking of God's Word and the administration of the Sacraments in a multitude of ways appropriate to a variety of times and places." The unstated conclusion is that the historic episcopate would close off this desirable diversity. Whether this conclusion in fact is valid is another question.

A merit of the Concordat is that it allows Lutherans to maintain their conviction that episcopacy and episcopal succession is not a necessity to fellowship even while moving the ELCA into the stream of episcopal succession. Such a move removes an obstacle to possible fellowship not only with Anglicans, but in the future perhaps with other episcopal churches. It also puts no new obstacles in the way of fellowship with nonepiscopal churches. If our desire is to be true to the ecumenical intent of the Augsburg Confession, which would have brought the Lutherans back into the fellowship of the wider Western church while preserving their commitment to the gospel and its implications, then the Concordat is a step in the right direction.

Gospel and Church: The Proposed Concordat between Lutheran and Episcopal Churches in the USA

WOLFHART PANNENBERG

In the historical confrontation between the churches of the Reformation and Rome, the Anglican church and the Episcopalian churches of the Anglican Communion have a special role. Anglican theology has been keenly aware of this potentially mediating role and of the responsibility arising from it. The traditional emphasis on the heritage of the patristic church in general and on the historical episcopate in particular provides the Anglican and Episcopalian churches with special opportunities and responsibilities in the contemporary ecumenical situation. They have taken up these opportunities and responsibilities in the Roman-Anglican dialogue on the one hand, and in the approach toward full communion with the Lutheran churches on the other. Therefore, the proposed Concordat is a highly significant ecumenical step, not only with regard to Lutheran-Episcopalian communion, but beyond that in the context of the relationship of the Reformation churches to the Catholic tradition of the church and especially to Rome and the Orthodox churches. In all of these relations, the question of ministry and its classical expression in the episcopal ministry is in the focus of ecumenical discussions. A possible solution of this issue in Lutheran-Episcopalian relations could therefore be of far-reaching ecumenical significance.

According to the Lutheran confessional position, agreement on the teaching of the gospel *(doctrina evangelii)* is the basis for church unity. Correspondingly, those involved in the third phase of the Lutheran-Episcopal dialogue in the USA have worked out a statement on the gospel and its implications. This very fine statement takes its

71

point of departure from the eschatological "grounding" of the gospel together with the significance of Jesus' resurrection for the church's proclamation that in Jesus Christ the "new age" of God has already begun, which the individual experiences in the act of baptism. From this point of view are developed the implications of the gospel for the understanding of God, of the church, of its relation to the world, and of its mission.

Remarkably, a consensus was reached on these matters, while no complete consensus was obtained in the study on the episcopal ministry and its place in the church. Although the commission agreed that the Lutheran confessional writings accept an episcopal ministry of oversight in the life of the church, some disagreement remained concerning the contention that such a ministry is essential in the church. This remaining disagreement was expressed in a dissenting report of two Lutheran members of the commission, who insisted that according to the Augsburg Confession "the Word of God rightly preached and rightly administered in the sacraments of Baptism and the Lord's Supper constitutes the sole and sufficient basis for the true unity of the Christian church."[1] It is not quite clear whether the dissenting report intends to say that the phrase from CA 7, by focusing on the teaching of the gospel and the administration of the sacraments, excludes the ministry altogether from what is essential to the unity of the church, or whether it only rejects such a claim for the historic episcopate as a particular form of that ministry.

Lutheran theologians have sometimes defended the contention that according to CA 7 the ministry as such does not belong to the basis of church unity. But that stands against CA 5, which says that God instituted the ministry of teaching the gospel and of exhibiting the sacraments. On the basis of CA 5 one has to assume that the reference to teaching the gospel and administering the sacraments in CA 7 includes by implication the ministry entrusted with such teaching and administration, to the effect that any consensus on the doctrine of the gospel and the administration of the sacraments also includes the ministry. But this leaves open the question as to the concrete historical form of that ministry. Thus perhaps the dissenting report

---

1. William A. Norgren and William G. Rusch, eds., *"Toward Full Communion" and "Concordat of Agreement," Lutheran-Episcopal Dialogue, Series 3* (Minneapolis: Fortress; Cincinnati: Forward Movement, 1991), p. 111.

rejects only the position that makes a concrete historical form of the ordained ministry, the historic episcopate, in distinction from other forms of that ministry, "a necessity for church fellowship and thus essential to the unity of the church."

Discussion of this question must seek to clarify the relationship between the rise of the episcopal ministry and other ministries in early Christianity. Only by doing so can one determine the relationship between the episcopate and the ordained ministry in general. Considering the importance of this question, it is astonishing how little is said on this issue in the document "Toward Full Communion." While the document mentions that Paul refers to "bishops and deacons" in Philippi (Phil. 1:1),[2] it does not attempt to clarify what these titles mean, especially the plural "bishops," which suggests, after all, that a plurality of "bishops" existed in that one city. Regarding the Pastoral Epistles, the document says only that they "envisage several orders of ministry," but again one misses some reflection on how these different orders of ministry are related to each other.

Recent exegetical work provided such clarification beyond the older finding that the office of bishops and deacons (as mentioned in Phil. 1:1) was rooted in the Pauline congregations, while the order of presbyters goes back to the Jewish form of administering the life of a congregation. John Reumann recently spoke of an "emerging view of scholars that the office of *episkopos* originated in the house church,"[3] meaning a group of believers regularly assembling in a particular private house. Reumann refers to earlier contributions on this issue by E. Dassmann (1984) and G. Schöllgen (1986 and 1988). To these names one should add Jürgen Roloff, who in his commentary on 1 Timothy traces the development from the early function of "bishops" as leaders in house churches like those at Philippi to the leadership in a local congregation in the early postapostolic period.[4]

These exegetical findings have direct bearing on the ecumenical problems at hand. One asks first what kind of entity is the "historic episcopate" (by contrast to later theories about it), and second, how it is related to the task of the church's ministry in general. The answer

2. Ibid., p. 38.

3. J. Reumann, "Contributions of the Philippian Community to Paul and to Earliest Christianity," *New Testament Studies* 39 (1993): 438-57, 449f. See his entire section on *episkopoi* and *diakonoi*, pp. 446-50.

4. J. Roloff, *Der erste Brief an Timotheus* (Zurich: Benzinger, 1988), pp. 171ff.

to the first question has to be that in the course of history several forms of episcopate emerged, not one, and that in the earliest history of the church the title "bishop" referred successively to the leader of a house church, the pastor of a local congregation, and finally the leader of the region surrounding a city *(diocesis)* or even of a province. The Protestant pastor, then, does not serve a ministry completely different form the "historic episcopate," but his ministry corresponds to one of the forms in the development of the early Christian episcopate itself. The Lutheran Reformers had some knowledge of this fact through Hieronymus, though it was mixed up with the question of the relationship between bishops and presbyters, a different though related issue.

Even more important is the second question of how the ordained ministry of the bishop is related to the ministry of the church in general. An answer can be found in the reasons behind the development of the title "bishop" in early Christianity. The rise of the bishop from the function of leading a house church among others within a city to the leading position in a local congregation seems to be related to a problem that the second and third Christian generations experienced: how to secure after the death of the apostles the continuity of the congregations in the line of their teaching.[5] The earlier forms of ministry in the young congregations could not easily meet this new task. The presbyters had originally no teaching function, the teachers no administrative authority. So finally the ministry of bishops was expanded and adapted to the task of preserving the congregation in the line of the apostolic gospel. In fact, then, the bishops became the "successors" of the apostles in that function, although the idea that the apostles formally transferred their authority to successors of their choice seems to idealize a more complicated historical process.

The result of these reflections is that the ministry of "bishop" as it developed after the death of the apostles was responsible for the unity of the church in each place with its apostolic origin, that is, with the teaching of the apostolic gospel. And this responsibility is met primarily by teaching the gospel. That the bishop presides at the eucharist is also related to the issue of unity: The unity of the congregation in the faith of the one gospel is in substance their unity in

---

5. See the discussion of this issue in my *Systematische Theologie,* vol. 3 (Göttingen: Vandenhoeck & Ruprecht, 1993), pp. 412ff.

Christ, whom the bishop represents in presiding at the eucharist as well as in authoritatively teaching the apostolic gospel.

If such is the essence of the episcopal ministry, that ministry can hardly be considered an unnecessary addition to the authority of the gospel itself, like the Dissenting Report seems to assume. The gospel is effective through the ministry that teaches it and thereby keeps the congregation united in the one faith that it inherited from the apostles and shares with the entire church.

Now it could be said that this is the pastoral ministry in distinction from the "historic episcopate." But it has been suggested already that this distinction is of secondary importance. What the churches of the Reformation called the pastoral ministry is in effect the episcopal ministry in one of its earliest forms.

The task of preserving the church and its unity in the faith of the apostolic gospel is to be met on all levels of the life of the church: not only on the local level, but also on a regional level with regard to a multitude of local congregations, and finally on the universal level of the life of the entire church. The ministry of regional supervision exercises basically the same function that the pastor fulfills on the local level. The matter is always unity in the apostolic gospel. The distinction between the local and regional levels of the exercise of that task are of secondary importance. It is always the same ministry, the ministry of preserving the church in the unity of the apostolic faith. That, however, is historically the task of the episcopal ministry in all its changing forms. This basic fact is blurred by the customary restriction of the title "bishop" to the ministry of regional supervision. But of course this function is a necessary one in the life of the church, if on all levels of its life unity in the faith of the apostolic gospel has to be maintained. Therefore, the Lutheran tradition was always open to the need for a ministry of doctrinal supervision beyond the local level. And since the task of such a doctrinal supervision is related to the unity of the church in the apostolic gospel, it is implausible that such a form of *episkope* is not essential to the unity of the church.

Therefore, in my judgment, the Concordat between the Lutheran and the Episcopal churches has a sound theological basis, even more so than the document "Toward Full Communion" has been able to spell out.

The Evangelical Significance of the Historic Episcopate

R. R. RENO

> Now I appeal to you, brothers and sisters, by the name of
> our Lord Jesus Christ, that all of you be in agreement and
> that there be no divisions among you, but that you be
> united in the same mind and the same purpose.
>
> 1 Cor. 1:10

Suddenly, much more quickly than most of us expected, we are faced
with a real decision about Paul's exhortation to the Corinthians. The
proposed "Concordat of Agreement" between the Episcopal Church
and the Evangelical Lutheran Church of America offers an opportunity for two splinters of a fragmented body to offer a living No to
Paul's question, "Is Christ divided?" However, this opportunity requires close examination. We must ask critical questions about the
Concordat, and these are not questions about bureaucratic feasability,
ethnic loyalties, or denominational identities. The decisive questions
are about the gospel. Does the Concordat propose overcoming the
divisions within the body of Christ with real promise? Does the
Concordat allow Episcopalians and Lutherans to say, with Paul, that
they belong not to Cephas or to Apollos or to Paul himself, but to
Christ? In short, does the Concordat meet the conditions of gospel
integrity?

This question about the conditions of gospel integrity is crucial,
for the very question of conditions dominates evaluation of the Concordat. As the ELCA Dissenting Report appended to the Concordat

clearly demonstrates, a certain view of Reformation doctrine rejects any and all condition for full communion beyond unity in Word and sacrament. The very purpose of the Concordat is to orchestrate revisions in canon law, in seminary training, and, most important, in episcopal ordination. These revisions are necessary for — conditions for — the ELCA and ECUSA to enter into full communion. Hence, the Dissenting Report dissents and rejects the Concordat as a violation of the "evangelical purity" of the gospel. The question of conditions is also central to murmurings of Episcopal dissent. Opposite from Lutheran dissent, this criticism finds the Concordat inadequately conditional. The proposed immediate recognition of the "full authenticity" of ELCA ordained ministry is viewed as an implicit denial of the Anglican condition of historic episcopal succession, and thus a major violation of Anglicanism's commitment to the "catholic fullness" of the gospel. The debate is, then, necessarily about *conditions,* and rightly so, for as Paul wrote to the Corinthians, the unity of the church is found in the very concrete and particular condition of Christ — his lordship and our discipleship.

My goal is to convince the reader that the Concordat has integrity, because it embodies the promise of Christ. It is Christ conditioned, and therefore is both evangelical and catholic. For Christ is both the purity and fullness of God's love. To sustain these claims, I shall reject the notion that the Concordat encourages a compromise between the "catholic fullness" of Anglicanism and the "evangelical purity" of Lutheranism. Instead, I shall argue that the central mandate of the Concordat — the absorption of the Lutheran ordained ministry into the historic episcopate — provides a striking opportunity to consider the worldly form of the gospel. This will involve identifying the conditions that the Concordat establishes for full communion, conditions that are precisely the glory of the gospel. As such, the way is clear to consider the historic episcopate as a fuller expression of Lutheranism's "evangelical" emphasis on the free word of grace in the gospel, and an opportunity to give evangelical depth to Anglicanism's "catholic" embrace of episcopal practice. Viewed in this way, the Concordat becomes a renewing challenge to both partners.

Evangelical Purity and Catholic Fullness

The ecumenical dialogue leading up to the Concordat uses a number of distinctions to guide Lutherans and Episcopalians toward full communion. The most basic is the distinction between an Anglican concern about the "catholic fullness" of the gospel and a typically Lutheran focus on the "evangelical purity" of the gospel.[1] When considering the Concordat, this conflict between "fullness" and "purity" comes into sharp focus, for at the center of that document is the historic episcopate. Episcopalians have a stubborn allegiance to the institution that gives them their name. For Anglicans, though the ministry of the bishop is, perhaps, a postapostolic development, this in no way compromises the need to conform to such a pattern, for the structure of the threefold ministry is no fall from original grace. Rather, the development of institutionalized ministry, and the ministry of the bishop in particular, is a growth in the grace of gospel fellowship. Bishops are part of the fugue of tradition that renders the basic theme of the gospel in its most beautiful aspect.

Not so, replies the Lutheran. The "purity of the gospel" — faith in the promise of justification — speaks against *requiring* bishops as a condition for true and godly church polity. Granted, Anglicans do not equate the historic episcopate with the gospel. Granted, Anglicans do not always speak in one voice about the significance and function of bishops. Yet, whenever we sit down to discuss full communion, observes the Lutheran, Anglicans always treat the historic episcopate as a necessity, a nonnegotiable. Flexible and imprecise as they may be on all other confessional matters, Anglicans consistently seem to make the historic episcopate into a condition for faithful church practice. But this is impossible. For to require bishops implies that something more than God's promise of justification in Christ is necessary for salvation, a promise proclaimed in Word and sacrament, and this violates the unconditional freedom of God's offer in Christ. So reasons the Lutheran.

Faced with this conflict between "fullness" and "purity," the ecumenical dialogue has lit upon two allied distinctions in order to

---

1. See "Toward Full Communion" in *"Toward Full Communion" and "Concordat of Agreement": Lutheran-Episcopal Dialogue, Series 3,* ed. William A. Norgen and William B. Rusch (Minneapolis: Augsburg; Cincinnati: Forward Movement, 1991), §7.

move beyond this impasse. Both attempt to explain how the sentiments of "fullness" and "purity" can coexist within a common definition of an apostolic or gospel-centered church fellowship. The first distinction is between the functional and ontological character of the ordained ministry, and the second is between the sign and substance of apostolicity.[2] Both distinctions are useful, yet neither is powerful enough to remove the dilemma facing Lutherans, and both tempt Episcopalians to ignore the evangelical challenge of full communion. We need to understand why these distinctions fail in order to prepare ourselves for a more radical solution.

When applied to the historic episcopate, the distinction between functional and ontological allows us to recognize that the historic episcopate is not *ontologically* constitutive of gospel faithfulness. Bishops serve the gospel promise, but they are not the promise itself. However, their sevice of oversight is valuable, perhaps *functionally* indispensible. Indeed, although they do not necessarily concentrate oversight in the person of a bishop, Lutheranism has always recognized the necessity of parallel functions — a public call to ordination, confessional conformity, an informal seminary magisterium for collegial exhortation and censure — lending support to the judgment that the function of episcopal oversight is woven into the fabric of the Christian community.

Just as the distinction between the functional and the ontological tries to balance "purity" with "fullness," so also does the distinction between sign and substance. This distinction suggests that the historic episcopate is not part of the *substance* of the church's apostolic witness, but rather is a *sign* of that apostolic witness. Yet again, it would seem that the Lutheran party of "purity" finds a way to affirm the importance and efficacy of the historic episcopate while still resisting a dilution of the gospel. This opens the way forward for the Lutheran adoption of episcopal ordination in historic succession as a second-order symbolic and functional rather than a first-order substantial or ontological form of the gospel (Conc, §3). Episcopal practice is adopted while Reformation commitments remain unviolated. At the same time, the Anglican party of "fullness" finds a way to affirm the "purity" of the gospel while still preserving a functional role and symbolic purpose for the historic episcopate. This opens the way

2. Ibid., §§12-13.

forward to a recognition of the "full authenticity" of Lutheran ordained ministry (Conc, §4). Lutheran confessional definitions are affirmed while retaining the functional and symbolic importance of episcopal polity. Thus, "fullness" recognizes "purity" and "purity" embraces "fullness."

Or so it seems. In fact, the two distinctions may allow, but they do not necessarily promote recognition or embrace. For both Episcopalians and Lutherans, the two distinctions threaten to exacerbate a dichotomy between polity and proclamation that already cripples the two churches. The two distinctions tempt rather than challenge. They tempt us to say that the Concordat and the resultant full communion need have no implications for our understanding of the *substance* of the gospel. They tempt us to think that the Concordat merely addresses second-order questions about how we *signify* the gospel. Such a temptation is dangerous, for it drains the evangelical integrity out of the Concordat. It allows us to think that the conditions for *communio in sacris* (e.g., eucharistic fellowship) are not intimately bound up with Paul's preaching of Christ crucified.

In order to avoid temptation and to sustain the evangelical integrity of the Concordat, we need to acknowledge directly and frankly that the Concordat does make the historic episcopate a condition of full communion between Lutherans and Episcopalians. And since eucharistic unity is an imperative of the gospel, the Concordat may be said to establish a condition for the fulfillment of that imperative — a conditon for the gospel. Neither Lutherans nor Episcopalians are particularly eager to hear this news. Lutherans confess that the gospel is "unconditional," and think that conditions for the gospel such as those imposed by the Concordat conflict with that confession. Episcopalians are less directly threatened, but in the end are perhaps less willing to accept the historic episcopate as a condition for the gospel. Episcopalians are too often unwilling to see or to allow their ecclesiastical practice to be infused and controlled by the gospel. Yet in both cases we must not avoid the fact that what we confess is intimately bound up with the way we live. And the point of this essay is to show how the gospel does not separate but rather brings together. Specifically, we need to recognize that the evangelical significance of the Concordat and its stumbling block, the historic episcopate, rests in the need to "go through" the condition of bringing Lutheran ministry under the sign of historic episcopal succession.

To make such a claim sensible to the Lutheran reader and challenging to the Episcopal reader, I need to show that *conditions* are integral to the gospel. Thus, I shall argue that a proper understanding of our justification in Christ concludes that the gospel glories in conditions: performative, christological, and soteriological. As I identify the conditions of the gospel I will show how the Concordat proposes a course of action that provides an opportunity to draw together proclamation and polity, what we confess and how we order our eucharistic fellowship.

Conditions of the Gospel

The Reformation doctrine of justification is shaped by the threat of Pelagianism. For the Pelagian, certain temporal conditions (i.e., "works") must be satisfied so that one might be justified. The clichéd Pelagian view pictures humans as litigious souls, pounding on the gates of heaven and demanding admission on the basis of the righteousness of their lives and the merit of their actions. Underneath this cliché is an important assumption: Our character and behavior have real standing in the eyes of God. Forensic metaphors flush out this assumption. For the Pelagian, at the bar of divine judgment, our actions are real and potentially decisive evidence either for us or against us. Our righteousness (or unrighteousness) counts. Such a possibility implies a basic continuum of divine and human existence. Recognizing this underlying implication is important, for the cliché of Pelagianism distorts the subtlety of its teaching. The Pelagian rarely argues that human righteousness is sufficient before the bar of divine judgment. The claim is more nuanced. Our efforts have a limited value or worth, but nonetheless, they are endorsed as necessary for justification. Though we need an advocate in Jesus Christ, we also must bear witness to ourselves through our own efforts and cooperation. However minimal, then, might be our righteousness, however puny our self-witnessing before God, our character and effort still remain as necessary conditions for the positive verdict of salvation. When we shift from the forensic metaphor to the language of promise, the Pelagian logic is clear. The promise of salvation in Christ must have an "if . . . then" structure. If we cooperate with grace and strive for righteousness, then we shall be saved. Fulfillment of the promise depends, at least in part, upon us. We must satisfy certain conditions.

The Reformation is a direct assault on the Pelagian assumption that human righteousness is comparable to divine righteousness and might, as a consequence, constitute a necessary condition for our salvation. At best, says Luther, our efforts are mere emptiness. At worst, they are self-damning. Our righteousness is not just minimal, it is irrelevant. Our presence before the judgment seat and the ultimate disposition of our case is purely gratuitous and absolutely dependent upon the righteousness of Christ. On the witness stand we can say nothing; Christ speaks entirely for us. Again, if we shift into the language of promise, the contrast with Pelagianism is plain. Where a conditional justification takes the form of an "if . . . then" promise, in Christ we encounter a "because . . . therefore" promise. Because the only begotten Son of God has died for our sins, therefore we are saved. The fulfillment of the promise has nothing to do with any requirements or conditions that we might satisfy. Instead, the efficacy of the promise depends entirely upon what God has done in Christ. Consequently, our destiny is unconditionally vested in Christ. This, for Luther, is the gospel.

I shall not argue that the Reformation insistence upon unconditional justification is correct. Extensive ecumenical discussion has identified a striking consensus about the *solus Christus* character of the Christian vision of salvation, a vision to which Lutheranism contributes the distinctive language of justification. Let us simply assume that the Pelagian position is untenable and turn our attention to the quite important question of whether promise of unconditional salvation in Christ rules out the sort of gospel conditions proposed by the Concordat.

In the first place, the gospel promise is unconditionally available and unconditionally triumphant. As a promise of the Lord of heaven and earth, the gospel of Christ necessarily triumphs over all impediments. Because the promiser has unconditional power to ensure fulfillment of the promise, the "because" is entirely sufficient to ensure the "therefore"; the gospel is utterly reliable. The unconditional nature of the promise accounts for the zest with which Luther asserts the immutability of divine foreknowledge in *De servo arbitrio*. To know that everything rests in God's predestining hands is, for Luther, a liberation. For this vests our future in the One whose will cannot be resisted, and, therefore, in the One whose promises may be trusted. This is the theological core of the doctrine of justification.

What is crucial for our assessment of the Concordat is that God's unconditionally triumphant love generates conditions! Precisely because the promise of justification takes a "because . . . therefore" form, things happen in our world that have the certainty and immutability of God's unconditional love. All the ambiguity of current chatter about the "eschatological dimension" of the gospel cannot corrupt the apostolic witness to the very real, present, and pressing "therefore" that follows the divine "because." Specifically, the unconditional promise of justification by faith creates and presupposes three types of conditions: performative, christological, and soteriological. If we can recognize these conditions as part of the glory of the gospel, then the Concordat's agreement to adopt the historic episcopate cannot be rejected simply because it takes the form of a condition or requirement for full communion.

The first condition is *performative*. The promise of God in Christ does not allow us to say that we are not ready to preach or that the world is not ready to hear. Nor does the triumphant promise allow us to sift out the offense and scandal of the gospel or to restructure the message to suit our spiritual needs. Because God's love is unconditionally available and unconditionally triumphant in Christ, we ought to preach that gospel of love without reservation and without modification. In other words, our commitment to the gospel in vigor and substance ought to be unconditional. Here, we discover what might be called the law of gospel performance: to proclaim fully and widely, accurately and promptly. The ecumenical dialogue leading up to the Concordat has clearly recognized this law as a basic condition for Christian communion. Unless the performative conditions are acknowledged, the gospel promise of God's love in Christ is not alive in the community. Both ecumenical teams have been able to discern a sufficient degree of commitment to gospel performance in both churches (in The Book of Common Prayer for Anglicans and The Book of Concord for Lutherans) to commend recognition of each as genuine apostolic communities.

Performative conditions are purely formal. These conditions have to do with our disposition toward the gospel — unconditional commitment — rather than with the content of the gospel. Thus, the Lutheran might acknowledge these performative conditions, yet reject the historic episcopate as another matter altogether. And this is quite justified, for adopting the historic episcopate entails much more than agreeing to inhabit the apostolic tradition with vigor. Such an agreement commits the ELCA to a quite particular form, a quite concrete and determinate dimension of the apostolic tradition, and that entails imposing substantive or particular conditions upon the gospel. Surely, thinks the Lutheran, *that* sort of condition impinges on the freedom of the gospel. Yet, a study of the christological and soteriological conditions of the gospel shows that substantive and particular conditions are exactly the ways in which God's promise of love is made real in our lives.

The christological conditions of the gospel emerge directly from the primary sense in which the promise of justification by faith is unconditional. These christological conditions establish the way in which the unconditional promise itself is made. Precisely because God's love for humans is unconditional, he has entered into a determinate course of action. God has committed himself to make that love unconditionally available and unconditionally successful. God has done, in other words, what is *necessary* in order to love unconditionally, and what he has done is chronicled in the Old and New Testaments. The crux of this particular course of action is summarized in the Nicene Creed.

> For us and for our salvation he came down from heaven: by the power of the Holy Spirit he became incarnate from the Virgin Mary, and was made man. For our sake he was crucified under Pontius Pilate; he suffered death and was buried. On the third day he rose again in accordance with the Scriptures; he ascended into heaven and is seated at the right hand of the Father. He will come again in glory to judge the living and the dead, and his kingdom will have no end.

In this sense, God is radically *conditioned:* conditioned by human life incarnate from the Virgin Mary, conditioned by suffering and death at the hands of Pontius Pilate, and conditioned by the commitment to come again in glory. These conditions do not violate or undermine the unconditional offer of justification by faith. On the contrary, they are the very conditions entailed by God's love. God *is* that Being Who so loved the world that he gave his only begotten Son that we might live in him eternally (John 3:16). Or, to translate into the structure of unconditional promise: "*Because* God accepts the human condition as and in the Incarnate Lord, *therefore* we are justified in his eyes." Such christological conditions are the consequences of God's utterly free and saving love, and these conditions — incarnation, suffering, death, and return — are the driving force, the "because," of the gospel promise.

Clearly, in this respect, we cannot deny that the gospel glories in quite particular and demanding conditions, especially the fateful condition of a certain first-century Palestinian Jew. Luther is alive to these christological conditions, and he expressly identifies the bondage of the Son of God to the man Jesus with the free offer of grace. Preaching on the Gospel of John, he writes, "You have already heard Christ refer to Himself as the Son of Man. With this term He wants to indicate that He is our true flesh and blood, which He obtained from the Virgin Mary and which contains eternal life. This is the article of justification." In other words, we are justified *because of* the particular, conditioned form of the Son of God in the man Jesus — by him and no other. Here, the Episcopalian concerned with the fullness of the gospel must feel the sharp point of God's entry into our lives in the form of God incarnate and Christ crucified. From this christological condition flow the performative conditions we considered above, conditions that Episcopalians might find absent in the life of their church, and the soteriological conditions that follow below, which challenge the Lutheran. In Luther's words, "The Holy Spirit insists that we never teach, know of, think of, hear, or accept any other god than this God [performative conditions], whose flesh and blood [christological conditions] we imprint on our hearts if we want to be saved [soteriological conditions]."[3] My claim is that the Lutheran concerned with evangelical purity and the Episcopalian concerned with catholic fullness must recognize that the historic episcopate might be exactly the sort of thing which the Holy Spirit imprints upon the life of the church.

Because of God's commitment to radical communion in the incarnation, certain soteriological conditions obtain. Paul suggests the nature of these conditions in his second letter to the Corinthians.

---

3. Both citations from *Luther's Works,* vol. 23 (St. Louis: Concordia, 1959), p. 129, quoted in David Yeago, "Gnosticism, Antinomianism and Reformation Theology," *Pro ecclesia* 2, no. 1 (1993): 47.

There he echoes an eschatological theme, the destruction of the "earthly tent" in which we presently find ourselves. However, this eschatological destruction is no demolition or exclusion of conditions. Instead, Paul emphasizes the accumulation of new and transforming conditions. He observes, "While we are still in this [earthly] tent, we groan under our burden; because we wish not to be unclothed but to be further clothed" (5:4). We seek not a lightning blast that might transport us from our current nomadic state in this world; rather, we are anxious for the quite wearable first fruits of the coming kingdom. Far from an eschatological limit that forbids the temporal presence of God's justifying action on our behalf, Paul seems to be suggesting that faithfulness involves an eschatological affirmation, a real sanctifying possibility *within* the life led inside the earthly tent.[4]

Paul continues in this same passage to elaborate the conditions of our new wardrobe. We are clothed in a quite specific manner: "The love of Christ urges us on, because we are convinced that one has died for all; therefore all have died. And he died for all, so that those who live might live no longer for themselves, but for him who died and was raised for them" (5:14-15). Here, Paul is nesting two "be-cause-therefore" promises. First, because Christ died for our sins, therefore we shall die to our sinful compulsions and in the place of the control of sin we shall live under conditions imposed by Christ. The control of sin is broken and the Lordship of Christ is established. The old conditions are destroyed and a new form of life is created. In other words, the christological conditions that God embraces in order to express his love creates conditions *in our lives*. Paul's second

---

4. Luther meditates on this possibility in his sermon on John 14:23-31:

This is indeed striking and lovely, and (as St. Peter says in 2 Peter 1:4), one of the precious and greatest of all the promises given to us poor, miserable sinners, that we are to be partakers of the very divine nature, and so highly honored that we are not only loved by God through Christ, and have his favor and grace as the highest, most precious of holy things, but we also have him, the Lord himself, dwelling wholly in us. For (Christ says) it is not to stop with love, that he takes his wrath away from us and has a gracious, fatherly heart toward us; rather, we are also to enjoy this love. Otherwise it would be a frustrated, lost love, according to the proverb about loving and not enjoying. (WA 21:458).

The reasoning is straighforward. For Luther, a *condition* of the success of divine love is that we, as recipients, enjoy that love by living in the very real, temporal possibilities of that love, "otherwise it would be a frustrated, lost love."

"because . . . therefore" promise provides specific content to this soteriological condition. His thinking takes this basic form: because God's unconditional love takes the form of Christ's death for us, therefore our new life shall no longer be for ourselves, but shall be a life for Christ. In short, the condition under which we are saved is as persons formed in Christ. This is the condition in which we receive our salvation: to live for Christ as he has died for us. And to live for Christ is not an inchoate, unformed possibility. Living for Christ involves a determinate form of worship (e.g., 1 Cor. 10:16-21) and service (e.g., 2 Tim. 1:8-14). In other words, the condition in which we receive our salvation is bound up with the reality of the church, a community of worship and service (Eph. 3:7-13; 4:1-16).

If Paul is right and we are to inhabit the free gift of salvation by conforming ourselves to Christ in worship and service, then Lutherans concerned with evangelical purity (rather than with Lutheran "identity" or "democratic principles" or any other ethno-cultural distractions) must be open, in principle, to the possibility that the historic episcopate might be a soteriological condition of the gospel. This does not settle the material question of whether, in fact, bishops are appropriately considered among the conditions of the gospel promise. (Later I shall suggest that bishops *should* be so considered.) The point is only that the gospel's immersion in conditions permits the inclusion of communal oversight as an enduring aspect of union with God in Christ. Further, Lutherans must be willing to do more than to accept the possibility of the historic episcopate in theory. Given the remarkable offer of full communion outlined in the Concordat, Lutherans concerned with evangelical purity must consider accepting the historic episcopate as a condition — symbolic, functional, or whatever — now!

Again, if Paul is right that the life of the church is a form of the gospel, then Episcopalians concerned with the catholic fullness must be deeply concerned with the question of whether ecclesiastical practices are genuinely and fully Christ-formed. Here, the point is that the gospel immersion in conditions, performative and especially christological, judges the various forms and expressions of communal oversight. Episcopalians cannot retreat from that judgment to the second order safety of "signs" and "functions." The substance of the gospel reaches into every aspect of the world, including the small corner of episcopal leadership. Moreover, the judgment of the gospel is not hypothetical. Given the confessional heritage of the Lutheran tradition, which the Concordat proposes the Episcopal Church draw into its practice of episcopal ordination, that judgment is real, tangible, and inescapable.

Fullness and Purity in the Concordat

We are now in a position to see the evangelical way forward for Lutherans and Episcopalians. Full communion is possible if Lutherans have sufficient faith to accept a fuller life in Christ. Full communion is possible if Episcopalian have sufficient life to accept a fuller judgment of faith in Christ. We need to look at both sides of the equation in turn.

The Lutheran Side

The Concordat mandates two significant changes in ELCA church order, both focused on the office of bishop. First, the ELCA must agree to revise its constitution to include all bishops, active or non-active, in the Conference of Bishops (§7). Second, the ELCA must promise always to include three Episcopal bishops, joining with three of its own in a common laying on of hands at the ordination of future ELCA bishops (§3). (The Episcopal Church must promise to do the same.) Both actions have multiple significance, but for Lutherans concerned with evangelical purity, the most important feature of both changes may be summed up in one word: durability.

Expanding membership in the Conference of Bishops signals the permanence of the episcopal office. Being a bishop does not depend upon having administrative duties, an office staff, and a seventy-hour work week. Rather, the bishop's office is evangelical, not functional. As such, we must recognize that calling individuals to the office of episcopal oversight is something God does, and when the call is consummated in ordination, a permanent condition is established. Retirement from administrative duties does not entail retirement from the episcopate. The gospel linkage is crucial. Just as God's decision to become flesh in Christ is a durable and lasting expression of his triumphant love, so also God's decision to call a person to the ministry of episcopal oversight is lasting. In affirming the durability of this call we cannot founder on the inevitable abuses of the office and the failure of personal character among individual bishops — perhaps God is calling such leaders as judgment and chastisement or even as a goad to the recovery of the apostolic tradition by those of us who have sat complacently on the sidelines. Instead, we ought to rejoice that God is willing to do things in our lives of which he will not repent. For surely, if God calls fools and charlatans to a permanent office that their sins cannot corrupt or efface, then perhaps we sinners may trust in God's more daring and costly call to eternal life. In this way, the change proposed by the Concordat invites Lutherans to trust both more purely and more fully in God's promise of justification by faith.

More dramatic and important than the change in how the ELCA treats existing bishops is the change in the way in which the ELCA consecrates. The Concordat speaks generally of the unifying role of the proposed joint consecration of future bishops, both Lutheran and Episcopal. However, any Anglican will recognize the unspoken, but crucial, concrete and specific consequence of this proposal for joint consecration. Within a generation, the ELCA will be led by bishops who have received their office from the hands of at least three members of the historic episcopate, and therefore, within a lifetime the entirety of the ELCA's ministry will have been reabsorbed back into the tradition of apostolic episcopal succession. What are Lutherans who have a passion for the evangelical purity of the gospel to make of such a consequence? Two aspects of the tradition of apostolic episcopal succession suggest themselves, and both proclaim loudly the truth about the gospel.

First, any consideration of apostolic episcopal succession cannot but be impressed by the observation that such a tradition is saturated with constancy. For Irenaeus, this character of the tradition of continuous episcopal succession was a crucial witness to the public and identifiable constancy of the gospel. Many commentators deride the anxieties about episcopal succession that fuel detailed historical searches for breaks in the apostolic chain. Perhaps this fixation is pathologically narrow, but the sentiment is surely evangelical. For is not the gospel a promise we can find in Scripture, in the preaching and teaching of the apostolic church, in the Holy Eucharist? We should be wary indeed of dismissing those who seek too narrowly, for we may well be judged for having sought not at all, for having "trusted in the Spirit" — such vain and overused words — but never immersing ourselves in the glorious details of what God has done in Christ, in the church, and in our own lives. Hardly, then, is apostolic episcopal succession a temptation away from the purity of the gospel. Instead, it is a tradition that drives us ever more deeply into the visible, constant, and public nature of the gospel. Such a practice forces us to confront the fact that like the succession of episcopal leadership, our faithfulness is open to investigation and scrutiny, and that in the final days we shall be so judged.

Second, the tradition of apostolic succession draws great attention to the requirement of succession through laying on of hands. Again, many commentators set aside the apparently crude notion of physical causality implied in this requirement, as if the act itself communicates a charism of leadership. However, we ought to be careful, for the requirement of laying on of hands would seem to be *exactly* the sort of condition God chooses in Christ and for us. The scandalous worldly features of the traditon of apostolic episcopal succession, the physical act of laying on of hands, echoes the much more scandalously worldly and physical features of Christ's obedience. Further, if we chuckle at the notion that God might use a bishop's hands to ensure the survival of his people, then we may all too easily chuckle when the gospel places demands upon our hands — to feed the hungry and cloth the naked. Will we not dodge *these* gospel imperatives with some self-serving line about how God does not establish conditions, does not call human hands into action to do his work? Far, then, from corrupting the evangelical purity of the gospel, the requirement of historical succession is an intensification of the penetrating power of the gospel.

The Episcopal Side

Just as the Concordat challenges the ELCA to accept the full condition of life in Christ, so also does it challenge the Episcopal Church, in a less pointed though perhaps more serious way. The first impression one has of the Concordat is that, unlike ELCA polity, the Episcopal Church changes very little. Aside from a strictly temporary suspension of the requirement of Episcopal ordination for ministry to allow a recognition of the "full authenticity" of Lutheran holy orders, Episcopal practice and polity will grind forward until that temporary suspension is rendered otiose by the absorption of Lutheran oversight into the historic episcopate. This first impression is itself a reason to think that the Concordat might change the Episcopal Church quite dramatically for Episcopal complacency about the conditions imposed by the Concordat focuses only on polity, and the characteristic Episcopalian myopia ignores the proclamation that the Concordat requires the Episcopal Church to accept. This narrowness of vision fails to see both the pattern of neglect in recent Episcopal history for that which has been given to the church by the apostles, and the utter centrality of that which the ELCA brings to full communion. The Concordat's proposed "conditions" for episcopal ordination directly confront this narrowness of vision.

The Concordat requires the Episcopal Church to invite at least three Lutheran bishops to the ordination of its own bishops. This invitation will commission these Lutheran bishops to discern whether the Episcopal candidate for the office of bishop will, in faithfulness, witness to, promote, and safeguard the unity and apostolicity of the church (§3). Further, these Lutheran bishops are expressly authorized to guide their discernment by the unaltered Augsburg Confession and Luther's Small Catechism (§2). This means that the future leadership of the Episcopal Church will be held to a confessional standard that has a real and concrete presence. Further, the Lutheran confessions are mandated as part of seminary training for Episcopal ordinands. One might expect, then, that these confessional documents might put some backbone into the education and selection of candidates for the priesthood. Unlike the ever shifting sands of Episcopal appeals to the hoary "three-legged stool" of Scripture, tradition, and reason, or vague allusions to the Book of Common Prayer, the confessional resources of the ELCA are far more explicit, inescapable, and useful as a standard for the ordained ministry, especially that ministry charged with oversight — the office of bishop. Thus, full communion will subject the Episcopal Church to far deeper and more durable confessional standards than at present. In this way, in seminary training and at every episcopal ordination, the Episcopal Church will be challenged to accept the performative, and even more decisively, the christological conditions of the gospel. Thus, the Episcopal Church may well come to know the evangelical purity and depth of true catholic "fullness."

*   *   *

There is a very good chance that the Concordat will fail — fail to be approved, or even if approved, fail to be enacted with any degree of evangelical integrity. We should not be optimistic, or at least, not optimistic because of a vitality or integrity in the life and faith of the ELCA or the Episcopal Church. Both churches suffer from bureaucracies committed to their own self-importance and survival, so much so that they are now desparately trying to find the "issue" to justify their existence. The "issues" are, in turn, increasingly estranged from the gospel. The genius of the Concordat rests in the minimal role to be played by the national bodies of the two churches. The decisive events proposed will take place at the altar, not in conference rooms. Further, the bureaucratic estrangement from the gospel is not accidental. Both churches suffer from a contemporary theological poverty. Lutheran poverty is heroic, an omnivorous dialectical "critique" of all worldly conditions of the gospel in which all of life is buried under the "freedom" of the gospel, a freedom from which there is no resurrection in discipline and service. Episcopal theological poverty is more transparent and cowardly, and takes the form of utter retreat before a panoply of "sensibilities" that now clamor for a "voice." In view of this poverty, one can predict that the greatest resistance to the Concordat will come from the seminaries of both denominations, for the evangelical nature of the proposal is a judgment against so much of what passes for theological education.

In short, there may well be insufficient faith in the ELCA to embrace the durable life of episcopal succession, and there may well be insufficient life in the Episcopal Church to respond to the durable faith of the Lutheran confessions. And if this is so, we ought then to suspect that neither church is genuinely anchored to its inheritance, and both churches are on their way toward becoming spectral echoes of the gospel rather than living, breathing and concrete witnesses. Given the likelihood of this slide toward a living death, our prayer should be that we shall be given the free grace of Christ to live in an evangelical future.

PART 2

CHALLENGE

Episcopalians, Lutherans, and Full Communion for Mission

GEORGE R. SUMNER, JR.

> [I pray] that they may all be one . . . so that the world may
> believe that you have sent me.
>
> John 17:21

Unity for a credible witness, and common witness conducing to unity: the connection is embedded in the New Testament itself. In more recent times, the launching of the ecumenical movement by the leaders of the world missionary movement reminds us of the association.[1] At present, the Concordat and its theological spadework found in *Implications of the Gospel* challenge the Episcopal and Lutheran churches to accept full communion, and to this end they employ the strategy of placing confessional differences in the context of a shared call to mission.[2] The missionary imperative should indeed be a strong rationale for Christian unity, and so a warrant for vigorous support of full communion between Episcopalians and Lutherans.

---

1. See Kenneth Scott Latourette's "Ecumenical Bearings of the Missionary Movement and the International Missionary Council," in *A History of the Ecumenical Movement 1517-1948,* ed. Ruth Rouse and Stephen Neill (Philadelphia: Westminster, 1954).

2. *Implications of the Gospel,* Lutheran Episcopal Dialogue Series 3 (Minneapolis: Augsburg; Cincinnati: Forward Movement, 1988) puts it this way: "In the often cited prayer of Jesus from the Gospel of John, the unity of the disciple community is to be visible so that the world can know and believe the messianic mission of the Father and the Son and thus participate in the future of the Spirit here and now" (p. 74).

Full communion for mission also means, however, that communion which hinders the proclamatory vigor of the church would be no service to the Lord. So mission must be a criterion as well as a rationale for communion, for it reminds Episcopalians and Lutherans of the kind of unity that they seek, one driving them both into the world to baptize in the triune Name (Matt. 28:19). Furthermore, mission can break an ecumenical logjam only where the word "mission" is ready at hand with its shape distinct and its consistency hard. Today, on the contrary, the concept evinces the same confusion of meaning as the theological scene at large. How then can we ensure that its invocation will bring clarity? In this essay I shall argue for three theses. First I shall distinguish the appropriate use of "mission." Where theologians gloss over this distinctive meaning, the ensuing communion can bear little fruit for the church. So, second, I will point out an example of this hazard in the argument of *Implications of the Gospel* itself. Third, I will suggest how, with a true and vigorous understanding of mission, the Concordat can become a real occasion for renewal of the faith and practice of the church.

A Definition of "Mission"

The church today needs a renewed sense of its proclamatory nature. So it must clearly conceive of evangelism as an indispensable dimension of mission.

We live in a time of theological disarray, when traditional claims about Jesus Christ, such as the finality of his revelation and the indispensability of his grace to save, are much in doubt. The decline of confidence in the wisdom of mission and evangelism conducted by the church in the name of Jesus Christ is connected to this confusion. For evangelism[3] is a practice that corresponds closely to the church's belief in the finality of the revelation in Jesus, in its applicability to all persons,

---

3. By "evangelism" I mean here the intention of the church as a whole, in a wide variety of its practices, to proclaim lovingly to its non-Christian neighbors the good news of Jesus Christ with the hope that by God's grace hearers may come to accept that message (and so evangelism will be understood as the proclamatory dimension of mission).

and in the stewardship of that "mystery" by the church (1 Cor. 4:1). In a milieu in which such belief is clouded or challenged, evangelism as proclamation serves as a pragmatic condition for serious theological affirmation of the finality of the church's christological claim.

Evangelism, rather than presenting the gracious offense of God's act on our behalf in Jesus Christ, has itself become particularly offensive for Episcopalians.[4] In part, the problem is a hangover from a Constantinian period when no one assumed that proclamation was truly necessary in a generally Christian country, and in part it stems from a certain standoffishness endemic in Episcopalians. Equally to blame is a caricatured notion of evangelism, associated with some of the more crude methods of fundamentalism. A further difficulty resides in the privatist, subjectivist, consumerist assumptions that we bring to the matter. We think naturally that "choice" is a good thing, and so a menu of religious alternatives strikes us as desirable. But the idea that the church as a particular religious community should put forth a claim in the marketplace for the truth of the gospel — respectfully, noncoercively, but a claim to truth nonetheless — offends our sensibilities. Such a claim implies that the choice made is of the utmost importance.

We shy away from evangelism not only because it embarrassingly makes a claim on our neighbor, but also because, in the process, it holds our own theological feet to the fire. The Order of Preachers had a saying that one cannot give what one does not have. Throughout the theological debates of our day, the categories of culture and experience hold sway in our parlance. Whatever nuances may once have existed in appeals to an Anglican "theology of the incarnation," bound closely to the doctrine of creation, they have vanished as the idea has leached down into ordinary church usage.[5] The examples are legion:

---

4. I leave Lutherans to draw conclusions about the applicability of this analysis to their own situation.

5. C. Robert Harrison, Jr., in his article "Competing Views of Evangelism in the Episcopal Church," *Anglican Theological Review* 75, no. 2 (Spring 1993): 226, cites the following line from a sermon of the Presiding Bishop, Edmond Browning, in defense of an "incarnational evangelism": "We do not take Jesus Christ to others. Rather we listen to others to hear where Jesus Christ is already at work in them." In terms of our argument, note how the second sentence could be true when used in a context of evangelistic practice. However, the first sentence would seem to provide just the sort of nonevangelistic context that would render the second sentence problematic.

a recent church document seeking to resolve the grievous divisions within Anglicanism has come up with the notion that theology ought to derive from a more vigorous and persistent appeal to "human experience."[6] Meanwhile a World Council of Churches conference exhorts us to "re-imagine" the tradition by the lights of our own imagination and without bounds.[7] Anglican treatments often understand mission as an "incarnational" solidarity with the socially marginal or as cross-cultural sharing, in order to avoid any preoccupation with witness (as if there were much danger of this). In such an environment, proclamation seems at best awkward and at worst imperialistic.

If our claims as Christians amount only to affirmations, projections, and emendations of our own culture and experience, then a public, serious evangelistic claim for Jesus Christ makes little sense. In the soil of emotivism evangelism is bound to shrivel. For are not my experiences my own, and is not culture relative to human situation and construction? Evangelism makes us uncomfortable, because it is a constitutive element of the Christian "form of life," attested throughout the New Testament, and yet in our theological world defined by culture and experience it ultimately makes no sense. Where personal experience reigns, without and within the church, discourse and debate devolve into the interchangeable airing of personal preferences, an endless daytime talk show, and the church shuts its ears to the call to the evangelistic task.

People can evade odious chores in many ways. We can stir up a dust-cloud of caveats, preconditions, questions with issues like the salvation of non-Christians, the adaptation of the proclaimed message, the need for tolerance, the question of church growth, and so forth. But there is a world of difference between a question posed in the midst of the task of evangelism and a question serving as evasion. Is it really humility that will share with a family member everything except what is most precious to us, or is it rather self-concern? If, as the old saying goes, evangelism is one beggar telling another where

6. The expression is found in the document called "Belonging Together," the report of a conference on Anglican unity sponsored by the Anglican Consultative Council and held in Alexandria, Virginia, in 1993.

7. The example, chosen virtually at random, is from a conference entitled "RE-imaging: A Global Theological Conference by Women for Women and Men," reported in *Episcopal Life* (January 1994).

there is a wonderful cache of food, theological conundra may lead us to acknowledge complex implications, but it cannot remove the truly humbling simplicity of the proclamatory imperative.

The real theological watershed concerning evangelism resides around the following questions: Is the church compelled by its very nature to proclaim? Is the object of that proclamation the crucified and risen Jesus Christ, whose identity is conveyed by the Scriptures? Where anyone truly hears that proclamation, is the response of conversion a matter of life and death? Must not such a proclamatory church challenge its hearers and itself again and again with the message of grace through faith over against whatever cultural works prevail at the moment? We do need to ask hard questions about evangelistic theology and method, but still the great divide is between those who answer Yes to these questions, and those who cannot.

A second tactic for evangelistic foot-dragging is redefinition. One affirms the need for mission, perhaps makes it a theological centerpiece, but understands it in a manner easily accommodating those answering No to the questions I have just listed. Those using "mission" in this way forget that proclamation is a necessary (though not all-sufficient) condition for its proper use. Otherwise "mission" comes to stand for an orientation toward general cultural trends or social goals, and eventually blends into the landscape. Those suspicious of the hyperinflation of the term "mission" in contemporary theology can recall the late Anglican missiologist Stephen Neill's saying that where mission is not at least evangelism it means nothing at all. We can find an instance of this theological slide away from proclamation in *Implications of the Gospel* itself; such argumentation may tempt us into a kind of communion devoid of evangelistic vigor. We need to confront and overcome this weakness in the argument for the Concordat, precisely because full communion holds the promise of a more robust evangelistic life for the churches.

Use of "Mission" in *Implications of the Gospel*

Uses of "mission" vitiating its evangelistic dimension perpetuate rather than challenge contemporary theological confusion. An example, ironically, may be found in *Implications of the Gospel* itself.

If mission entails evangelistic proclamation, how does the Lutheran-Episcopal dialogue's appeal to mission as a basis for full communion stack up? I believe that, in fact, it fails the test by providing a tangle of meanings for "mission," one of which elides the evangelistic dimension. I will defend this claim by a more detailed exegesis of the text.

Implications of the Gospel, the theological consensus for the full communion proposed by the the Episcopal-Lutheran Concordat, trades heavily on the strategy of emphasizing unity for common mission: "They [the baptized] are the community of the reign of God and are continually sent into the mission of the Christ on behalf of the reign of God."[8] The document lays out the wider, eschatological perspective into which the Episcopal-Lutheran dialogue is placed. The church is the community that shares Jesus' mission as it witnesses to and lives out the promise of a new future in that kingdom, a promise proclaimed by Jesus and anticipated in his resurrection. Such a move serves several purposes: It preserves traditions like the episcopate precisely to the extent that they subserve something larger, namely the kingdom present in Christ. Such a simultaneous relativization and affirmation seems an astute ecumenical move. Likewise the emphasis on the future induces the traditions to find their unity "ahead" of them. All of this is accomplished by appeal to eschatology, a major theme in modern New Testament criticism, and an academic inheritance common to the contemporary traditions.

Such an argument borrows from several major currents in twentieth-century theology, accounts of which may be helpful to clarify the reasons for such moves in *Implications of the Gospel.* The emphasis on eschatology, which reaches back to the early stage of dialectical theology (e.g., in Karl Barth's *Epistle to the Romans*), functioned originally as a stunning rediscovery of the sovereignty and transcendence of God and therefore as a protest against cultural captivity and accommodation of the church. It served to affirm the finality of Jesus Christ at the same time that it fittingly rendered the church that witnesses to him provisional and questionable.

One (of many) theological offshoots of this changed climate in theology was a renewed association of mission with eschatology. Here too the liberal associations of the missionary movement with Western

8. *Implications of the Gospel,* p. 39.

100

culture were roundly renounced and the origins of mission in Christian life "between the times" were unearthed. Characteristic of this change was the shift from an understanding of "the kingdom of God" as progressively built on earth to one of witnessing to its free and "perpendicular" arrival. In the post–World War II era these turns to eschatology and mission as central theological concepts converged in the development of the concept of the *missio Dei*. The goal was to surpass narrow, pietistic tendencies toward the conversion of individuals and toward the advancement of church institutions for their own sakes. A more dynamic view of the God who is at work in history was sought. No longer was it a matter of the church having a mission, but rather of the mission (of God) having (as an instrument) the church.[9] Consistent with the original meaning of God's "missions," the triune nature of God, as the One whose nature is to redeem and consummmate what he has created, was invoked. This served to couple the unique identity of the Christian God with the widest scope of divine interest in world history.

Missio Dei was originally intended to say something about the nature of the church, namely that it participated in God's kingdom come in Christ precisely as it witnessed to this surpassing reality. In this sense "kingdom" and "church" were correlative terms employed to place the community between Christ and world, resurrection and parousia. The original meaning of *missio Dei* depended on this *Gestalt* of terms, and served as a way of keeping them in right theological relationship.

Ambiguities in the idea of *missio Dei* emerged almost immediately after its first use, however, and divergent interpretive paths led to strikingly different missiological results. Even as the term was being hoisted onto its pedestal at the international mission conference at Willingen, West Germany, in 1952, cracks were already appearing in its casting.[10] In fact the superiority of God's mission could apply equally well to the freedom of God's Word in the church (in a classical Reformation sense), to the outward-oriented vigor of the church's

---

9. A good example of the latter is found in Jürgen Moltmann's *The Church in the Power of the Spirit* (New York: Harper & Row, 1977), pp. 10f.

10. A good account of the conference is found in James Scherer, *Gospel, Church, and Kingdom: Comparative Studies in World Mission Theology* (Minneapolis: Augsburg, 1987), pp. 95ff.

life, or to the central focus on God's interest in struggles for liberation in the world.[11] In the last case it was a short step to declare that the church was an optional instrument of God's work, that indeed God had no interest in the church as a continuous institution. *Missio Dei* proved to be a handy tool for a thorough secularizing, politicizing tendency in mission thought in the 1960s.[12] The expression took on a meaning at cross-purposes with any discernable connection with proclamation.

The emphasis on the *missio Dei*, on the coming kingdom of God for which the church is servant, underlies the argument in *Implications of the Gospel*, and the very same ambiguity of meaning may be found in its usage. The earlier sections of the document, which deal with the doctrines of God and the church, emphasize the witness to the unique, eschatological, salvation-historical event of Jesus' death and resurrection. His history is both the world's fulfillment and the decisive act of God on the world's behalf. In this case the term "kingdom" must refer to the risen Christ himself,[13] from whom it solely derives its content.

However, as we move into the document's treatment of the world and of mission (sections IV and V), a different theme emerges. Here the kingdom can be described in general terms as "freedom for radical newness," an attitude that Jesus exemplified and that we can share as we enter into the same mission he embarked on, the service of the kingdom. Now the *missio Dei* that the church subserves is described in a distinctly different way. In this case his resurrection has initiated a new epoch in which the church is enabled to continue that same mission by the Spirit, who is identified as "the Spirit of freedom and openness to the future."[14] The task of the church is "to witness

11. An example of the first option may be found in Georg Vicedom's *Missio Dei* (Munich: Christian Kaiser, 1958), and an example of the second in Lesslie Newbigin's *Household of God* (London: SCM, 1953). The third option is pervasive; J. C. Hoekendijk, *The Church Inside Out* (London: SCM, 1967), is but one example.

12. See H. H. Rosen's *Missio Dei: An Examination of the Origin, Contents, and Function of the Term in Protestant Missiological Discussion* (Leiden: Inter-university Institute for Missiological and Ecumenical Research, 1972).

13. On the idea of Christ as *autobasileia* (as "himself the kingdom"), see especially Joseph Cardinal Ratzinger, *Eschatology: Death and Eternal Life*, vol. 9 of *Dogmatic Theology* (Washington: The Catholic University of America, 1988), pp. 8ff.

14. One can tellingly compare *Implications* here with the document resulting

to God's future on behalf of the reign of God."[15] Christ no longer embodies that future, but tells us about it.

What, after all, does "freedom for radical newness" mean? I am reminded of the householder who swept one demon out, only to find seven sneaking in the back door. Theological vacuums are illusions; as anyone who has tried in meditation to "think about nothing" knows, an "open" mind may just mean thinking about this and that; "radical newness" always implies some content or other.

Part of the confusion may lie inherently in theological appeals to "the future," appeals that continue to be popular in theology at large. Such a concept implies a contrast to the usual grooves along which our own thinking runs; it points to a receptivity to the unprecedented coming presumably from God's eschatological creativity. But straightway we realize that the modern age is itself readily characterized by an appreciation of history, change, and freedom. "The future" slides easily from being *ganz anderes,* "totally other" (so that we can only speak of it as it is revealed to us in Jesus Christ), to being a characteristic dimension of our modern human experience offering a ready "point of contact" for talk about God. It is in this vein that the writers of *Implications of the Gospel* tell us that a theological horizon of "God's future" is eminently useful apologetically, as it is so readily "meaningful . . . in the context of a secular worldview."[16] The "otherness" of the category "the future" may be formally preserved, but it has been materially evacuated. From this perspective, advocacy of the "radically new" turns out to be neither.

In light of such a *volte-face* we can understand how the theological strategy of shifting emphasis to "the future," originally intended as a protest against cultural captivity, can come to foster the "affirmation of the world."[17] The transcendent and dialectical notes are silent. We come full circle back to the "kingdom" of the Social Gospel, albeit in a new form. In fact, *Implications of the Gospel* makes a tacit appeal at

---

from the Anglican-Reformed dialogue, *God's Reign and Our Unity: The Report of the Anglican-Reformed International Commission* (London: SPCK, 1984), which attempts the same strategy of placing confessional differences in an eschatological, missionary perspective, but limits itself more stringently to this first mode of discourse, namely Christ's personal embodiment of and continuing identification with "God's future."

15. *Implications,* p. 39.
16. Ibid., p. 62.
17. Ibid., p. 63.

this point to a liberal consensus across denominational lines on a variety of cultural and political ideas. In light of the watershed concerning evangelism that I described above, uses of "mission" in the document fall simultaneously on both sides of the divide. This allows one to finesse the question of the indispensability of proclamation and conversion, to sidestep the blunt centrality of Jesus' question at Caesarea Philippi.

The use of eschatology for "affirmation of the world" is a dramatic example of the primacy of the category of culture at the root of the quandary over the proclamatory, evangelistic dimension of mission. Once mission has become commitment to the "radical newness" of "the future," there is no reason why such mission need involve the challenging and gracious news of Jesus Christ (other than as a fellow pilgrim toward the future). In short, the Concordat is here buttressed by an argument that, although having ecumenical and political appeal, hinders theological, ecclesiological, and evangelistic renewal.

Does this mean that the very idea of the Concordat is ill-conceived from a missiological point of view? Not at all, since we can readily understand it as a practical response to the need for communion precisely in the service of the Christian missionary imperative. As a concrete opportunity presented to us it shares in the inescapable necessity of that imperative. In fact, the fundamental service the Concordat can render to mission helps to disclose its true promise, allowing us to overcome the limitations of the theological consensus described in *Implications of the Gospel.* Our churches need the Concordat because we need to grow into common missionary vocation, too often neglected of late. Thus, I now turn to the elucidation of the promise and possibility of the Concordat for the renewal of proclamation in the church.

The Concordat and Renewal in the Church

If evangelism is a pragmatic condition for serious theological commitment to the finality of Jesus Christ, the fuller communion between the Episcopal and Lutheran churches could become an occasion for understanding this connection anew.

Episcopalians need the Concordat precisely because they need to hear the incisive witness of Martin Luther. Perhaps other voices from the tradition could help equally well, and surely that voice is not synonymous with the contemporary Lutheran church. But I cannot think of a more likely source of renewal, especially with respect to the proclamatory dimension of the church. The issue is not what Martin Luther, in his different, distinctly Constantinian, historical setting, thought about mission.[18] Nor is the central issue found in old wrangling over confessions and episcopal succession. The power and primacy of the preached Word, the theology of the cross, "by faith alone," the insistence on "letting God be God"[19] — these are the theological *desiderata* that could help to make possible a comprehension of mission, and invigorate the practice of mission. For attention to Luther directs us back to the very questions most central to mission, and over which, in today's landscape, one can most easily stumble.

At the very heart of Luther's theology is proclamation of God's gracious Word of promise. The One who is that Word, Jesus Christ, incarnate, crucified, risen, "for us," cannot be separated from the Scriptures in which he is "brought forth," nor from the preaching of that Word to us sinners. So the Word heard and the Spirit by which it is heard cohere as an "indissoluble unity."[20] Likewise Word and faith are for Luther correlative terms, denoting as they do God's promising address to us and our response, a gift of grace. Word, Spirit, and faith constellate about proclamation, the place that God has designated that humankind may find him.

For our purposes we need to highlight several implications important to Luther. First of all, Luther stressed that, just as God in Christ came and comes to human beings who possess nothing in themselves to conjure up God, likewise the Word comes from without. We can never reduce its work to some mere confirmation or articulation of what was already within us: "We must hold to the conviction that God gives no one his Spirit or grace except through or with the external Word which comes before."[21] This externality

---

18. On the question see Scherer, *Gospel, Church, and Kingdom,* chap. 2.

19. I have borrowed the expression from Philip Watson, *Let God be God! An Interpretation of the Theology of Martin Luther* (London: Epworth, 1947).

20. Paul Althaus, *The Theology of Martin Luther* (Philadelphia: Fortress, 1966), p. 38.

21. This quotation, from the Smalkald Articles (III.8.3), is cited in ibid., p. 36.

requires that God's Word be proclaimed, for how will they hear without a preacher, one who is sent?

This reminds us of the underlying roadblock to mission today, the prevailing assumption that God is directly accessible in creation itself, in our selves, in nature, in the religions of the world, and so forth. In such a case, Christianity becomes but one more "cultural gift,"[22] its only role one of confirming what is already and patently present. In such a case, the missionary imperative is a vestige best excised. Luther had an equally robust theology of the Creator at work in all things. But he claimed, also, that in keeping with the "folly of the cross," we can only approach the Creator as revealed "under the opposite," through the cross, against the grain of our own sinful resistance and distortion of the Creator God for our own ends. How much theological talk, often anti-missionary in spirit, is toppled by this little word: "He deserves to be called a theologian, however, who comprehends the visible and manifest things of God seen through suffering and the cross."[23] Luther, in the spirit of Paul, asks us how we can truly hear of the inner longing of creation (as we wish) without first believing the word of the cross. "And how are they to believe in one of whom they have never heard?" (Rom. 10:14).

We would misunderstand proclamation if we supposed that its burden could be relegated solely to a few designated preachers, or if we supposed that the church could be reduced to the pointillism of isolated events of speaking and hearing (in which case church reunion would indeed be pointless). On the contrary, we do better to conceive of the community as a whole as proclamatory, since it derives its very identity from God's promising Word, and conducts its life in the wake of God's calling to be a priestly nation. This understanding too finds support in Luther's writings, for he stressed that the universal priesthood was the possession of the community and laid on all the obligation to witness: "A Christian not only has the right but the duty to teach the Word of God; and he fails to do so at the risk of his own salvation." This explains (in part, along with the circumstances of Luther's time), his lack of emphasis on mission, since every Christian

22. The phrase is used in Denise and John Carmody, *Native American Religions: An Introduction* (New York: Paulist, 1993).

23. "Heidelberg Disputation," thesis #20, found in *Martin Luther's Basic Theological Writings,* ed. Timothy Lull (Minneapolis: Fortress, 1989), p. 43.

was a steward of God's proclamatory mission: "God has been so gracious to us that he has stuffed every corner of the world full with God's word." As a result, Luther insisted that "the gospel shall without ceasing sound and resound through the mouths of all Christians."[24]

To our contemporary ears all this talk of externality, scandal, and an evangelistic community may seem to confine God's gracious will, indeed the very nature of God. But for Luther it affirmed the freedom of God to come to us in a way we would never have dreamed, a way we in ourselves reject as impossible. To find God in the proclaimed Word is to see that God can come to us humbly, but freely, so that God is accessible without being liable to being manipulated.[25] A renewed awareness of the church as a community created by and proclaiming the Word "lets God be God" as much for us today as for Luther and his contemporaries.

I have suggested how the theological vision of Luther could sharpen the sense of an evangelistic imperative for the churches. Yet, practice renews theory as much as theory guides practice. Missionary and evangelistic practice is conducive to placing a communion of Episcopal and Lutheran churches on a more solid theological footing. Of course, we cannot expect grand projects. In the present climate of ecumenical thought, with a greater skepticism about "top-down" solutions, we ought rather to imagine localized intentional activities at the level of "structured fellowship" between parishes and dioceses. Such shared Christian life may create the conditions for full communion that make a difference.[26]

The first context for renewed missionary practice, potentially fostered by the Concordat and conducive to its success, is as narrow

---

24. These words of Luther are quoted in Althaus, *Theology,* pp. 315, 318.

25. A creative and eloquent restatement of Luther's point is found in Eberhard Jüngel, *God as the Mystery of the World: On the Foundation of the Theology of the Crucified One in the Dispute between Theism and Atheism* (Grand Rapids: Eerdmans, 1983), sect. 11, "The Word as the Place of the Conceivability of God."

26. For the recommendation of local "structured fellowship" as the way to make ecumenical progress today, see *Facing Unity: Models, Forms, and Phases of Lutheran-Roman Catholic Fellowship* (Geneva: Lutheran World Federation, 1985). The experience of disappointment in large-scale programs for missionary renewal, however theoretically valid and well-intended, is widespread among Episcopalians; "Mutual Responsibility and Interdependence" and "Partners In Mission" are two examples, from the 1960s and 1970s respectively.

as the local parish and as ancient as the early centuries of the Christian community. A series of practices traces the steps in the process of Christian initiation: evangelism, catechesis, the identity-rendering seal of baptism, vocation for service within and beyond the community.[27] The contemporary church already shows interest in various of these stages, especially the catechumenate and the Easter Vigil, as well as spirituality and the "discerning of gifts." Too often, however, catechesis has to do with "our own story" rather than immersion in the scriptural story, and Christians do not always discern that the process as a whole presupposes proclamation, conversion, and the priestly, cruciform character of the baptizing community.

This limited vision and lack of vigorous proclamation need not be so. Imagine yoked parishes committed to joint evangelism in their shared bounds. The means could be as varied as the locales: training in personal evangelism, preaching missions, spiritual talks, community meals, concerts, calling on new members, and the like. Imagine furthermore our churches commonly committed at the local level to a newly rigorous catechumenate, and the reverberating effect that the disciplines of Bible reading and personal prayer, instilled there, would have, not only on the newly baptized, but on the baptizing community as a whole. Only where such joint local renewal of evangelism and diaconal ministry exist would *communio in sacris* (sharing in the holy things) take on its proper plenitude of meaning, since the *primum sacrum* (holiest thing) we hold in common is the *evangelium* (the gospel).

The second context for renewed missionary practice is as wide as the globe itself and, in a sense, is new for the Christian community. Neither Cranmer nor Luther could have imagined being members of worldwide communions of churches. We should furthermore note that our respective sister churches are often neighbors: in south India, in east Africa, in Papua New Guinea, and so forth.[28] In the Episcopal

---

27. For an account of evangelism that builds on the Anglican liturgical tradition (and compatible with the view presented here), see Stephen Sykes, "An Anglican Theology of Evangelism," *Theology* 84 (1991).

28. It is worth noting that, in the early period of the missionary movement, Anglican mission societies employed Lutheran personnel in several locations. The Church Missionary Society sent Krapf and Rebmann to east Africa in the early nineteenth century, while the Society for the Propagation of the Gospel even had Lutheran missionary pastors confirming in southern India in the late eighteenth

Church, at the same time that rhetoric about globalization has risen, actual commitment to overseas partners is declining.[29] Imagine local dioceses yoked in renewed and common commitment to non-Western sister churches. Imagine that our own churches, in addition to sending, might increasingly receive missionaries into our own midst (just as "South-South" exchanges have in recent years increased), with the serious intent to learn anew something about evangelism.

One benefit of such a joint commitment might be a clearer vision precisely of our own ecumenical interdependence. If we think of the church primarily as a global web of communities of the crucified, risen Christ, scattered throughout the world,[30] then from such a catholic (i.e., worldwide) and evangelical perspective, justification and episcopacy serve in the most complementary way.[31] For the task of expressing the one gospel of Christ appropriately in local terms, without allowing that gospel to be overwhelmed by its surrounding culture, presents itself in each place. It was against just such an over-whelming that Martin Luther fought, and the doctrine of justification can serve as a rule for this on-going task of discernment. On the other hand, we can think of bishops, in keeping with their function in the early church, as both guardians and symbols of the universal gospel that sprang from the same Christ but was handed over to all the nations. When so understood in its global implications, mission can serve as a helpful context for conceiving the compatibility of the confessions themselves.[32]

---

century! A brief account of such cooperation may be found in Bengt Sundkler's *The Church of South India: The Movement Towards Union 1900-1947* (London: Lutterworth, 1954), chap. 1, "The Nineteenth Century Background".

29. As I write, the virtual gutting of commitment to missionaries for overseas partners is being discussed at the national level of the Episcopal Church (due to a budgetary crisis). This is a dramatic symptom of the missionary amnesia of the ECUSA.

30. I am borrowing here from George Lindbeck's idea of an "interlocking network" of communities in "The Church," in *Keeping the Faith: Essays to Mark the Centenary of Lux Mundi,* ed. G. Wainwright (Philadelphia: Fortress, 1988), pp. 198f.

31. In this connection, we should realize that the strategy of the Episcopal-Lutheran Concordat is in large measure dependent on the arrangement of the Church of South India, where the exigencies of witness in a predominantly non-Christian environment required the church to rethink their confessional separation. Unfortunately, after much discussion, the Lutherans of south India decided not to participate.

32. Here again the example of evangelical pietism provides an interesting, if

*   *   *

Robert Jenson's words a decade ago about ecumenical prospects common to Episcopalians and Lutherans apply equally today:

> [We] live . . . by the same mixture of fundamentalism, helplessness before every wind of doctrine, tag-ends of denominational tradition, and occasional saving theological and proclamatory miracles. . . . We will make progress only as we recognize that what we have to do is to make interim arrangements between segments of a disintegrating form of the church, to try to make the birth of a new form a little easier.[33]

We should judge the Episcopal-Lutheran Concordat with just such a modest goal in mind, for then it has a real contribution to make. The time is ripe for a wholehearted return to the word of the cross, and so for a new grasp of the proclamatory implications of being the "ecumenical" and "evangelical" people of God. Mission must be a rationale, a criterion, and a practical context for steps toward fuller communion by such a people. To be sure, accepting the Concordat in such a spirit would require the acknowledgment of our own weakness and so our need for one another to learn how to fulfill such a calling, to answer the Great Commission anew: Now *that* would be the "openness to the future" bestowed by the risen Christ. Then the Concordat would truly be an occasion for the kind of christological and evangelistic renewal that the churches, singly and together, so urgently need.

---

ambivalent, precedent. For it comprised christocentric focus and evangelistic intensity, and, in large measure, a common pietistic background made cooperation across confessional lines possible. Pietism's ecclesiological shortcomings, however, allowed such cooperation often to bypass actual ecclesial structures.

33. See Eric W. Gritsch and Robert W. Jenson, *Lutheranism: The Theological Movement and its Confessional Writings* (Philadelphia: Fortress, 1976), p. 175.

Episcopal Oversight and Ecclesiastical Discipline

PHILIP TURNER

A similar problem faces both Anglicans and Lutherans, namely that the succession in the presiding ministry of their respective churches no longer incontestably links those churches to the *koinonia* of the wider church.

The Niagara Report, paragraph 58

Thesis

The "Concordat of Agreement" soon to be presented for ratification to the governing bodies of both the Episcopal Church U.S.A. (ECUSA) and the Evangelical Lutheran Church in America (ELCA) is the product of over a quarter-century of prayer, study, and dialogue. If ratified, full communion between the two churches will soon be established.

I write in support of the Concordat and in hope of full communion. I write also to respond to a concern that deeply troubles many Lutherans — one that has not received the attention it deserves. I hope to cast the objection in a different and more helpful light and in so doing ask if the matter at issue is not in fact one that troubles the life of both churches. If indeed the problem is common it does not in itself constitute a reason to reject the Concordat. Instead it presents a central issue that the two churches, if they enter into full communion, must address jointly.

111

The objection is that the historic episcopate, upon which the ECUSA insists as a condition for full communion, and which by the terms of the Concordat would become a part of Lutheran polity, seems, in the case of the ECUSA, to have been unable to maintain "incontestably" the apostolicity of life and witness the office is supposed to effect. In short, the objection is that, in spite of the historic episcopate, the life and doctrine of the ECUSA are in such disarray that its links with the one, holy, catholic, and apostolic church are in question.

In a number of places the Concordat anticipates the objection and seeks to address it. Thus, its proposers acknowledge the fact that the historic episcopate is but a sign of apostolicity, and that it can become an empty sign. This frank acknowledgment grants that the apostolic message and way of life may be lost even when the historic episcopate forms the centerpiece of an ecclesiastical polity. Thus, no magical powers are being claimed by either Episcopalians or Lutherans in respect to the effectiveness of this particular institution. Further, neither party is claiming that the historic episcopate is a necessary implication of the gospel.

However, in respect to the more specific charge that faithfulness to the apostolic witness within the ECUSA is indeed in question, the Concordat states that, though disobedience mars the life of *both* churches, Lutherans and Episcopalians alike share the apostolic faith in all of its essentials, and that, despite the imperfections found in both churches, each recognizes those essentials in the worship, formularies, sacraments, and common life of the other.

Though this judgment is certainly contestable, I am in thorough agreement with it. Nevertheless, as both *The Niagara Report* and "Toward Full Communion" suggest, it is plausible to arrive at a different conclusion.[1] The proposers of the Concordat themselves admit, for example, that those responsible for doctrine and discipline find themselves unable to assure in a way that is "incontestable" the fidelity of their respective denominations to a tradition of life and doctrine that accords with the witness of the apostles.

The most helpful response to what, by mutual admission, ap-

1. See *The Niagara Report: Report of the Anglican-Lutheran Consultation on Episcope 1987* (London: Church House Publishing, 1988), p. 33, and William A. Norgren and William G. Rusch, eds., *"Toward Full Communion" and "Concordat of Agreement,"* *Lutheran-Episcopal Dialogue Series 3* (Minneapolis: Augsburg; Cincinnati: Forward Movement, 1991), p. 79.

pears to be a common problem is to ask if it has a common source. The history of episcopal oversight within the ECUSA traced below suggests that it does.[2] By exposing what this common problem is, the history suggests that the basic issue in respect to the historic episcopate is not its apparent ineffectiveness within the ECUSA but the erosion of a moral tradition upon which the effectiveness of this and all other forms of ecclesial oversight depend. The history suggests further that this moral tradition is now under attack by another — one that is suspicious of any form of oversight that has as its stated purpose the protection and furtherance of *common beliefs and practices*.

I can summarize the two traditions in the following way.[3] The original one holds that the very purpose of authority is to further common beliefs and practices in situations where, because of the exigencies of historical circumstance and the limitations of human knowledge and good will, the common life of a people is strained or threatened. This tradition assumes both that there are common beliefs and practices to be guarded and furthered and that there are certain persons who have virtues (spiritual, moral, and intellectual powers) that make them better able than others to undertake this work. Accordingly, those given powers of oversight ought to be persons who understand the foundational beliefs and practices of a people better than others. They ought also to have the virtues required for a public life dedicated to the protection and furtherance of a commonwealth. If those in authority do not have these virtues, the koinonia of the church will weaken and perhaps fragment into schismatic factions.

It follows then, that according to what I shall call the originating moral tradition of authority in the church, those in and those under authority are both stakeholders in a common enterprise. Thus, those in authority have a responsibility to order the life of the church in

2. I would like to express appreciation for the work of Ms. Lauren Lyon, a student of the Yale Divinity School, who has traced these events with great care and insight in an as yet unpublished paper presently entitled "An Analysis of the Disciplinary Actions in the House of Bishops of the Episcopal Church between 1966 and 1991" (hereafter cited as Lyon, 1992). I have been saved much time by her accurate description of the events in question in this paper.

3. For a more thorough discussion of these two traditions see Philip Turner, "Authority in the Church: Excavations Among the Ruins," *First Things* (December 1990): 25-31.

ways that accord with and further koinonia. For this reason also, those under authority have a duty to express disagreement and if necessary disobey if the directives of those in authority violate common belief and practice in a persistent and/or egregious way. Thus, the originating tradition joins the ethics of oversight and the ethics of dissent and civil disobedience through a single purpose, namely, the protection and furtherance of koinonia.

What I shall call the new tradition, or the tradition of bureaucratic/prophetic authority, begins from a very different premise. It assumes that authority exists because koinonia is not possible. Public life in all its forms is marked by an irreducible pluralism. In these circumstances, authority functions not to guard common beliefs and ways of life but to ensure that all shades of opinion are allowed expression and provided access both to political office and to social benefits.

The assumption of irreducible pluralism that lies behind this view of authority is accompanied by another, namely, that social life may be characterized without qualification as a struggle for power. In this struggle, the weak are marginalized by the strong. Within these circumstances, an additional form of authority is called for — one that is best termed "prophetic." If bureaucratic authority exists to ensure fair treatment for all shades of opinion and all styles of life within a pluralistic social universe, the function of its companion, prophetic authority, is to unmask the injustices of power (which are hidden by tradition and maintained by authority) and to establish the rights of individuals both to their own opinions and to their fair share of social reward.

In ways that will become clear enough, prophetic authority is constitutionally suspicious of all forms of authority save its own. It is prone to make unqualified moral claims for assent to its insights and prescriptions. Because it always claims the moral high ground, prophetic authority has immediate appeal and is usually successful in its attempts to create social ferment. However, a high price must be paid for its success. When situations arise that some, perhaps many, believe call for oversight and discipline, those responsible for their exercise find themselves without sufficient popular support and without a coherent set of ideas and virtues that make oversight and discipline either possible or intelligible. Conversely, those who feel compelled to follow conscience and in so doing claim the prophet's mantle have no means of making it clear that their dissent or disobedience is offered in the name of a common good rather than a private ideal. In short, the eclipse of what I have called the originating tradition by the newer one leaves everyone, be they liberal or conservative, with inadequate means for honorable and constructive institutional review and change. In turn, the inaccessibility of adequate means for institutional review and change leads not to rich diversity but to an increasing number of internal schisms.

The Pike Affair

I shall try to establish the claims set out above by tracing the way in which the House of Bishops and the General Convention of the ECUSA have, during the past twenty-five years, sought to address three issues that profoundly affect its doctrine, discipline, and order. The story begins in 1966 when procedures were initiated in the House of Bishops to bring Bishop James Pike to trial for heresy. The presentment of charges noted, among other things, that Bishop Pike said, "The Church's classical way of stating what is represented by the doctrine of the Trinity . . . is not essential to the Christian faith."[4]

Bishop Pike's statements on doctrine and other matters caused no small uproar, but the majority of bishops believed that a heresy trial would prove disastrous for the public image of the church.[5] Accordingly, the Presiding Bishop urged the signatories to the presentment to leave the matter to a more informal process in the House of Bishops. They agreed, and he appointed an ad hoc committee to review the matter and report to the House of Bishops at its next meeting. The report of the committee can be taken as a good summary of the mood of the bishops at that time. It reads in part:

> It is our opinion that this proposed trial would not solve the problem presented to the church by this minister, but in fact would be

4. James Pike, *A Time for Christian Candor* (New York: Harper & Row, 1965), p. 204.

5. See W. Stringfellow and A. Towne, *The Bishop Pike Affair* (New York: Harper & Row, 1967), p. 129.

detrimental to the church's mission and witness. . . . This "heresy trial" would be widely viewed as a "throw back" to centuries when the law in church and state sought to repress and penalize unacceptable opinions . . . it would spread abroad a "repressive image" of the church and suggest to many that we are more concerned with traditional propositions about God than with faith as the response of the whole man to God. . . . Having taken this position regarding a trial, nevertheless, we feel bound to reject the tone and manner of much that Bishop Pike has said as being offensive and highly disturbing within the communion and fellowship of the church. And we would disassociate ourselves from many of his utterances as being irresponsible on the part of one holding the office and trust that he shares with us. . . . He has certainly spoken in a disparaging way of the Trinity.[6]

In adopting this statement, the House of Bishops voted also by a margin of 103 to 36 to censure Bishop Pike.

Thus, strictly speaking, in the case of Bishop Pike, the House of Bishops fulfilled its responsibility under the constitution of the ECUSA to discipline its members. Nevertheless, the disciplinary act of the House of Bishops was both mild and highly qualified. First of all, though he had renounced one of the most basic doctrines of the church, Bishop Pike was in no way inhibited in the exercise of office. Second, the move to censure did not condemn the substance of what Bishop Pike had said about the Trinity. It was concerned instead with what might be the public response to a heresy trial and with the "tone and manner" in which the bishop had spoken. Third, a minority report took the view that, though Bishop Pike's remarks had been hurried and ill-considered, they nonetheless were well meant, even admirable. The minority report reads, in part, as follows:

> Bishop Pike has been disturbing, admittedly. Often in his dialogues with the faithless, with youth, with adherents of other religious faiths, he has spoken precipitously and with some risk. He would have preferred more time for consideration, but the page of our day does not allow us much time. We believe it is more important to

6. Minutes of the House of Bishops 1966 in the *Journal of the General Convention* (New York: Office of the General Convention), p. 27.

be a sympathetic and self-conscious part of God's action in the secular world than it is to defend the positions of the past, which is a past that is altered with each new discovery of truth. . . . Bishop Pike has faced, often hurriedly, the demands, intellectual and theological, of our time in history, and we commend him for doing so. If he has to be a casualty of the Christian mission in our day, we regret that this is so.[7]

As most know, the "Pike affair" did not end with the censure of Bishop Pike. In 1968 Bishop Pike formally left the Episcopal Church. He died shortly thereafter. In 1970 the House of Bishops, as is their custom, took notice of the death of a former member, passing the following memorial:

> Many in the church were and are hurt and bewildered at the seeming inability of our normally inclusive community to understand James Pike in his pilgrimage, so that at the end he felt forced to renounce our brotherhood; now, therefore, be it
> Resolved that the House of Bishops give thanks to God for the life and prophetic ministry of James Pike and recognize the depth of our loss in the dying of this creative and compassionate man.[8]

One might say many things about the bishops' response to the "Pike affair." The most obvious is that the official statements and remarks by the bishops in large measure display what I have called the newer tradition. Thus, the bishops, despite their vows to guard the doctrine of the church, believed that a heresy trial would give the church a bad name with the wider American public, and it might inhibit theological exploration and reformation required by fidelity to the church's mission in a secular age. The resolution of 1970 seems to indicate, furthermore, that after the elapse of a remarkably short period of time, the bishops of the Episcopal Church had come to the conclusion that even their censure had proven unfortunately exclusionary and harmful.

What are the assumptions that lie behind these views? The most

---

7. Ibid., p. 31.
8. Minutes of the House of Bishops 1970 in *Journal of the General Convention* (New York: Office of the General Convention), p. 79.

basic is certainly that heresy is itself a suspect notion. Why? The majority report of the theology committee suggests that to discipline severely even a heretical bishop would give the church a bad name with the general public, illegitimately repress and penalize "unacceptable opinions," and identify faith with "traditional propositions" rather than with "the response of the whole man to God."

The minority report goes further and suggests that a concern about heresy hinders the mission of the church. Such an interest manifests an undue concern to defend "positions of the past." It thereby fails to recognize that the past "is altered with each new discovery of truth," and, in so failing, inhibits the ability of the church "to be a sympathetic and self-conscious part of God's action in the secular world." The memorial resolution of the House of Bishops suggests, furthermore, that discipline for heresy both silences prophecy in the church and reveals an unacceptable inability to include individuals, especially individual bishops, whose particular pilgrimage may take them in directions other than those marked out either by the fundamental doctrines and practices of the church or by their oath to order the life of the church in accord with these doctrines and practices.

As one reviews the record, the newer tradition at first stands out. However, from time to time the original tradition appears. It reads in a very different way. According to the original tradition, bishops occupy an office that requires them not only to maintain the unity of the church but to do so in such a way as "to banish and drive away . . . all erroneous and strange doctrine contrary to God's Word."[9] By implication, some duties of office may require the sacrifice of certain personal opinions and predilections. This view produced the most contrary note in an otherwise mild act of censure; that is, the bishops wished to disassociate themselves from many of Bishop Pike's utterances "as being irresponsible on the part of one holding the office and trust he shares with us."

This review of the record indicates that because of the "Pike affair" two views of authority and discipline surfaced. According to one, discipline represents an attempt to silence prophecy and inhibit individual insight and liberty. As such, attempts to discipline resist the

9. This vow had to be taken by all bishops consecrated, as was Bishop Pike, in accordance with the ordinal in the Book of Common Prayer adopted by the General Convention of the ECUSA in 1928.

providential movement of God in history and so betray the real purpose of oversight. According to the other, discipline is necessary to preserve communion and to honor established procedures for institutional review and change as the church waits in the midst of great storm and stress for the return of Christ.

The Ordination of Women

The debate over how the church ought to view the first ordinations of women to the priesthood serves to reveal more about the basic assumptions that lie behind each of these positions. This second issue of oversight and discipline surfaced in 1974 when three retired bishops ordained to the priesthood eleven women deacons. These ordinations were performed after a motion to ordain women priests had failed at two consecutive General Conventions (1970 and 1973). Review of the record reveals a variety of clashing opinions about how these acts ought to be judged. In an open letter to the church, the three ordaining bishops claimed that their act was an obedient and prophetic protest against oppression and an act of solidarity with those oppressed (in this case, women).[10]

A number of Episcopal bishops saw things in yet another light. In response to what they believed to be a gross violation of church order, at a special meeting in August 1974, twenty-three bishops charged the ordaining bishops with violation of the Constitution and Canons of the ECUSA, the rubrics of the Book of Common Prayer, and their ordination vows.

Seeking once more to avoid a trial, the House of Bishops, at this meeting and at a subsequent one in October of the same year, adopted resolutions critical of the ordaining bishops' behavior. The resolutions in question "decried" (but did not censure) the action of the bishops as a breach of collegiality. The second of the two went on to question the validity of the ordinations themselves and to call for no further ordinations until the matter had been settled one way or another by the General Convention.

Because there was no inhibition of the offenders, some bishops

10. *The Living Church* (August 18, 1974): 5.

thought that the resolution was insufficient. Thus, at the same meeting they filed another set of charges. In accord with the canons, the Presiding Bishop set up a committee to review them. The committee gave its report in March 1975. They found that canonical offenses had been committed and that the acts involved "teaching publicly a doctrine contrary to that held by the Church." In the body of their report, the committee went on to raise what is arguably the most fundamental issue of order and discipline these irregular ordinations presented. The committee asked "whether this church's understanding of the nature of the church and the authority of the episcopate permits individual bishops, appealing solely to their consciences, to usurp the proper functions of other duly constituted authorities in this church."[11]

By canon law, a charge of false teaching brought against any of its members must be addressed by the House of Bishops. Once more, however, the House of Bishops chose not to proceed to trial. In his opening address at the next meeting of the House in September 1975, the Presiding Bishop, John Allin, said, "We cannot get involved in a judicial process . . . because we don't have that sort of energy." The Theology Committee of the House of Bishops did, however, respond in detail to the findings of the investigative committee that had been filed at the previous meeting. In contradistinction to the previous report, the Theology Committee stated that they found no scriptural or theological barrier to women's ordination. Nevertheless, in coming to this conclusion, the Theology Committee stated what might have proved (but did not) an important principle for the adjudication of this and other similar cases of ecclesiastical disobedience:

> In our judgment there is an immediate and formal correlation between the powers of the ordained ministry and the community within which that power is exercised . . . each refers to the other in order to be itself; neither is itself in isolation from the other. . . . While a bishop is called to exercise prophetic witness . . . , he is not free to appropriate the sacramental structure of the Church to his own views within the Church.[12]

11. Minutes of the House of Bishops 1975 in the *Journal of the General Convention* (New York: Office of the General Convention).

12. Minutes of the House of Bishops 1976 in the *Journal of the General Convention* (New York: Office of the General Convention), p. B-319.

Despite the resolutions passed and the reports given, all critical of the bishops' actions, by the time the House of Bishops met again in October 1975, Bishop George Barrett had ordained four additional women deacons to the priesthood. As in the first case, the ordaining bishop had no diocese. This time, however, all but one of the women involved had completed the requirements that must be met before ordination within the ECUSA. The House of Bishops, nonetheless, reacted swiftly with a vote not to "censure" but to "decry" the action of Bishop Barrett. They did, however, vote to "censure" the three original ordaining bishops, namely, DeWitt, Corrigan, and Wells.

In 1976, with these actions fresh in mind, the General Convention adopted a resolution authorizing the ordination of women. As a result, the ordination of women became a recognized practice. Nevertheless, the question of discipline for previous acts of ecclesiastical disobedience remained. In 1978, the House of Bishops returned to the subject and passed a motion reminding the church of the censure of bishops DeWitt, Corrigan, and Wells. A motion that would have barred them from any further deliberations of the house failed, but in its place the following resolution passed:

> Resolved, that the Secretary notify Bishops DeWitt, Corrigan and Wells that it is the mind of this House that they betrayed the trust that the church placed in them in their consecration; and have broken their fellowship with the House of Bishops and that the Presiding Bishop and/or such other Bishops as the Presiding Bishop may designate should raise, with the bishops who have been censured, questions concerning their continued participation in the deliberations of the House, and report the results of such discussion to the next meeting of the House.[13]

At the beginning of the next meeting of the House of Bishops, the Presiding Bishop reported that he had "productive meetings" with the offending bishops. No further actions have since been taken in respect to these matters either by the House of Bishops or the General Convention. The matter of the legitimacy of the ordinations performed by the bishops was left to the discretion of individual dioceses.

13. Minutes of the House of Bishops 1978 in the *Journal of the General Convention* (New York: Office of the General Convention), p. 258.

None of the women were required to be ordained according to the established procedures of the ECUSA and the dioceses in question.

As with the "Pike affair," it would be untrue to say that, in the case of the "irregular ordinations," no disciplinary action was taken by the House of Bishops. It is, however, true that no actions were taken against the women ordinands and that the discipline taken in respect to the bishops was, once more, mild and arguably ineffective. Indeed, one must ask if the precedents laid down in the case of the "irregular ordinations" have not spurred other acts of ecclesiastical disobedience, namely, the increasingly frequent though unauthorized ordination of practicing homosexuals. These acts will be the subject of attention in the concluding section of this essay. Before turning to them, however, it will prove instructive to ask once more what the actions of the House of Bishops reveal about the two traditions this history displays and what they suggest about the assumptions that lie behind them.

Two Views of Oversight and Discipline

First, the original tradition holds that bishops are particularly responsible for the good order of the church, and, to this end, they make vows to God before the church. The very purpose of these vows is to inhibit personal freedom in respect to doctrine and order. For this reason the offending bishops were originally charged with violations of the canons and their ordination vows. For this reason also the charges brought against the offending bishops "decried" their breach of collegiality. The point would seem to be that unless the defenders of order follow the order they are to defend and so also refuse to act without the assent and cooperation of their fellow bishops, there can be no dependable order at all. Each bishop in effect becomes judge in his own case and in so doing undermines the point of the vows by means of which he received his title and authority.

The comments of the initial board of inquiry set up by the Presiding Bishop suggest certain presuppositions that lie behind the insistence on the part of the bishops who brought charges upon the importance of canonical order and the binding authority of vows and collegiality. They asked whether the nature of the church and the nature of the authority entrusted to bishops "permits individual bishops, appealing solely to their consciences, to usurp the proper functions of other duly constituted authorities in this church?"

The response of the Theology Committee to the investigative committee report suggests that its authors held similar views. The majority report of the Theology Committee stated that "there is an immediate and formal correlation between the powers of the ordained ministry and the community within which that power is exercised." It went on to insist that a bishop "is not free to appropriate the sacramental structure of the church to his own views."

Certain presuppositions about order, authority, office, and discipline make such statements intelligible. Together they make up the tradition of authority that has guided the thinking of catholic Christians from the beginning. According to this tradition, authority in all its forms is a form of social control that lies between raw power on the one hand and the simple ability to exert influence on the other. To have authority (as opposed to influence), one must be licensed both to command and enforce (take disciplinary action), and yet (in a way different from the exercise of raw power) the commands issued and the acts of enforcement that may follow must fall within a commonly recognized moral and legal order.

Thus, according to the originating tradition, authority exists to further commonly held beliefs and ways of life in circumstances where unanimity lies beyond immediate reach. With reference to the church, authority exists "between the ages" or "for the time being" to maintain the communion of saints that between this age and the next remains in a less than perfected state. In other words, the authority of bishops exists to further the common belief and life of a "good enough" church while the members thereof (who before God remain *simul justi et peccatores*) await the return of Christ and so a time when all rule and authority disappear because God will be all in all.

In their determinations, therefore, those responsible for the oversight of the life of the church must make prudential judgments about how best to further common beliefs and ways of life during a period when the church is buffeted both from within and without. Since they live in the tension between this age and the next, those who make these determinations must on the one hand uphold Christian belief and life, and yet also take account of the fact that we know in part and that we remain always justified sinners. To paraphrase

Bishop Kirk of Oxford, ecclesiastical oversight and discipline are always prudential matters that do not lend themselves to deductive reasoning. In the exercise of oversight and discipline, one must deploy the virtue of prudence and in so doing strike a balance between rigorism on the one hand and antinomianism on the other.[14]

Before proceeding, one more thing needs to be said about the originating tradition. If a communion of saints that lives by faith in God's mercy rather than trust in its own perfection is to be maintained over time, authority must be linked to a system of offices that exist within an order or polity. If, as a moral notion, authority serves to promote the legitimate use of power within a commonwealth, polity and office serve to promote the orderly and perduring use of authority within the same. The major constitutional work of a church, therefore, is to assure that authority is adequately linked to office within a polity, and that authority, working through office within the rules of a polity, indeed promotes, with due allowance for human limitation and sin, what is common rather than foreign to Christian belief and life.

These assumptions serve to explain the action of those bishops who brought charges against the ordaining bishops. They imply that when one responsible for the doctrine and order of the church acts in a way that serves to undermine either, it is incumbent upon those who also hold positions of authority to take notice and decide upon a prudential course of action. Failure on the part of those who hold authority to address a threat to the faith and common life of the church indicates either a dereliction of duty or (more seriously) a de facto rebellion, revolution, or schism.

These assumptions about communion, authority, power, office, and polity also suggest what ought to be the course of action followed by someone who, like the ordaining bishops, feels unable for conscience' sake to follow a particular dictate of authority or a particular law of polity. If the disagreement is not one that requires rebellion, revolution, or schism, and yet morally demands disobedience, then the person acting disobediently has an obligation first of all to use all reasonable legal means to get the unacceptable ruling changed. Failing this he may assume a duty to be ecclesiastically disobedient but, should he actually do so, he is also obliged both to expect and accept punish-

14. See Kenneth Kirk, *The Vision of God* (London: Longmans Green and Co., 1931), pp. 4-10, 111-73.

ment. Exhaustion of all reasonable and legal means for change and acceptance of punishment are necessary ways to make it clear that an act of ecclesiastical disobedience is not in fact a rebellious, revolutionary, or schismatic one.[15]

The record reveals that the original account of authority and discipline is still present within the ECUSA. It reveals also that it is being submerged by the newer tradition. Thus, the protesting bishops in the case of the first ordinations of women justified their action by direct reference to the "Lordship of Christ" and to the "sovereignty of the Holy Spirit." They implied, therefore, that their action was a direct act of obedience to a divine command to show solidarity with people who, by the order of the church, were being denied both "freedom" and "dignity."[16]

More light is shed upon this other point of view by a letter written to the House of Bishops by the four women ordained by Bishop Barrett. The women offered this justification for their participation in ordinations that the House of Bishops had said should not occur: "To await another vote by the General Convention which has twice defeated the ordination of women to the priesthood *in principle* is to affirm the concept that discrimination against women may be practiced in the church until the majority changes its mind and votes."[17]

It would appear that, for the women involved, their act of ecclesiastical disobedience was taken after due process, in their judgment, had failed as a means of protesting unjustifiable discrimination against women. The issue in their minds, and in the minds of the protesting bishops, appears to have been that the order of the church was itself at this point immoral and from that time on should (again in respect to the ordination of women) no longer be considered binding upon conscience.

To this point, we can understand the actions of both the bishops and the women they ordained to be acts of ecclesiastical disobedience rather than schism. However, two factors obscure the nature of the

15. For a contemporary account of the ethics of civil disobedience that applies as well to ecclesiastical disobedience see James Childress, *Civil Disobedience and Political Obligation* (New Haven: Yale Univ. Press, 1971).

16. *The Living Church* (August 18, 1974): 5.

17. Cited by Lyon, 1992, p. 12.

case. First, by not insisting that the women in question be reordained (this time following the due processes of the church) the House of Bishops, despite their act of censure and their statements of disapproval, left it unclear as to whether there had indeed been a serious violation of order. This impression is given greater weight by the unwillingness of the bishops to censure or otherwise discipline Bishop Barrett, who contravened the express order of the House of Bishops that no further ordinations take place until General Convention had approved.

Second, because the disciplinary actions of the House of Bishops were less than clear in their intent, no issue was forced with the protesters. They were presented with no opportunity to make clear to the church whether or not they viewed their acts as acts of ecclesial disobedience or of rebellion, revolution, or schism.

My own guess is that neither ecclesiastical disobedience nor schism were on the minds of the protesting bishops and the women ordinands. It may well have been that both simply believed God to be on their side and that time would show them to be right because everyone would follow their lead. With the conviction firmly in mind that they were obeying a divine command (a conviction clearly stated by the protesting bishops), they could have believed also that no submission of their act to judgment on the part of the church was appropriate. No ecclesial verdict on the matter was called for because God himself had given the command and would himself provide the verdict in due time.

If this had been the stated opinion of the bishops and the women they ordained (which it was not), their detractors would no doubt have reminded them that even Paul submitted his decision to baptize Gentiles to the Jerusalem Council, and that Anglican polity instantiates a belief that personal convictions about divine commands ought always to be brought before the church for confirmation.

In my view, the confusion that surrounds this case stems neither from schismatic intentions nor from a lack of awareness that discipline might be called for, nor from a disputed appeal to prophecy. The confusion stems rather from the fact that both parties involved were insufficiently aware of the richness of the originating tradition about communion, order, authority, discipline, and ecclesiastical disobedience to which they were jointly heir. As a result, both parties lacked the resources of moral discrimination afforded by that tradition. Had they been more aware than they appear to have been, each party to this dispute might have been able to make their point with greater clarity and effectiveness. Indeed, their dispute might have served to edify rather than to divide the church.

Another problem as well might have stood behind this clash of two points of view. The originating tradition contains an account of those virtues necessary for its continued health and effectiveness. This part of the originating tradition touches on the spiritual gifts and powers of soul necessary if the historic episcopate is to prove an effective sign and guardian of the apostolic witness.

According to the originating tradition, order, dissent, and disobedience are all intended to foster communion in the truth and life of Christ. As such, each depends upon the presence in the church of those powers of soul by which Christ makes koinonia possible. The fact is that harmonious common life depends more upon the presence of virtue in a community than it does upon fair procedures.

The fourth chapter of the Epistle to the Ephesians contains as good a summary of these necessary strengths of soul as we possess. They are, among others, humility, meekness, patience, forbearance, eagerness to maintain unity, truthfulness, kindness, tenderheartedness, and forgiveness (see, e.g., Eph. 4:1-3, 15, 32). To these "fruits of the Spirit" should be added the "natural virtues" of prudence, courage, temperance, and justice.

These homely virtues give thickness to the idea of love, the great virtue that makes it possible for the church in fact to follow in the teaching and example of the apostles. They root the doctrine of the church in the soil of everyday life, and in so doing give it concreteness. They, most of all, make it possible for the church to maintain its communion, order, and discipline without schism in the midst of fierce disagreement.

These remarks seem necessary for more than theoretical reasons. Bishop Allin's remark that the House of Bishops did not have "the energy for a judicial process" suggests the disturbing possibility that neither its members nor the members of the church for whose order the bishops were responsible possessed the gifts and virtues necessary to confront their differences in a disciplined and direct manner. In reviewing the record, it is tempting to be overly critical of what appears to be a certain timidity on the part of the bishops. Nevertheless, if the originating theory of authority sketched above has any validity, those

127

in authority exist in a dialectical relation with those among whom their authority is exercised. If a community has let its moral traditions about the exercise of oversight and the imposition of discipline decay and if, at the same time, the powers of soul necessary for the exercise of authority decline, then authority, despite its best intentions, simply cannot function as it ought. In such circumstances, a prudential and effective response to an act of ecclesiastical disobedience would by definition lie beyond the intellectual and moral reach of both the bishops and the church as a whole.

If indeed the ECUSA was (and is) confronted with such a crisis, then perhaps the best and most prudent thing the House of Bishops could have done at the time was to do what they did — put together a pastiche, a bit of bricolage, made up of bits and pieces culled from the two traditions to which I have referred. The majority of the House may have thought that their responsibility for oversight (and so communion) lay in patching things up as best they could while waiting for a better day.

The Unauthorized Ordination
of Gay and Lesbian People

At this point I cannot demonstrate whether these were in fact the intentions of the House of Bishops. No matter what their intentions may have been, their actions amount to a pastiche and the question that arises concerns the wisdom of the compromises struck.

Cruel though it seems, it can be argued, despite the posthumously expressed regrets on the part of the House of Bishops, that the disciplinary actions taken in the "Pike affair" were effective. Under censure, Bishop Pike chose to leave the Episcopal Church and declare himself out of communion with people whose discipline he did not accept and whose beliefs he did not share. Nevertheless, the unauthorized ordination of gay and lesbian people that followed hard on the heels of the "irregular" ordination of women at least raises questions about the effectiveness of the House of Bishops' response to these ordinations. A review of the record makes it difficult to escape the conclusion that a growing number of Episcopal bishops and clergy, claiming the prophet's mantle, seem willing to act according to their own likes and convictions and to do so without fear or expectation of discipline.

The first of these ordinations was performed in 1977 by Paul Moore, Jr., Bishop of New York. During the height of the controversy over women's ordination, he ordained a professed and practicing lesbian to the priesthood. In response, at their next meeting, the House of Bishops received a report that said, among other things, that "the ordination of an advocating and/or practicing homosexual . . . involves the Church in a public denial of its own theological and moral norms on sexuality."[18] A minority report was also submitted.[19] After hearing the reports, a resolution was proposed, stating that the House of Bishops "disapproved" of the action taken by the Bishop, Standing Committee and Commission on Ministry of the Diocese of New York.[20] After some debate, this motion was tabled. Bishop Moore then submitted a letter of apology to the House, which was subsequently incorporated into the minutes.

In the end, no disciplinary action was taken. Nevertheless, at the General Convention in 1979 a resolution was passed that said, among other things, "we believe it is not appropriate for this Church to ordain a practicing homosexual or any person who is engaged in heterosexual relations outside marriage."[21] In reaction to the majority vote, twenty bishops signed a letter that stated their view that the action of the General Convention was "recommendatory and not prescriptive," and announced that, in the name of "apostolic leadership" and "prophetic witness," they would not implement the resolution in their dioceses.[22]

In retrospect, what strikes one as remarkable about the dissenter's statement is its implied claim that anyone who so chooses can consider a resolution of the General Convention that is clearly intended to prohibit the introduction of a new practice into the church to be "recommendary" rather than "prescriptive." This claim is particularly striking because the new practice of ordaining women had just been introduced into the ECUSA by resolution. No one seemed

18. Minutes of the House of Bishops 1977 in the *Journal of the General Convention,* (New York: Office of the General Convention), p. B-184.

19. Ibid., pp. B-185-88.

20. Ibid., p. B-192.

21. Ibid., pp. B-96-97.

22. Ibid., p. B-112

to notice that if dissenters can simply assert, as they did, that a resolution is recommendary rather than prescriptive, others can do the same when they find themselves in the minority. If such a view were to prevail, one would be faced with governance by assertion rather than by due process.

Despite these remarkable implications, as far as I can determine no reply was made to the dissenting bishops' assertion. Indeed, in more recent cases, bishops ordaining either gay or lesbian people have in fact justified their actions by asserting, as did the originators of the claim, that the General Convention resolution in question is merely recommendatory.[23]

That the majority of the House of Bishops did not at that time consider the resolution merely recommendatory is indicated by the fact that there were no publicized actions contrary to the General Convention resolution taken by any of the bishops for a decade. Nevertheless, on December 16, 1989, the Bishop of Newark, John Spong, amid considerable public fanfare, ordained to the priesthood a man who was known to have been in a long-term homosexual relationship.

On this occasion, the first reaction did not come from an officially constituted committee of the House of Bishops but from an unofficial committee known as the Presiding Bishop's Council of Advice. This council, made up of representatives from each province of the ECUSA, "disassociated" itself from Bishop Spong's action, and, while noting that a number of bishops were not in agreement with the General Convention resolution on the ordination of homosexuals, noted that they, the Council of Advice, "believe that good order is not served when bishops, dioceses, or parishes act unilaterally." They concluded that they believed as well that "good order is served by adherence to the actions of General Convention."[24]

It should be noted that the rebuke issued to Bishop Spong was considerably milder than those given the offending bishops in the case of women's ordination. It is also important to note that the admonitions given about the importance of order and of adherence to the

23. See, e.g., the statement by the present Episcopal Bishop of Chicago in *Christianity Today* (January 1994). In an interview, the bishop defended his decision to ordain a certain number of practicing gay people on precisely this ground.

24. Minutes of the House of Bishops 1990 in the *Journal of the General Convention* (New York: Office of the General Convention), pp. 501-502.

actions of General Convention were of little effect. In June 1990, Bishop Walter Righter ordained a known and practicing homosexual, as did Bishop Ronald Haynes in June 1991. Though a motion to censure bishops Righter and Haynes failed, the House of Bishops in 1991 did pass a motion that mentioned no names but acknowledged "the pain and damage to the collegiality and credibility of this House and to the whole Church when individual bishops and dioceses ordain sexually active gay and lesbian persons in the face of repeated statements of this House of Bishops and the General Convention."[25]

It is widely acknowledged that since that date other ordinations of practicing homosexuals have occurred, but no disciplinary actions have been taken. Furthermore, it is increasingly simply asserted by dissenters that the resolution of General Convention in respect to the ordination of gay and lesbian people has only the force of a recommendation. That this claim goes unchallenged appears to indicate that twenty bishops, giving voice over a decade ago to their own dissent, have by simple declaration been able to work a change in Episcopal polity that has received no ratification by the body whose operation it was originally meant to challenge.

Thus, over the last quarter of a century the House of Bishops of the ECUSA has been confronted by statements and actions on the part of individual bishops that fly in the face of established doctrine, morality, and order. In the first case, a bishop left the church after an act of censure. In no case, however, has a bishop been removed from office or in any way inhibited in the exercise thereof. Further, the disciplinary actions of the bishops have become increasingly weaker, moving as they have from censure to statements that "decry" an action or "disassociate" other bishops from it. Each reaction seems weaker and less effective than the one before. One must ask, therefore, about the prudence of a pattern of oversight and discipline that, in the face of obvious challenges to the doctrine and discipline of the church, goes no further than an increasingly mild and qualified expression of disapproval. One must ask if this pattern of response does not signal both the decay of tradition and the decline of virtue within an entire church and a de facto break in its communion — an internal schism whereby warring factions make use of a single organizational structure but in fact do not seek to maintain communion by means of it.

25. Ibid., pp. 321-22.

Conclusion

What conclusions ought to be drawn from this history and its analysis? A number of inferences can be made, but one presents itself with particular force. Even if it is true, as the Concordat asserts, that the doctrinal formulations and liturgies of the ECUSA and the ELCA present no issues of sufficient weight to divide the church, and even if each church is prepared to recognize the ministry of the other as being in the proper sense apostolic, the preceding examination of oversight and discipline within the ECUSA raises the question of whether or not the moral tradition that in part defines and in part preserves "the communion of saints" is sufficiently vital to preserve the apostolicity of the church within its forms.

Lutherans have tended to focus on confessional agreement as a means of ensuring apostolicity. Episcopalians have turned to the historic episcopate and liturgical form to achieve the same purpose. My study suggests that apart from the moral tradition sketched above, episcopacy cannot be effectively linked to apostolicity. The question of course is whether the same can be said about establishing a link between confessional adequacy and apostolicity. It would take another study to answer this question, but I suspect that the same moral tradition is just as necessary for maintaining the apostolicity of a confessional church.

If this observation is correct, it serves to provide a partial explanation for the remark from the *Niagara Report* with which this essay began. After lengthy studies of the two churches, the framers of that report on *episcope* said of both Episcopalians and Lutherans "that the succession in the presiding ministry of their respective churches no longer incontestably links those churches to the *koinonia* of the whole church."[26] If this observation is correct, as it appears certainly to be in the case of the ECUSA, it leads to a rather unexpected question, namely, Exactly what is the ecumenical importance of the proposed Concordat?

Clearly, the long history of dialogue between Lutherans and Anglicans has produced among its participants a conviction that any differences in doctrine, worship, or church order that exist between the two are of insufficient weight to warrant either to exclude the

26. *The Niagara Report,* p. 33.

other from full communion. The agreements about doctrine, baptism, eucharist, and ministry that have been reached by representatives of the ECUSA and the ELCA represent a milestone in ecumenical relations. They ought to be a cause for rejoicing.

Few, however, are rejoicing. Why? The history traced above suggests a disturbing possibility, namely, that forms like the historic episcopate, or the shape of the liturgy, or the Augsburg Confession can remain in place yet be ignored or subverted and denied from below. If doctrine and discipline can be ignored or subverted in this way, and if the moral tradition that makes effective oversight and discipline possible falls into decline, then a much to be desired ecumenical event, full communion between the ECUSA and the ELCA, may still leave the question of apostolic succession in its proper sense unresolved. It may well turn out that the deep issue before these two churches soon (I hope) to be bound in full communion is the same for both. With all the agreements about doctrine, baptism, eucharist, and ministry in place, it might (and I believe it will) prove to be the case that those who are responsible for the oversight of the doctrine and common life of the two churches find themselves, because of the decline of the moral tradition necessary for the exercise of episcopal oversight and discipline, unable to protect either church from the distortions of doctrine and discipline now powerfully present in both.

The Cost of Communion: A Meditation on Israel and the Divided Church

EPHRAIM RADNER

Israel, a Figure of the Christian Church Conformed to Christ

The purpose of this essay is to place movements toward ecumenical communion like the Concordat within the context of scriptural prophecy; it is to read them, in other words, in terms of the future signaled by the divine promises offered in the Bible's discussion of communal division and integration. The prophetic context I will explore in particular is that of Israel, understood to be the figure that historically embodies the Christian church's present endeavors to overcome denominational separation.

I should emphasize first that my remarks derive from a firm judgment as to the Concordat's rightness as part of God's plan for Christ's church. Still, in adopting the material of scriptural prophecy to this discussion, I am also calling into question many of the Concordat's temporally and socially limited premises, justifications by its framers that rely on affirmations of denominational readiness within supposed historical evolutions. Prophecy speaks of a divine decree imposed on the often *un*willing. Thus, what an appeal to prophecy on this matter calls into question in particular is the pervasive presumption of the ecclesial integrity of those denominations coming to the Concordat, as well as the assumption that the proposed arrangement for "full communion" will act as a ratification of that integrity. Whatever lip service is paid to an acknowledgment of our past shortcomings, the possibility of the Concordat's proposed structural

134

changes in Lutheran and Episcopal ordination and oversight has been founded on the sense that each denomination already possesses the status of "churches in which the Gospel is preached and taught" and that each already stands united in the "One, Holy, Catholic, and Apostolic Church."[1] Within these assumptions is an idealist strain that the given reality of unity, already accomplished, simply awaits its apprehension. But these assumptions are necessarily subverted by a glance at the scriptural vision of disunity as the historical judgment against unrighteousness. A prophetic understanding of denomination-alism answers with a curt No the question as to whether divided churches can, by definition, possess integrity at all.

The obviousness of this judgment on the divided church's lack of integrity has been obscured by a novel unwillingness, over the last few centuries, to view the Christian church as figured prophetically in the people of Israel. At the time of the sixteenth-century Reforma-tion and Counter-reformation polemics, all groups insisted on the integrity of their *own* party as "church," whatever their opponents' failures. (Ecumenical "progress" is now marked by the generous ex-tension of such an appellation to others.) That there be *some* Christian body rightly designated as "church" at any given time was, in any case, an article of faith linked to a common belief in the "indefectability" (if not infallibility) of Christ's ecclesial body: "the gates of Hades will not prevail against it" (Matt. 16:18). In addition, however various were the theological reasonings involved in such an assertion, a common exegetical practice supported it. That is, the Christian church was seen as having supplanted the limited and broken fortunes of the Old Testament's Israel. This "supersessionist" attitude, whereby the scrip-tural narratives of Israel's failures were excluded from references to the Christian church, appears to have been a peculiar accomplishment of the Reformation era, and one well-suited to the self-justifying claims of a factionalized Christendom. While patristic commentators from Origen and Theodoret through medieval scholars like Hugh of

---

1. See "Toward Full Communion," in William A. Norgren and William G. Rusch, eds., *"Toward Full Communion" and "Concordat of Agreement," Lutheran-Episcopal Dialogue, Series 3* (Minneapolis: Augsburg; Cincinnati: Forward Movement, 1991), pars. 25-27 and 82-91, for examples of how the progress of dialogue is fueled by the principle of "recognition," according to which each party is called primarily to see in the other a church that is, of itself, fully "church." The sin against unity from this perspective is the sin against the recognition of integrity within diversity.

St. Victor could continue to read the Old Testament prophets in their discourses on the fate of Israel for good and ill as speaking figurally about the Christian church's history as well, we find Luther, Calvin, Donne, and Bellarmine adamant about limiting these prophesied visions to the fate of the Hebrew people that the Christian church had supplanted, useful in the present only as examples of moral obstinacy divinely requited.[2]

This exegetical separation of Israel and the Christian church, mercilessly raised to the level of dogma by historical criticism, left an enormous gap in the churches' powers to explain their own division. Virtually no New Testament text explicitly deals with the reality of schism and separation within the church, and with the resulting lack of scriptural resource, we have seen how contemporary ecumenical rationales can search after only vague theological principles to sustain their efforts — dominical encouragements to mutual love, the "nature" of the eucharist, Trinitarian "relations," and so forth. These rationales often float freely, divorced from any understanding of the divinely informed character of our intrinsically problematic ecclesial existence as a fractured body.

The alternative that I shall advocate is to let go altogether of the exegetical supplanting of Israel by the church, and to return to the New Testament's — and (albeit inconsistently) the undivided church's — own willingness to see in Israel the figure for the Christian church's historical formation. My goal here is to gain some kind of clarity about the demands, frightening in some respects, facing our churches as they in fact pursue communion in even the limited forms envisaged by the Concordat. We must see how the reality of the church's division, as well as the promise for its restoration, is given in the form of Israel's own existence. And in so doing we must also see how the figure of Christ's own life must give shape to whatever disciplines of ecclesial existence we engage as faithful responses to the search for Christian unity.

What would such a prophetic exploration of division and unity

---

2. "Supersessionism" of a kind that viewed Christians as taking the place of Jews *within* Israel was, of course, something constant in the history of the church. The point is that, however much traditional Christian exegesis was anti-Judaic in its assignment of non-Christian ethnic Jews to a condemned position within the nation of Israel, until modern times Israel itself was still always affirmed as continuously existent in the historical body of the church.

in the church look like? Two fundamental premises underlie the New Testament's own discussion of the divided church. First, the historical reality of the church's fragmentation is located within a specific era, what Scripture predictively identifies as the "last days" of demonic assault, within which the followers of Christ are violently, and not all successfully, drawn into conformance with his own redemptive life and death. This is the context that informs both standard ecumenical proof-texts like John 17:23, just as it is made explicit in the single New Testament text that concretely deals with the reality of schism and separation within the church, 1 John 2:18ff. Thus, we must claim this era as our own. The second premise asserts that the prophetic bridge by which the church's life in the endtimes, including her division, is biblically explicated lies in the figural fulfillment given to all scriptural promises in the person of Christ, a fulfillment in which the church, his body, participates. Christ stands as the mediating figure by whom the church is linked to the prophetic contours of the Old Testament's witness, and he stands as the access by which the whole of Scripture is directed by God to speak to the church.

I propose, then, that we build on these two premises by looking to Israel as the form of the church. Through Christ, who provides the salvific shape to Israel's redeemed life as prophesied in the Old Testament, the Christian church exists as Israel's historical continuation (not replacement), for whom at the end of the ages, all that has happened to God's people in the past has taken place in a "figural" *(typikos)* and instructional fashion (1 Cor. 10:11). As Christ's body, the church's life is prophesied through the life of Israel "of the flesh," which forms her parallel through time (see Rom. 11), and her predictive symbol for the Last Days (e.g., Rev. 12). Thus, the shape and fate of the Christian church's life in disunity is given formal order in the scriptural life of Israel, a fact attested to implicitly by the church's continued liturgical use of the Psalter (e.g., Ps. 80) or of texts like Lamentations. An examination of Israel's own fragmentation and restoration to unity, according to Scripture's witness, ought then to provide a prophetic illumination to the shape of our own ecumenical endeavors in these latter days. This is my proposal, and to this task I now turn.

Prophetic Parallels between
Divided Israel and the Church

Reading the division of the Christian church in the prophetic terms of Israel's life requires at least two activities. The first is a retrospective identification of the historical parallels that already establish the figural conformity between the peoples of the two testaments, a discernment, in short, of prophecy fulfilled. This activity, however, goes beyond a mere assertion of the applicability of certain Old Testament textual referents to the church's temporal life in a general way. Applying these elements of Israel's history to what can be observed already of the church's experience is an act of penitential confession that derives from the particular shape of present ecclesial distress. Therefore, unless we submit to the concrete resemblances of scriptural figure as part of a movement in self-knowledge, we cannot grasp the promises embedded in those figures. Having admitted such resemblances, then, a second activity can be assumed: following the prophetic contours of the figures themselves into the church's future, pursuing them with the cautious expectation that springs from that peculiar mixture of fear and hope which surrounds the Scripture's historical promises. To see how the church's history in the past fulfills the figure of Israel in Christ is an act of penitential faith that thereby permits us to discern and to welcome our divinely revealed future. Thus, when Paul, in the manner of a psalmic benediction, calls down peace and mercy upon the Christian church as the "Israel of God" (Gal. 6:16), he does so in the light of his own conformance to his crucified Lord: "From now on, let no one make trouble for me; for I carry the marks of Jesus branded on my body" (Gal. 6:17). Only by living in this detailed conformity, from which the prayer for peace and mercy springs more as longing, can the church recognize herself as Israel and behold her life in the form of Israel.

Notice now what this double vision — to the past's prophecies fulfilled and to the future's promises of conformity as they await us — must mean when we actually come to read the life of Israel figurally in terms of the Christian church's history of schism. The prophet Ahijah's prediction of the dismemberment of Solomon's kingdom is symbolized in the tearing of a garment into pieces (1 Kings 11:29ff.). But this symbol of dismemberment is taken up through Jesus' own accomplishment of Solomon's messianic character (cf. the use of Ps.

72 in Matt. 2:11 and Luke 1:68) and given its most pointed, if altered, expression in the fate of his own clothing distributed at the cross. Thus, when Paul asks concerning the factions at Corinth (1 Cor. 1:13), "Has Christ been divided?" he uses language reminiscent, through the crucifixion's intervention, of just that first disintegration of Israel in the wake of Solomon's sin and Jeroboam's revolt prophesied by Ahijah. The church is tied to this past, through the body of her Lord, and when early Christian exegetes like Origen tried to understand the heretical conflicts tearing apart the church, they could, in the Person of Christ, turn to the divided Kingdom of Israel as the prophetic figure for the church's present woes and future healing.

Keeping in sight this christological bridge protects one from the self-justifying predictive correlation of free-floating events. We must rather see their linkage as figures of promise and judgment only in terms of the cross's redemptive assumption of sin. The church looks to Israel's past in order to acknowledge her own present, a present that must be described primarily, as oriented in the cross of Christ, in the language of subsuming penitence. If we are to see, for instance, the Reformation's institutionalization of ecclesial division within the history of Israel's partition into separate kingdoms of Samaria and Judah, of North and South, we cannot simply be content to note the parallels of righteous dissatisfaction that lay behind these revolts against entrenched structures of oppression (see 1 Kings 12). It may well be that the specifics of these events fall cleanly within the dynamics of rational or strategically justifiable social evolution; here historians and perhaps ecumenical documentarians properly pursue their craft. But the figural character of the events as scripturally given to the church points elsewhere, to their location within a larger movement of human sin's painful adoption by the form of divine mercy. This view discloses the demise of Israel as the shape given to judgment's curse within a redemptive scheme, a demise that has no purpose or justification beyond this. Therefore we can evaluate the church's own division no differently.

Beginning with the self-seeking call for a king on the part of the people (see 1 Sam. 8), the movement toward Israel's partition and ultimate destruction as an independent kingdom had its roots in the abandonment of God for the sake of human pride's satisfaction. The sins of Solomon and Rehoboam, against which the people "righteously" revolted in setting up the northern kingdom (the revolt was divinely sanctioned in this regard) were themselves a form of punishment visited upon the nation as a whole, whose reach in fact lay far beyond the fragmentation of Solomon's royal legacy. These particular sins were to form the borders of Israel's extended communal experience, bearing with them the final results of the country's destruction at the hands of foreigners and the people's ultimate decimation and exile. The constant warfare between Samaria and Judah (1 Kings 15:6f.) turns out not to be the misspent opportunity for cooperation between diverse communities. Rather, the nation's internecine violence is shown to be but the inevitable outplay of a single community's chosen destiny apart from God, that had its roots in the people's earliest rebellions against their Redeemer.

When the church seeks herself within the form of Israel's history, she must therefore seek herself not simply within the individual parallels of revolt and division, but in the more basic current of sin's determining reach as it is divinely ordered. This is the burden of the summary of 2 Kings 17, in which the final destruction of Samaria by Assyria, held in parallel to Judah's own imminent fall, is related as the culmination of the united Israel's history of treason and idolatry, set in motion already at the Exodus from Egypt hundreds of years before. The fact of division and the fate of a divided kingdom themselves form the historical tributaries to this wider and prior tide of a single people's character. Indeed, the particularities of the two kingdoms' histories are significant only as the outcome to such a previous movement, whose current is its own judgment. Within this judgment on sin stands the whole of Israel as a unity, and her partition can only remark upon that unity by *not* claiming for its parts particular roles susceptible to specific praise or blame.

If we are to be faithful to the prophesied pattern of our life as Israel, then we cannot construe the denominational history of the church in terms of comparative goods and ills, as if one could measure the benefits and losses given by the formation of this or that denominational experience or tradition. Instead, in parallel with the fragmentation of Israel, the church's divisions are to be seen as a judgmental commentary on the single whole of the People of God, the parts of which are identifiable precisely as they form a common complaint for the body in its single entity suffering the curse of human rejection. Any seeming advantages reaped from division, any seeming contributions offered to the store of the church's faithfulness by individually divided communions and members of such communions, are shown in the figure of Israel to be but the passing instruments of a furthering wrath, deceptive in their immediate attractions to the demands of the moment, but finally burdensome elements in Christ's figural duration. Claims therefore made to specific "Lutheran" or "Anglican" "gifts" to communion are bound to prove illusory in this light.[3] We have nothing to offer each other outside the self-knowledge that can see our own fate as that of a body ravaged for the cause of human sin.

Further, to recognize the fulfillment of these figures of Israel in the Christian church is to see in what direction the promise of redemption is to move. If the destruction of Samaria by Assyria and the scattering of its people into exile (2 Kings 17) along with the fall of Judah, the murder of its leaders and people, and the razing of Jerusalem and the Temple at the hands of the Babylonians (2 Kings 24) together stand as the inevitable end to a previous communal unrighteousness, then the overcoming of Christian division cannot be substantively advanced through the manipulations of restorative strategies, such as the Concordat. If such strategies are to play any useful role, they will do so as they are inscribed within the larger context of this inevitability of judgment that alone, we are assured, is made the vehicle for healing through its embodiment in the form of the Christ. Here, a series of prophecies like Zechariah 11–14 reminds us that, as they touch upon the historical existence of Israel, the efficacy of "grace" and "union" finds its ambit within the figure of the shepherd who is struck, "that the sheep may be scattered" (13:7), the One whose own life given brings for the sheep a day of purgation. This is a day in which the church now lives. And only at the end of such a day will holiness extend as a common feature to a gathered flock.

A clear retrospective grasp of the figural relationship between the fate of Israel and the Christian church's division, then, reveals the fulfilling form of Christ. In his shape we can then discern the meaning of the promised restoration of God's people to unity (e.g., John 16:32, which precedes Jesus' famous prayer for the disciples' "oneness"). And

---

3. At issue here is not the ecumenical debate over whether "diversity" or "uniformity" ought to inform the shape of a reconciled church. Rather, we must ask whether, in our present configurations as separated churches living under judgment, we are in any position properly to discern or to evaluate the positive aspects historically embedded in either principle for the future form of Christ's body.

unless we can see this mediating form of Christ, whose body both gathers up the details of Israel's historical life and joins them to the substance of his baptized children, it will be hard for us to make sense of the few Old Testament prophecies about the reunion of Israel and Judah, brief and scattered words that would otherwise dwell uneasily within the shadows of their darker contexts, instead of lightening a future path of hope. For example, the singular text of Jeremiah 50:4, far from disappearing amid surrounding and overwhelming verses concerning the divine anger to be exercised against Babylon, can reveal its full meaning only within the course of God's articulated and dismantling rage set against a city that stands as the sharpest figure of human rebellion:

> Declare among the nations and proclaim . . . , Babylon is taken, Bel is put to shame. . . . For out of the north a nation has come up against her; it shall make her land a desolation, and no one shall live in it; both human beings and beast shall flee away. In those days and in that time, says the LORD, the people of Israel shall come, they and the people of Judah together; they shall come weeping as they seek the LORD their God. (Jer. 50:2-4)

The darker aspects of Jeremiah's prophecy thus offer a deeper light in their connection with the life-giving judgment against evil made by God in the person of Christ.

Nothing more clearly attests to the eschatological character of the church's division than this particular setting by Jeremiah of the promise of Israel's reunion within the prophecy of Babylon's fall. For while other texts in the New Testament (e.g., Rom. 11) point to the prophetic parallel within history of Israel and the church, Revelation especially shows the followers of Christ to form the people Israel in their fullness, precisely as they are arrayed in suffering — as "martyrs" — against a Babylon whose downfall marks the completion of Christ's temporal will for those who love him (see Rev. 7, 12, 14, 18). If the divisions of the church derive from the final attacks of Antichrist in the last days, the healing of those divisions lies even more inextricably bound up with the patience of the church given over to the expiring assault of a wickedness aimed upon Christ's Little Ones. The restorative promise of Jeremiah, therefore, in its rent Babylonian clothing, points to the shape already assumed by the city's victorious conqueror: "triumphing over them by the cross" (Col. 2:15, NIV).

Prophesied Elements of Unity

Here, then, I will explore the more prospective elements of the prophetic figure of Israel for the church's future life. By seizing upon the mediating figure of Christ as the fulfillment of Israel's historical fate for the church, in the breadth of its communal burden of sin, the historical shape of Israel's reunion is also made the predictive stamp for the church's future healing. Embedded in the prophecy against Babylon, the very instrument of divine punishment aimed at a beleaguered Israel, Jeremiah's prediction of restoration is freed from the level of abstract promise. Instead, the hope of reunion points to the necessary historical transformation that Israel must undergo, a transformation that will take place within her temporal vicissitudes so that she might discover the restored life of her divinely assured communion. Since they are no longer a divided people driven by pride, the return from Babylon is accomplished in national unity because it represents a new shape given to the people, accomplished in "weeping" and as an enslaved remnant seeking the face of the Lord. This new shape is a promised shape, held up for the church, which James (1:1) and Peter (1:1; 5:13) address as Israel herself and which is directed into a coming time of strife and fugitive resistance (see Rev. 12, 14).

To see the church restored to her full unity, to see even her division properly rebuked in minimal steps like the Concordat's proposal, is to behold the form given to this new shape by the figure of Israel's straggling return from the shattered remains of an oppressor whose gift was the weight of total transfiguration. To behold this prophesied penitential form, however, is also to await its coming, to understand the inescapable aspect of its pertinence already made exigent in the person of Christ, and annointing the church's future by virtue of her bond to the Lord. Here, our efforts to find our way into a future for our churches beyond disunity must be distilled into a simple call to fellow members of divided denominations not to run away from the inevitably wrenching and structurally destructive metamorphosis this prospect will entail.

Three elements must guide our prospective discernment, precisely because they are aspects of the prophesied future fulfillments of the church's figural history given in Scripture: the destruction of denomination, the formation of a remnant, and a reunion in constricted penitence. I will now examine each element in turn.

143

The Disappearance of Denomination

The destruction of denomination was a most obvious result of the Assyrian and Babylonian defeats and exiles: The kingdoms of Samaria and Judah disappeared completely. While in later years reference is occasionally made to the "house of Judah" and the "house of Israel," it is only as two groups whose future is now linked without reference to their past identities. In general "Israel," "Jacob," or "Zion" become interchangeable terms for a people reunified through the destruction of its previously distinguishable and independent parts. "Here we are, slaves to this day," in Nehemiah's words, and whatever material identities they once possessed as separate groups now belong "to the kings whom you have set over us because of our sins; they have power also over our bodies and over our livestock at their pleasure" (Neh. 9:36f.).

Within the figure of Israel, such a loss of denominational distinction is bound to three experiences whose prophetic content points to the church. First, the loss of distinct "names" follows the numerical decline of the communities in question. Not only were large numbers killed in both the Assyrian and Babylonian assaults, but the years of exile and intermarriage that resulted saw the disappearance of countless Jews who had once attached themselves to the particular kingdoms of North and South. When the census is taken at the return, it only bears out the earlier prophecies that but a fraction of the nation would survive in any specifiable manner. Second, the years of exile saw, as an extension of the slow degradation of Israel's original religious calling that had brought upon it its dispersal, a continued loss of ethnic and devotional identity. Finally, and most evidently, the denominational disappearance of the divided kingdom coincided with its material demise: political structures, economy, cities, temples, objects of value — all of these were systematically destroyed by the victors, with the detritus siphoned off for foreign use.

This prophesied loss of denominated character will perhaps come as no surprise as separated churches ponder the promises of full communion, let alone reunion. But the figural import of its accomplishment ought to challenge us. Not only does continued use of names like "Lutheran" and "Anglican," in light of Paul's comments in 1 Corinthians 1:12ff., make only blasphemous sense, but the details of denominational disappearance, as figured in Israel, should make us pause. Is a precipitous decline in our own numbers not something to

144

be expected within the figure of unity? If so, then the current concerns with denominational "growth" are equally blasphemous, since they are aimed at institutions destined for destruction, whose progress is tied to the propagation of a divided church that may, in fact, be no church at all in the end. Whatever evangelism may mean in the divided church of the end times, its association with an increase in denominational membership is surely perverted. Indeed, were a causal connection able to be drawn between positive evangelistic efforts and the decline in numbers in our denominations, we could be more assured of our faithfulness and of the firmness of God's promises than if the reverse were the case.

More relevant to the actual energies expended by our institutional leaders and ecumenical representatives must be the prophecy that our denominational disappearance will be effected by a loss of distinguishable identities. The proper maintenance of a peculiarly *Christian* identity may in fact be dependent on the loss of such particular identities as divided churches. Shall a restored Israel hold on to the courts of Samaria, to its high places, its dress and manners? Yet not only do we see an upsurge among theologians and church leaders in the struggle to "define" something as egregiously beside the point as "Anglicanism," but we see ecumenical programs structured around the ecclesial nonsense that "communion" among separated churches must be based on the maintenance of their "traditional identities." However much such "diversity" may be necessary and justified sociologically, it is the product of a divine judgment upon unrighteousness, and its future, prefigured in the Babylonian captivity and figured in Christ, is therefore consigned to the conflagration of a uniformity imposed by historical events, welcome or not. If we are to cease from living as denominations with distinct histories and practices, with distinct attitudes and outlooks, we can only do so in the knowledge that to be called "children of the living God," we must first submit to the appellation "Not my people" (Hos. 8ff.), to the removal of histories and claims, as the basis for receiving a new history and a new shape of common life.

The disappearance of denomination is, as with the melted gold of a burnt Jerusalem, finally best embodied in the demise of those material structures which themselves uphold the temporal figment that a divided church is untethered from the weight of God's conforming purpose for his body. In the face of this prophecy of material dispersal, we may await with rejoicing the closure of our buildings and offices in favor of new organizational arrangements for worship and for work; we may look forward to the completion of our seminaries' creeping decline into insolvency and irrelevance under the illusion that they must perform like secular universities ("just as the nations"!); we may pray with expectation for the itinerant oversight of pastors and bishops no longer wedded to the demands of sustaining bureaucratic apparatus; we may finally hope for the moment when, influenced by such changes in the deployment of our material resources, we see the "names" of our churches crumble before the entry of economic and ethnic outsiders heretofore granted their diversity only without our walls.

The Formation of a Remnant

Even while the loss of denominational distinction remains the most obvious element of Israel's prophetic figure for reunion, the second aspect of her restoration is perhaps the more substantive: the formation of a remnant. Throughout the predictive texts bearing upon her return (Isa. 4:2f.; 10:20ff; Jer. 23:3; 31:7; Ezek. 6:8-10), the positive feature consistently given to Israel is that of a "remnant," not simply in terms of her reduced numbers, but more especially as pertaining to the actual character of her faith. Clearly, the positive nature of this figure derives from the actual experiences bound up with the loss of distinctive names of identity, and the material scaffolding of separation. Thus, the historical reality of Israel as a numerical remainder founds the theological outlook of books like Ezra and Nehemiah. Yet the winnowing of Israel does so not by driving the people's leaders away from a contemplation of the weight of the nation's suffering in division, but, through constant remembrance, her reduction as a people leads them to the discovery of a renewed unity in the reinvigorated Law and cult. United Israel as a remnant depends on linking such remembrance with the vocation to righteousness. One can see this linkage in the way that both Ezra and Nehemiah (and Daniel) articulate the survival of Israel as a conjunction of confession of sin and devotion to the practical shape of Torah.

Ezekial, perhaps more than any other writer, is the prophet of the nation as remainder, giving voice to the shape of the people's health granted in exilic form. In chapters 33–39, for instance, we hear him

146

describe three layers to a popular call to of holiness. First, he challenges the nation to care for the righteousness of its people and pastors, and reiterates the connection between such care and the historical fate of Israel, which we have already seen in its figure of division and destruction. By contending for a righteousness in contrast to the nations as a whole, Ezekial refashions the notion of identity, detached now from denominational and material marks, in terms of a general distinctiveness from the wickedness of a surrounding culture. The holiness of God, understood in the form of his Name, is made the basis for the nation's constituted self, and its remembrance both in confession and reverence becomes the activity by which Israel's renewed integrity is consistently formed and reformed. Finally, the actual receipt of divine holiness "in spirit," already validated and celebrated, becomes for Ezekial the last measure by which the people are brought into conformity with the judging and redeeming character of their God.

Taken together, the prophecy of the remnant thus outlined points to the formation of a particular community defined in terms of forms of life distinguishable from its environment, and identifiable with aspects of God's life already given flesh in the fate of the nation: accountability, prayer, moral integrity — the formation of communal virtue in such a way as to set a boundary between the realm of God's disciplined devotion and the world still set against such service. All of this becomes the deliberate focus of a people whose restoration in holiness is nothing but a form of moral survival under the crushing blows of inimical history. That the New Testament (e.g., 1 Thess. 3:11–4:12) emphasizes the same points in language of purity as strict as Leviticus's, recasting the figure of the remnant into the shape of the church in the last days, only underscores the significance of this positive character in which the unity of the church is to come into being. And the New Testament does so by reminding us of the purgative and refining effect that the church's historical existence must exert upon her members as they come to understand themselves in relation to the temporal world around them.

This is an important point to consider, especially as ecumenical discourse has tended to advance the cause of rapprochement through devaluing the distinguishing language of holiness and moral boundaries. To urge the disappearance of the churches' denominational definitions is not to proclaim the ascendency of "inclusive" standards based on least common denominators of either belief or behavior.[4] Just the opposite. Only as churches revert to the forming of a remnant distinguished in its Christian conformities from the world's practices and particularities, concerned like Daniel with the character of apostasy's allurements and, like Ezekial, with the integrity of its teachers and leaders and its people's collective commitments, only as the edges of this reversion are allowed to follow the route of the nation's demotions and diminutions, only in such a movement will it be possible to say that divisions are being taken away.

A formation in holiness such as this must follow distinctive paths. The figure of the revived Law in Ezra that clothes the form of restored Israel meets its "fulfillment" in the person of Christ and in his words given through his apostles, words that nevertheless retain their clear demarcating power of guidance for the life of the church, regulating teaching, prayer, and conduct in a strict, if not necessarily codifiable, manner. No matter how we handle the resulting dialectic between "normative doctrine" and gospel "openness," the prospect for the church's future unity hinges upon the inculcation of a culturally distinctive holiness.[5] Sociologists would probably link this process to a "sectar-

---

4. See, e.g., William Countryman, *The Language of Ordination: Ministry in an Ecumenical Context* (Philadelphia: Trinity, 1992), pp. 35ff., where the New Testament "inclusivity" of Jesus is deliberately contrasted with a rigid and "exclusivistic" Old Testament understanding of holiness as "purity." Countryman, who was part of the Episcopal delegation that produced the final Lutheran-Episcopal Dialogue documents, uses this contrast as a justification for relativizing denominational differences, pointing to it as the basis of a more fundamental moral relativization inherent in a gospel whose "expansiveness, openness, and accessibility" are seen to undermine the concern of the church with the bounded formation of righteousness as reflective of God's presence in judgment and mercy. But just this kind of analysis illegitimately divides the gospel into competing testaments, using liberal concerns for the social outsider to the same modern end of cutting the church off from Israel. Although marshalled for laudable ecumenical purposes, the outcome to this kind of thinking is familiarly denominational in its rejection of prophetic Israel's promise for a unified church: The principle of "accessibility" ends by obscuring the necessarily prior destruction of structures in the church into which anyone might be welcomed; the call to "expansiveness" ignores the inevitable transformation of God's people into a remnant; the virtue of "openness" refuses to stoop to the humble constriction of a nation rendered penitent in its submission to the limits of holiness.

5. The looseness with which documents tied to the Concordat refer to this "dialectic" can only cause concern. See William A. Norgren and William G. Rusch, eds., *Implications of the Gospel, Lutheran-Episcopal Dialogue, Series 3* (Minneapolis: Augsburg; Cincinnati: Forward Movement, 1988), pars. 64ff.

ian" dynamic of group formation, but if so, then the vagueness with which the Concordat itself approaches the shape and force of communal structures of oversight within the participating denominations must seem less than penultimate. The Concordat here simply refuses to point out the hard road to holiness. For the ability both to articulate and to implement a particular form of life, definite in its theological and moral boundaries, cannot be expected as the "natural" outcome of ecclesial communion, something left "to be worked out as the Spirit moves." We cannot simply wait for it, since such formation is a visible tool divinely imposed by history for etching the outlines of a transfigured community. Such clearly defined communal discipline of life and speech is not the "fruit" of communion, but is its root and trunk.

The Limits of Constricted Penitence

This leads to the third element of prospective conformity that will greet the church's figural fulfillment of Israel's form: reunion in constricted penitence. That a reinvigoration of the Law and cult were at all possible for the remnant people of both Diaspora and return was due to a particular turn of communal attitude, one exemplified in the repeated "confessions" for the nation given, among other places, in the books of Ezra, Nehemiah, and Daniel. To be a people of remainder, as we have noted, was bound to the act of remembrance, and the "return" embodied by Israel's restored unity is one made to an "enslaved" condition of memory: the Law, with its promises, is discovered within the continual representation of the people's sin and suffering, as they led from the spurning of God's love through the waywardness of the two kingdoms and their destruction. This backward turn to the past's revelations, given in the weight of historical forgetfulness and divisive affliction, provides the context in which a definition of normative commitment can take shape. Within the particular epoch of restoration, cleaving to this past out of which the shape of the Law and the revived cult is organized, becomes the special mark of prophetic fulfillment. Far from promoting a blind traditionalism, the invention of the historical "norm" in the Second Temple derived from a grateful submission to limits divinely set by the circumstances of punishment and penitence. As such, the careful promulgation of Law and regulated practice of devotion are limits only

149

contingently necessary to the time of Israel's penitence. They are not primitivist universal principles of interpretation. It might have been otherwise with a faithful Israel; it may yet change. Yet for the present, such a backward turn is the shape of Israel's unity.

In the church's figural accomplishment of this prophetic posture, the constrictions of such a retrieval of the past are all the more forcefully imposed in these last days. Thus, in 1 John 2:24, the search for unity amid the divisive attacks of Antichrist at the "last hour" is characterized especially by a grasp of "what you heard in the beginning," and the church's integrity is revealed in an "abiding" at that origin. Here, the terms of "orthodoxy" demand a renewed currency, as measured by the teaching and practice of the still undivided church of antiquity, not so much to be mimicked as to set the bounds for the discourse of a proper ecclesial remnant. And without the deliberate assumption of this collective bequest from the past as the prophetic determinant of the church's contemporary speech, we consign ourselves to living our Christian existences in a kind of willful ignorance of what God is doing to us. Blind to the events shaping our participation in the body of Christ, we become, in Paul's words, a "fragrance from death to death," though in the mercy of God, our church's unfolding fate might be for us instead a savor of "life to life" (2 Cor. 2:16).

Were constricted penitence accepted as the posture of denominations moving toward communion, then the kinds of worries over the theological vacancy of the documents surrounding the Concordat and the unreined structures proposed in its wake would fail to disturb. In any case, because it is something prophesied, such a constricted posture will embrace the church one way or another, as we are simply forced by circumstance to cast away all thinking that has perverted the initial gift undergirding orthodoxy. And as alien and impossible as constricted penitence might seem to us, this is one point of hearing prophecy: to see ourselves as we are and will become. We can here catch a glimpse of the future shape of our community: Joining with Ezra, we will recognize fifteen hundred years of the church's theologies as inescapably implicated in historical deviation, whose providential role will be revealed as being the expositor of what is worthy by way of contrast (see 1 Cor. 11:19). If Christ is glorified when betrayed and raised on the cross (John 13:31), so too will be his church in her cruciform history (John 21:19). In seeing this, the second point of prophecy will then be reached: to behold the glory of God figured in the history he has wrought. In a drama where denominational identities will inevitably wither or be cast down, parties to the Concordat might expect that a self-conscious retrieval of the apostolic faith, gleaned unashamedly from an acknowledged past, will provide the outline for the work of ecclesial restoration.

*   *   *

It may well seem, of course, both too grand and too awful a thing that the small denominations of American Episcopalians and Lutherans have a future revealed within the shape of Israel's history. But it is only too grand, if we persist in using the Jewish nation as but a detached and foreign cipher for something as untarnished as a still awaited "kingdom of God"; and only too awful, if we take the details of Israel's life as starkly characteristic of our own. The proposed Concordat between the two denominations ought surely to settle more comfortably somewhere between these two reactions of distaste. Or so we might wish. Yet without the figural identification given to us in Israel, the Concordat will also settle into something whose harmlessness will only contribute to the premonitions of inadequacy that rightly greet us in the face of a prophetic future. Only in the shape of Israel does the church take on the form won her by her Lord. If the promise of such conformity as this is to include the ecumenical actions of divided churches in its grasp, then even these churches themselves will be called to submit to the pressures of its figural embrace. If the Concordat has a place within this promise, it is in the shadow of just such awful grandeur as this saving clasp, in which denominations disappear, a remnant is formed, and Christians confess their necessary reliance upon a past not yet deformed by their history.

In view of these considerations, an adopted Concordat has, as a practical act, at least two possible outcomes. Either it takes its place within the unfolding drama of the church's configuration in the form of her Lord, in which case the Concordat will prove one small element of the faithful dissolution of denominational pride on the way to a much more profound reformed restoration of the church within the prophetic parameters established above. Or the Concordat can be left outside this drama altogether, as a (pretended) resting place or (false) embodiment of restored communion, set apart from our churches'

151

inescapable exilic transformation, which is taking place whether we like it or not. In which case, it will simply be irrelevant, along with most of our other supposed ministries of the age.

PART 3

OPPORTUNITY

Magisterium: Unity and Substance

J. A. DINOIA, O.P.

Like many other features of contemporary church life, the unity proposed in the Lutheran-Episcopal Concordat invites social-scientific
analysis. Is there a consensus sufficient to give the Concordat legitimacy? What kinds of bureaucratic structures will promote or retard
the success of the Concordat? What will the consequences of adopting
the Concordat be for congregational hiring, seminary education, and
denominational structures? Though such questions may be pressing,
they cannot proceed independently of a theological assessment of the
ecumenical union proposed by the Concordat. This essay elaborates
a basic principle of such an assessment — participation in the divine
life of trinitarian communion.

The triune God who is the source and focus of the church's life
both transcends and encompasses the social realities of the community. Although it must take a social form, the church is properly
speaking not a social construct but a divine creation.[1] It constitutes
the visible expression of the divine grace by which created persons are
drawn into communion with each other in the eternal communion
of the uncreated Persons of the blessed Trinity. Precisely as a worldwide community, it is the sign of and summons to the universal
communion that God foreordained as the destiny of humankind in
Jesus Christ. For this reason, functional assessment of ecclesial structures cannot proceed independently of theological assessment. As

1. See Johann Auer, *The Church: The Universal Sacrament of Salvation* (Washington: The Catholic University of America Press, 1993), esp. pp. 7-14.

social realities, ecclesial structures already embody a "supernatural-ized" level of human existence: an imperfect, yet nonetheless real, participation in the divine life of trinitarian communion.

This participation is accomplished by Christ's grace at work in the hearts of believers. Fellowship with Christ — realized through his incarnation, death, and resurrection — constitutes our initiation into the life of trinitarian communion: He who is Son by nature makes us sons and daughters by adoption. Participation in this trinitarian communion thus involves a union with God both personally in reconciliation and conversion, and interpersonally in the sacraments, liturgy, and communal life of the church. This participation takes an active form through the faith, hope, and love that it enables and that are its expression.

As central to Christian faith as are teaching and proclamation are patterns of receptivity. We receive God's truth in faith, and the teaching of the community must train us in these patterns of receptivity. The community must seek to cultivate in its members the intellectual and moral dispositions appropriate to the gift of divine communion. In its broadest sense, "magisterium" denotes those organisms or mechanisms of ecclesial life which take responsibility for this cultivation. This magisterial function is not optional or merely recommended. Magisterium is precisely that which makes what is heard a cause of our participation in trinitarian communion.

It is not the place of the sole Roman Catholic contributor to this volume to offer uninvited recommendations to Lutherans and Episcopalians as they struggle with the challenges and opportunities posed by the Concordat. But it seems clear that the structures and institutions created or reshaped by the Concordat must include some form of genuine magisterial function if Lutheran-Episcopal union is to be faithful to the truth, acknowledged by the report "Toward Full Communion," that communion is God's gift to the church. Both the Lutheran and Episcopalian traditions possess resources for reflection on this issue.[2] The manner in which these resources could or should

2. On the gift of full communion, see William A. Norgren and William G. Rusch, eds., *"Toward Full Communion" and "Concordat of Agreement," Lutheran-Episcopal Dialogue, Series 3* (Minneapolis: Augsburg; Cincinnati: Forward Movement, 1991), esp. pp. 72-81. On church doctrine, see William A. Norgren and William G. Rusch, eds., *Implications of the Gospel,* Lutheran-Episcopal Dialogue series 3 (Minneapolis: Augsburg; Cincinnati: Foward Movement, 1988), pp. 52-58. For Lutheran conceptions of magisterium, see the essays by George A. Lindbeck, Gerhard O. Forde,

156

be recovered in present circumstances is something for Lutherans and Episcopalians to determine. My objective is to offer a Roman Catholic perspective on the theology of the magisterium that may be helpful to Lutherans and Episcopalians as they seek jointly to embody in ecclesial life the pattern of receptivity that is fundamental to the enjoyment of the gift of trinitarian communion.

Receiving the Gift of Truth

Since "faith comes from what is heard" (Rom. 10:17), the teaching and learning activities of the church are essential to the cultivation of ultimate communion. Together with hope and love, faith is an element in the personal engagement and intercommunication with the triune God that the life of grace makes possible for human persons. The teaching activities of the community — with the magisterium occupying a unique place among them — contribute to engendering and sustaining faith.

In revelation through Scripture and tradition, the church has received the gift of God's truth, namely, the truth that God himself initiates ultimate communion with human persons. The church is — in Walter Kasper's felicitous phrase — "the place of truth."[3] To hear the truth, to learn it, to teach it, to believe it — these are basic activities in the church.

Eric W. Gritsch, and Warren A. Quanbeck in *Teaching Authority and Infallibility in the Church: Lutherans and Catholics in Dialogue VI,* ed. Paul C. Empie and T. Austin Murphy (Minneapolis: Augsburg, 1980), pp. 101-58. For Anglican views in comparative light, see Joseph W. Witmer and J. Robert Wright, eds., *Called to Full Unity: Documents on Anglican–Roman Catholic Relations 1966-1983* (Washington, D.C.: United States Catholic Conference, 1986), pp. 223, 253-82. For some current Protestant perspectives on teaching authority, see the papers by John B. Cobb, Jr., David C. Steinmetz, George Lindbeck, Carl Braaten, and Joseph C. Hough, Jr., in "Teaching Offices of the Church and Theological Education," *Theological Education* 19 (1983): 33-99. For a historical perspective, see G. R. Evans, *Problems of Authority in the Reformation Debates* (Cambridge: Cambridge Univ. Press, 1992). For a Catholic view of some aspects of the discussion, see Avery Dulles, S.J., "Moderate Infallibilism: An Ecumenical Approach," in *A Church to Believe In* (New York: Crossroad, 1982), pp. 133-48.

3. Walter Kasper, "The Church as the Place of Truth," in *Theology and Church* (New York: Crossroad, 1989), pp. 129-47.

As the recipient of the gift of "first truth," the church is bound to commend this truth to its members and to proclaim it to persons outside its ambit. In other words, a teaching role belongs to the whole community as such, both with respect to its own members and with respect to the wider world. "We also believe, and so we speak" (2 Cor. 4:13). Christian instruction occurs at many levels, beginning with that provided by the family and the local community who are the first teachers of the faith. Parents, pastors, catechists, and religious teachers furnish initial instruction in the Christian faith for children and adult new members of the community. Preachers, lecturers, and popular authors provide Christian instruction in a variety of media and forums. Theologians and other scholarly specialists perform a distinctive instructional service for the community through their dedication to a life of study, reflection, and authorship. Finally, the pope and the bishops — both together and singly — exercise their apostolic office through authoritative teaching of different degrees of solemnity. Authentic teaching and learning thus continue throughout the community on a variety of occasions and at several levels.[4]

This structure of teaching and learning illumines something of the unique role played by the magisterium within the teaching activities of the community. For in this structure is embodied a central feature of the mystery of the truth present in the church: This truth is a gift, not an acquisition whose discovery and possession can be claimed as a human or even an ecclesial accomplishment. Revelation is itself a grace. Hence, in a real sense no follower of Christ can assume the role of teacher: With respect to the divine truth, there is only one Teacher, and everyone else is a learner. This structure of human receptivity in the face of the superabundant grace of God is fundamental to every aspect of Christian communal and individual existence. It has an important place in the teaching and learning activities of the community as well. Openness to authoritative teaching on the part of members of the church replicates the structure of receptivity that characterizes human dispositions in the face of divine gifts. Just as the apostles received the gift of truth from Christ, so do bishops accept it from the apostles, the community from the bishops, pupils from their teachers, congregations from their pastors, children from their parents, and so on. The teaching and learning

4. See Ladislas Orsy, S.J., *The Church: Learning and Teaching* (Wilmington: Michael Glazier, 1987).

activities of the community thus reflect the radical receptivity with which all persons in the church accept the word of the Divine Teacher and place their faith in him as "first truth."

The gift of God's truth establishes the reality of ultimate communion in the church. Yet the teaching activities of the community play a part in commending this truth. What is more, according to Catholic doctrine, the teaching of the pope and bishops — the official magisterium, properly speaking — plays a decisive role.

"Faith comes from what is heard, and what is heard comes by the preaching of Christ" (Rom. 10:17). Encompassed within the grace of ultimate communion, the learning that transpires in the community remains personal and interpersonal. Acceptance of the word of the Divine Teacher is a personal acceptance of the triune God. The faith that it engenders and sustains is a theological virtue: God as "first truth" is its primary and immediate object.[5] The teaching activities of the community play an important part in the genesis of faith. But in the act of faith itself, it is God himself who is attained. Because of faith in God, the individual believer accepts all that the community teaches about him. What the church proposes in its teaching is acknowledged as the contents that must be believed on the basis of the interior grace of faith that accepts God himself as "first truth." The act of faith is "essentially an act of union."[6]

---

5. This paragraph adopts a Thomistic position on much-debated topics within Catholic theology, namely, the formal object of faith and the role of church teaching in the genesis and act of faith. See Thomas Aquinas, *Summa Theologiae,* 2a2ae.1, 10. For a general orientation to the debate and for a compressed argument for the Thomistic view, see Thomas C. O'Brien, appendices 2 and 3, in Thomas Aquinas, *Summa Theologiae,* Blackfriars ed. (New York: McGraw-Hill; London: Eyre & Spottiswoode, 1974), 31:186-204. On 2a2ae.1, 10, see Yves M.-J. Congar, O.P., "St. Thomas and the Infallibility of the Papal Magisterium," *The Thomist* 38 (1974): 81-105. Extensive discussion with references to the scholastic controversy can be found in Reginald Garrigou-Lagrange, O.P., *De Revelatione* (Rome: F. Ferrari, 1929), 1:458-514, and, with less detail, in his *The Theological Virtues,* vol. 1, *Faith* (St. Louis: B. Herder, 1965), pp. 51-84, 154-55. For a brief discussion of some of this material, see Rene Latourelle, *Theology of Revelation* (New York: Alba House, 1966), pp. 181-85. In "The Teaching Office of the Church," *Theological Investigations XII* (London: Darton, Longman & Todd, 1974), p. 24, Karl Rahner makes the crucial point succinctly when he says that, ultimately, the Catholic Christian "believes in the authority of the teaching office because he already believes in God."

6. Joseph Ratzinger, *Principles of Catholic Theology* (San Francisco: Ignatius Press, 1987), p. 329.

J. A. DINOIA, O.P.

Communion with the Triune God

The fundamental core of the narrative the church recounts is that the triune God has undertaken to be in communion with humankind. Christ himself affirms this: "If a man loves me, he will keep my word, and my Father will love him, and we will come to him and make our home with him" (John 14:23). The fundamental truth about this ultimate communion is that it is a personal one: Each person is invited to enjoy the communion of the Persons of the blessed Trinity and, in this way, a transformed communion with all other persons.

The church's narrative of human history and society is essentially trinitarian in structure.[7] It recounts the stages by which this ultimate communion has been pursued and achieved by God, and where its final consummation lies. To employ a central Pauline motif, through Christ human persons come to enjoy by adoption the triune familial life that Christ the Son enjoys by nature. Since the grace that comes through Christ overcomes human finitude and sin, it entails both enablement and restoration. It involves enablement because enjoyment of trinitarian communion is "natural" only for uncreated persons; created persons can enjoy it only by grace. Thus human life in grace is life lived at a new level, one enabled by the triune God for the sake of communion in the trinitarian life. The grace of Christ involves restoration as well. No sinner can begin to enjoy ultimate communion without reconciliation and conversion in continual conformity to the cross.

But if this communion is personal, it must also be *inter*personal. It affords nothing less than human engagement and communication with the triune God in knowledge and love. Faith, hope, and charity are properly "theological" virtues because they permit precisely this level of engagement with God. The life of faith, hope, and love in grace is the life of ultimate communion begun here on earth.

Those raised up with Christ and in Christ are joined to each

7. This discussion depends at many points on Thomas Aquinas's theology of grace; see especially *Summa Theologiae,* 1a.43, 3; 1a.62; 1a.93; 1a.95; 1a2ae.109-114; 1a2ae.62; 2a2ae.1-46; 3a.8; 3a.46-49; 3a.53-57; 3a.60-62. See also "Some Aspects of the Church Understood as Communion," *Origins* 22 (June 25, 1992): 108-12; J.-M. R. Tillard, O.P., *Church of Churches: The Ecclesiology of Communion* (Collegeville: The Liturgical Press, 1992), and *Chair de l'Eglise, Chair du Christ: Aux Sources de l'Ecclesiologie de Communion* (Paris: Cerf, 1992).

other by the Spirit. No human community can have the depth of the communion of those called in Christ to share the life of the Spirit in the church. No sinful community can have the reconciliation that overcomes obstructive human pride, factionalism, and selfishness. Through the sacramental and liturgical life of the church, Christ's grace remains a permanent source of vitality and renewal for the community that is, in a true sense, his body. In this way, ultimate communion becomes the foundation of authentic human community. Part of the church's mission in the world is to summon all human persons to share in this communion and to resist the social and political constraints that obstruct its cultivation. The church thus has a story to tell not only to its members but to the whole human race. This story's divinely assured happy ending will come only when the entire human race is united in communion with the triune God.

In this perspective, we can understand all of the activities of the church — including its teaching activities — only when we see them as directed toward fostering ultimate communion. This is the context in which a properly theological account of the role of magisterium can be advanced.

Sustaining Receptivity

For the most part, the church's teaching and learning activities have the objective of shaping the lives of its members with a view to the present and future enjoyment of ultimate communion with the triune God and with other human persons in ever-deepening charity. Through these teaching activities, the community seeks to cultivate the intellectual and moral dispositions appropriate to this enjoyment, to enhance understanding and appreciation of its profound meaning, and to commend it to nonmembers. In the course of teaching about these matters, the community inevitably will be engaged in proposing its doctrines. The ensemble of Catholic doctrines encompasses the entire range of beliefs and practices that serve to shape life in a distinctively Catholic Christian pattern. The new *Catechism of the Catholic Church* furnishes an overall view of what the body of Catholic doctrines includes. Such doctrines answer questions about what must be believed, which courses of action should be pursued and which

161

shunned, which interior dispositions must be cultivated and which avoided, and so on, in order to enjoy the life of ultimate communion to the full. Much of the teaching activity of the community, including the authoritative teaching of the magisterium, is concerned with questions of this kind.

But another range of questions can arise. These are concerned not with what must be believed and undertaken in order to grow in the life of grace and charity, but with how it can be known reliably that such things should be believed and undertaken. The magisterium has been especially concerned with questions of this second type. Indeed, as I shall show, the doctrine of the magisterium can itself be construed as a partial answer to questions of this second form.

William A. Christian, Sr., has suggested that, in response to these two sorts of question, the teaching activities of religious communities generate two broad types of doctrines: "primary doctrines" and "governing doctrines."[8] According to Christian, primary doctrines respond to the first set of questions. Thus, in its primary doctrines, a religious community commends the beliefs and practices that constitute its distinctive pattern of life.

Governing doctrines, on the other hand, respond to questions of the second type, such as the following: Is this really a doctrine of our community? Do we have procedures for deciding? Is this doctrine more important than other doctrines? Does what we teach about this matter mesh with what we teach on other topics? How do our doctrines relate to new information or new discoveries in science or history, or to new techniques in medicine and research? What is the bearing of our doctrines on issues that they do not explicitly address or did not even envisage? Is it appropriate to develop understandings that seem implicit in our doctrines? Should we count these new understandings as doctrines? Who in the community is authorized to say one way or the other? These and similar questions relate to issues of the authenticity, ranking, consistency, derivation, and scope of a community's doctrines. In developing answers to questions of this type, a community generates and expresses what Christian calls "doctrines about doctrines" or, more simply, governing doctrines.

8. William A. Christian, Sr., *Doctrines of Religious Communities: A Philosophical Study* (New Haven: Yale Univ. Press, 1987), chap. 1.

The history of the Catholic community and of other Christian communities has afforded many occasions for developing and invoking governing doctrines. Particularly germane to our topic is the fact that questions of the authenticity of its primary doctrines have been pressed upon the Catholic community almost without interruption for the past two hundred years. Thus, for example, more systematic attention has been given to the doctrine of revelation by both theologians and official church bodies during this period than in all the previous centuries taken together. Largely in response to the challenge of modern philosophers and historians, the Catholic Church has been compelled to articulate as official doctrines its operative but often largely implicit teachings about the sources of the truth of its primary doctrines.[9] Throughout this period, the church has gradually formulated a range of governing doctrines concerning the authenticity of its doctrines: to show that its primary doctrines (and governing doctrines as well) authentically express what is contained in Scripture and tradition, that Scripture and tradition themselves constitute the single source of revelation, that revelation involves in a real sense a divine communication mediated through prophets and apostles, that the scriptural record of this revelation is inspired, that the liturgical and doctrinal tradition embodies communally authorized readings of the Scripture, and that the church under the bishop of Rome is divinely guided in its formulation of primary doctrines about faith and morals.

Again, the pattern of receptivity that is fundamental to the human response to divine grace is instantiated. In Catholic understanding, the preservation and continuance of the church in truth are emphatically not to be ascribed to human achievement. That the church remains the place of truth is a divine gift. Whenever the church forsakes its receptive mode in the face of the gift of divine truth, it risks unfaithfulness and falsification. The much-misunderstood doctrine of infallibility affirms the church's confidence, not so much in the adequacy of its grasp and expression of the truth, as in the abiding grace that engenders authentic receptivity — or faith — in otherwise fallible and self-assertive human communities.

9. For the distinction between official and operative doctrines, see George A. Lindbeck, *The Nature of Doctrine* (Philadelphia: Westminster, 1984), p. 74.

J. A. DINOIA, O.P.

Emergence of "the Magisterium"

The now almost restricted use of the term "magisterium" as a designation for the official teaching authority of the church is a relatively recent development.[10]

In scholastic usage, the term was more likely to have referred to the teaching authority of university faculties of theology than to that of the pope and the bishops. But we should not imply from this semantic fact that the pope and the bishops came to be recognized as authoritative teachers in the community for the first time only in the nineteenth century. On the contrary, historians have demonstrated that their role as authoritative teachers was recognized from the earliest Christian times.[11] As successors to the apostles in their leadership of the church, the pope and the bishops were seen to exercise this official teaching role particularly, but not exclusively, when assembled in council or synod to decide on some disputed point of doctrine. Precisely in exercising this role, they relied heavily on the assistance and counsel of non-episcopal theologians and, beginning in the scholastic period, the distinguished theological faculties of the Christian world. The theologians and doctors were themselves the subject of a governing doctrine: Consensus among the doctors was an important criterion to be invoked in judging the authenticity of new doctrinal or theological proposals. For much of the period from the medieval emergence of university theology until the end of the eighteenth century this situation prevailed with minor variations throughout the Catholic world.[12]

10. Yves M.-J. Congar, O.P., "A Semantic History of the Term 'Magisterium,'" in *Readings in Moral Theology 3: The Magisterum and Theology,* ed. Charles E. Curran and Richard A. McCormick, S.J. (Ramsey, N.J.: Paulist, 1982), pp. 297-313.

11. In *Infallible? An Inquiry* (Garden City, N.Y.: Doubleday, 1972), Hans Küng argued that theologians rather than bishops are the inheritors of the special teaching role exercised by the prophets and teachers of the New Testament. Francis A. Sullivan, S.J., convincingly refutes this contention in *Magisterium: Teaching Authority in the Catholic Church* (Mahwah, N.J.: Paulist, 1983), pp. 35-51.

12. For this and the following paragraph, see Avery Dulles, S.J., "The Magisterium in History: Theological Considerations," in *A Church to Believe In,* pp. 103-17. For the New Testament, see Joseph A. Fitzmyer, "The Office of Teaching in the Christian Church According to the New Testament," in *Teaching Authority and Infallibility in the Church,* ed. Paul C. Empie, T. Austin Murphy, and Joseph A. Burgess (Minneapolis: Augsburg, 1978), pp. 186-212. For this and subsequent periods, see

The French Revolution, the Napoleonic Wars, and the rise of European state nationalism combined around the beginning of the nineteenth century to bring an abrupt end to such collaboration between theologians and the papal and diocesan curias. The secularization of the universities and the collapse of the theological faculties was accompanied by a drastic decline of the religious orders that had exercised theological leadership in the church for centuries (especially Dominicans, Carmelites, and Jesuits). The result was a kind of "magisterial vacuum." Just when the church faced a range of critical intellectual challenges, many of its primary teaching mechanisms were weakened or neutralized. In response to this situation, beginning at least with the pontificate of Gregory XVI, the papal teaching office — increasingly termed simply "the magisterium" — came into new prominence among the teaching activities of the church. Within a few decades, it became the focus of the conciliar definition of infallibility.

In the light of the analysis presented in the foregoing section, it is clear that this evolution represented a response to the growing need for a clearer articulation of the community's governing doctrines. In circumstances in which the authenticity of Christian doctrines was a matter of persistent controversy, it was natural, as we have seen, that doctrinal developments addressing this issue should take place along several fronts at once: the nature of revelation, the interpretation of Scripture, the authority of tradition, and the scope of the church's teaching office. Each of these topics was central to the agenda of Vatican Council I in 1870 and, in varying degrees, has remained prominent.

In the Constitutions on Divine Revelation and on the Church, Vatican Council II attained a new level in this developing articulation. While reaffirming the central teachings of Vatican I, these constitutions located the teaching office of the church in the broad context of the community's governing doctrines and of its teaching activities as it

---

Eugene LaVerdiere, "The Teaching Authority of the Church: Origins in the Early New Testament Period"; John E. Lynch, "The Magistery and Theologians from the Apostolic Fathers to the Gregorian Reform"; Yves M.-J. Congar, O.P., "Theologians and the Magisterium in the West: From the Gregorian Reform to the Council of Trent"; Michael D. Place, "Theologians and Magisterium from the Council of Trent to the First Vatican Council"; and T. Howland Snaks, "Co-operation, Co-optation and Condemnation: Theologians and Magisterium 1870-1978," in *Chicago Studies* 17 (1978): 172-263. For a general perspective, see Patrick Ranfield, *The Limits of the Papacy: Authority and Autonomy in the Church* (New York: Crossroad, 1987).

continues Christ's prophetic role. This new stage is strikingly reflected in the new Code of Canon Law (promulgated in 1983). In contrast to the previous code, in which references to the teaching office were distributed throughout the canons, the new code provides a unified and systematic treatment of the teaching activities of the community in an explicit endeavor to implement the directions indicated by Vatican II. The teaching responsibilities of all members of the church are considered in turn after the discussion of the magisterium.[13]

From the vantage point of the end of the twentieth century, it seems clear that the definition of papal infallibility at Vatican I was but an early stage in the church's continuing endeavor to articulate a consistent set of governing doctrines in the face of modern challenges. Viewed in this context, the nineteenth-century emphasis on the official magisterium will appear, not as an unwarranted inflation of papal power at the expense of other teaching authorities in the church, but as a necessary aspect of a developing articulation of the community's governing doctrines.

Christian convictions in this area are challenged by deep-seated modern notions of religious individualism and personal autonomy. These notions make patterns of receptivity extraordinarily difficult to explain and to inculcate. Even the most modest exercise of doctrinal authority will seem unintelligible or intrusive to the membership of many Christian communities today — whether these communities possess inchoate or fully developed governing doctrines of "magisterium." In the face of just such a challenge, Christian communities must affirm their faith that human beings cannot create the truth but must receive it as a gift.[14]

The modern Catholic doctrine of the magisterium can be understood as an attempt to make this affirmation. The doctrine is in major part a product of ongoing developments in which the church has sought to articulate its governing doctrines with a view to the

---

13. In his commentary on Code of Canon Law, Book III: Teaching Office of the Church, James A. Coriden makes this point; see James A. Coriden, Thomas J. Green, and Donald E. Heintschel, eds., *The Code of Canon Law: A Text and Commentary* (Mahwah, N.J.: Paulist, 1985), pp. 545-89. See also Karl Rahner, "Theology and the Church's Teaching Authority after the Council," *Theological Investigations IX* (London: Darton, Longman & Todd, 1972), pp. 83-100.

14. This is a central theme of the recent encyclical of Pope John Paul II, *Veritatis Splendor* (Washington, D.C.: United States Catholic Conference, 1993).

patterns of receptivity that express a faithful response to the gift of truth. In this doctrine, the church has given official formulation to its confidence that, by God's grace, it will be preserved from error and maintained in the truth when it proposes to its members and to the wide world the primary doctrines by which it seeks to foster the life of ultimate communion. Among the teaching activities of the community, only that exercised authoritatively by the pope and the bishops is understood to be divinely guaranteed in precisely this way. As successors of the apostles, only the pope and the bishops have the authority to determine in a definitive way the authenticity of what is proposed for belief and practice in the church.

In essence, this determination consists in affirming that what is proposed accords with the revelation in Scripture and tradition by which the church itself is constituted and to which it must be obedient. This grace-given power extends to the determination of other matters addressed by governing doctrines: whether a particular proposal is consistent with other things that the community holds, whether one doctrine has priority over others, whether a proposed doctrinal formulation represents a legitimate development of the tradition, and so on. If through faith in God the believer assents to truths about him as these are expressed by the church, then the church engages its teaching activities in a distinctive mode when it seeks faithfully to affirm the truth about the "first truth."

Magisterium and Dissent

If ultimate communion, and hence unity of faith, are the principal objectives that the church pursues in its teaching activities, then surely dissent from the common teaching is likely to be seen as a serious threat to communion. And, in some cases, it has proven to be so. But in the perspective of this essay, we can view dissent as a providential occasion for continued development in the Catholic community's governing doctrines.

In the decades following Vatican Council II, the chief impetus for ongoing development of the theology of the magisterium has come from the challenge posed for the church by dissent from its teachings. Indeed, much of the literature upon which I have drawn here is the product of the debate arising from the promulgation of the encyclical *Humanae Vitae* in 1968. Dissent from the teaching of this encyclical provoked a major crisis in Catholic allegiance to the magisterium.[15] While the strain on the visible communion of the church has been considerable, the controversy surrounding dissent has had a beneficial outcome in stimulating historical research and theological reflection on a wide range of issues bearing on the nature of the magisterium.

This debate has accelerated developments on several fronts. Perhaps the most significant outcome has been a thoroughgoing reconception of the relation of theologians and the magisterium. Historical studies have demonstrated the central "magisterial" role played by Catholic theological faculties prior to the nineteenth century. The Catholic community has struggled to reappropriate the doctrinal bases of collaboration between theologians and the magisterium, and to formalize such collaboration in the vastly altered ecclesial and academic contexts of contemporary societies. A central feature of this reappropriation has been a renewed awareness of the creative role of the theologian in contributing to the understanding and formulation of the Christian faith. The magisterium itself has sought to articulate an "ecclesial role" for theologians within the frame of an ecclesiology of communion.[16]

15. See Joseph A. Komonchak, "*Humanae Vitae* and its Reception: Ecclesiological Reflections," *Theological Studies* 39 (1978): 221-57; and Avery Dulles, S.J., "*Humanae Vitae* and the Crisis of Dissent," unpublished address at the Twelfth Bishops' Workshop, Dallas, Texas, reported by the Catholic News Service, March 11, 1993. For a positive assessment of the encyclical and its impact, see Janet Smith, *Humanae Vitae: A Generation Later* (Washington, D.C.: The Catholic University of America Press, 1991). See also Joseph Komonchak, "Issues Behind the Curran Case," *Commonweal,* Jan. 30, 1987, 43-47.

16. For this paragraph, see Glenn W. Olsen, "The Theologian and the Magisterium: The Ancient and Medieval Background of a Contemporary Controversy," *Communio* 7 (1980): 292-319; Yves M.-J. Congar, O.P., "A Brief History of the Forms of Magisterium and Its Relations with Scholars," in *Readings in Moral Theology* 3, ed. Curran and McCormick, pp. 314-31; Avery Dulles, S.J., "The Two Magisteria: An Interim Reflection," in *A Church to Believe In,* pp. 118-32. In *Imagination and Authority: Theological Authorship in the Modern Tradition* (Minneapolis: Fortress, 1991), John E. Thiel has shown the importance of the shift in conceptions of theological authorship from the classical to the modern periods. Congregation on the Doctrine of the Faith, "Instruction on the Ecclesial Role of the Theologian," *Origins* 20 (July 5, 1990): 117-26, and "Social Communications and the Doctrine of the Faith," *Origins* 22 (June 18, 1992): 92-96; Francis A. Sullivan, S.J., "The Theologian's Ecclesial Vocation and

In a related development, a much-debated issue concerns the force to be accorded to magisterial teaching in theological inquiry. Here, again, the community has been able to draw upon traditions of reflection in which classical and scholastic theologians sought to rank the authority of the different levels of sources bearing on theological inquiry. Discussion of this issue has advanced Catholic understanding of the community's governing doctrines and may provoke further developments in the official (as distinct from simply operative) formulations of such doctrines, particularly in refining the distinctions between different levels of magisterial teaching. This discussion is driven by controversy about the appropriateness and extent of a theologian's disagreement with magisterial teaching. In connection with this controversy, theologians and official teaching bodies in the church have experimented with provisional formulations of the levels of magisterium (especially the difference between ordinary and extraordinary exercise of the teaching office), the nature of the teaching office of diocesan bishops and their national conferences, and the degrees of acceptance (faith, assent, "obsequium") that are due to the distinct levels of magisteral teaching.

Increasingly, theologians have recognized the relevance of theoretical studies on the nature of authority for intra-Christian reflection concerning the relation of the exercise of religious authority in the realm of religious knowledge. Church officials and concerned theologians have argued that, while privately expressed disagreement with church teaching may be appropriate and even necessary in certain circumstances for ongoing development of official doctrine, public dissent undermines the church's communion. Others have questioned the viability of the distinction between public and private dissent, given the nature of modern communication. There is a marked trend toward reserving the term "dissent" for public dissent that takes activist and politicized forms. In this context, official initiatives have involved the institutionalization of specific controls (canonical mission, profession of faith, oath of

---

the 1990 CDF Instruction," *Theological Studies* 52 (1991): 51-68; Leo J. O'Donovan, S.J., ed., *Cooperation between Theologians and the Ecclesiastical Magisterium* (Washington: Canon Law Society of America, 1982); Cardinal Joseph Ratzinger, "The Church and the Theologian," *Origins* 15 (May 8, 1986): 761-70; U.S. Bishops' Conference, "Doctrinal Responsibilities," *Origins* 19 (June 29, 1989): 97-109.

fidelity) by which the community can stipulate the ecclesial role of the theologian.[17]

Debate on these issues has been extremely lively, and promises to yield a more highly refined articulation of the church's governing doctrines as they bear on the teaching activities of the magisterium. In principle, there is no reason why so productive a debate should harm the visible communion of the Catholic Church, so long as it is characterized by restraint and charity on all sides.

Magisterial Function in Full Communion

Christians confess the reality of a stunning divine initiative: the transformation of human life and society such that persons in grace can enjoy communion with the Persons of the Trinity and a transformed communion with each other. The governing doctrines of the church seek to preserve the unity of faith that in part constitutes the created, yet supernatural, basis for this communion. But the communion itself is a divine gift, with nothing less than the triune God as its source and focus.

In a historic endeavor to overcome some of the divisions that have separated the recipients of this gift, the Lutheran-Episcopal Con-

---

17. For the bearing of the magisterium on theological inquiry, see J. A. DiNoia, O.P., "Authority, Dissent and the Nature of Theological Thinking," *The Thomist* 52 (1988): 185-207; Avery Dulles, S.J., *The Craft of Theology* (New York: Crossroad, 1992), chaps. 7, 10, 11; Aidan Nichols, O.P., *The Shape of Theology* (Collegeville: The Liturgical Press, 1991), chap. 18. See also Avery Dulles, S.J., "The Teaching Authority of Bishops' Conferences," in *The Reshaping of Catholicism* (San Francisco: Harper & Row, 1988), pp. 207-26; U.S. Bishops' Conference, "The Teaching Ministry of the Diocesan Bishop," *Origins* 21 (Jan. 2, 1992): 743-92; Ladislas Orsy, S.J., *The Profession of Faith and the Oath of Fidelity* (Wilmington: Michael Glazier, 1990). For studies of the nature of authority with direct bearing on the role of authority in religious knowledge, see Joseph M. Bochenski, O.P., *Autorität, Freiheit, Glaube* (Munich: Philosophia Verlag, 1988), and *The Logic of Religion* (New York: New York Univ. Press, 1965); Yves Simon, *A General Theory of Authority* (Notre Dame: University of Notre Dame Press, 1962, 1980), esp. chap. 3; Richard T. DeGeorge, *The Nature and Limits of Authority* (Lawrence, Kans.: The University Press of Kansas, 1985). For a theological appropropiation, see Joseph Komonchak, "Authority and Magisterium," in *Vatican Authority and American Catholic Dissent,* ed. William W. May (New York: Crossroad, 1987), pp. 103-14.

cordat lays out a program for the mutual recognition of ministers and, eventually, for full communion. The Concordat thus represents a momentous ecumenical initiative, with implications for the whole of a now divided Christendom.

Lutherans and Episcopalians must ask themselves whether this communion will continue to be sustainable by an articulated substantive unity in faith. In the *Implications of the Gospel,* representatives of the two communities were able to affirm a wide area of present doctrinal consensus. An implication of the argument advanced here — one with which Lutheran and Episcopalian theologians and leaders would presumably agree — is that this doctrinal consensus constitutes a response to the gift of gospel truth. None of us is a teacher in his or her own right, but all are learners at the feet of Christ. What we have received in faith, we hand on to faith. Will the structures of the post-Concordat Lutheran and Episcopal churches embody this pattern of receptivity? Will there be room, in other words, for a sustained "magisterial" function in the reshaped or newly created institutions that follow upon the Concordat?

This question is one that Lutherans and Episcopalians must answer for themselves. My underlying assumption here is that the Roman Catholic experience of the past two hundred years may be instructive for Lutherans and Episcopalians who are inclined to reflect on this question. The developing role of the official magisterium in the Catholic Church in the nineteenth and twentieth centuries constitutes, as I have argued here, a judicious pastoral response to the particular sorts of problems created for the church by a range of political, social, and intellectual revolutions.

It may be that this development will be seen to illumine the experience of other Christian communities as they struggle to articulate an authentic and faithful response to the gift of divine truth in the face of modern challenges to the very possibility of such truth. In the past, Protestant communities relied upon the operative though implicit "magisterial" role of renowned divinity and seminary faculties and distinguished theologians to assist them in this endeavor. But, in the United States at least, the erosion of liberal Protestant culture, the flight of theology from formerly elite Protestant universities, and the ascendancy of teachers of religion with no special allegiance to the Christian tradition are factors that may give rise to a situation markedly parallel to that of the Catholic Church in nineteenth-century Europe.

This type of situation, as we have seen, gives urgency to a Christian community's reflection upon its governing doctrines and to the development of institutional structures to ensure its fidelity to the gift of truth it has received.

Lutherans and Episcopalians possess rich traditions of reflection on precisely these issues. But their experience has made them understandably suspicious of any talk of magisterium. Lutherans typically protest that a magisterial function can all too readily become the "guardian of institutional ideology."[18] Episcopalians, on the other hand, might object that a magisterial mechanism would inhibit the diversity they so rightly prize. These are important objections. How they might be resolved is a matter for Lutherans and Episcopalians to determine as they deploy their traditional resources in the post-Concordat situation. A friendly Roman Catholic observer might be permitted to remark that these objections, far from excluding a magisterial function, seem rather to presuppose it. The strongest defense against the ideological captivity of the church is an institutionalized form of reflection that continually calls its membership and its leadership to faithfulness and obedience to an evangelical truth that transcends and challenges the church as a whole. Cultural and theological diversity, on the other hand, will be welcome rather than threatening in a church alert to maintain the unity of the communion in one faith. Thus, a magisterial function can serve rather than undermine both faithfulness and diversity.

Whatever institutional form it might take, a magisterial function is arguably essential to the visible communion embodied in the church. Through this function, the church brings to expression the underlying patterns of receptivity that characterize its situation in the face of the gift of trinitarian communion. "Magisterium" denotes those mechanisms of ecclesial life by which Christian communities — Lutheran, Episcopalian, and Roman Catholic alike — take responsibility for the cultivation in their members of the patterns of receptivity that are fundamental to the enjoyment of this communion.[19]

18. *Implications of the Gospel,* p. 53.
19. Substantial portions of this essay appeared in a paper under the title, "Communion and Magisterium: Teaching Authority and the Culture of Grace," *Modern Theology* 9 (1993): 403-18. I am grateful to R. R. Reno and Romanus Cessario, O.P., for suggestions that helped me in revising that paper for this volume.

The Lectionary as
Theological Construction

CHRISTOPHER SEITZ

In this essay I want to look at the present lectionary from the standpoint of biblical theology. In the context of Lutheran-Episcopal discussions, my concern is twofold. First, would this not be a good time to reconsider the logic of the lectionary that both of us employ and that both of us have inherited from others? My second concern is more fundamental and is covered in part by my frequent reference to the lectionary *and* biblical theology: How are we to communicate the gospel when this involves making selections from the Bible to be read in public assembly? What is "the gospel"? Is "the gospel" fundamentally related to the literary witness of the four Gospels of the New Testament and, if so, how does this witness relate to the remainder of the Christian canon? Does the present distinction between Epistle and Gospel influence conceptions of "the gospel"? How does the Old Testament proclaim "the gospel" — if in fact it does so at all? In short, how does the shape of the present lectionaries affect the church's proclamation of "the gospel"?

In what follows I will make some preliminary remarks about the lectionary from the standpoint of biblical theology and the practical problem of general biblical illiteracy facing the churches. I will then consider the emphasis of the present lectionary, and make an argument in favor of two rather than three readings. Following this I will briefly examine the theological and hermeneutical implications of freeing the Old Testament to be heard in immediate reciprocal relationship with the New Testament. In the final section I will make several suggestions about how a different lectionary might take form, in the light of this essay.

My larger thesis is that the lectionary offers the greatest possibility for rejuvenating serious interest in the Bible as the source of the church's life and identity before God, for the broadest possible constituency. That one can speak of such a possibility at all is due to the astonishingly widespread adoption of some sort of lectionary scheme by a broad assortment of denominations, many of whom would once have denounced any notion of prescribed readings (and along with it, the very concept of a church year). Further, I believe that far more is done in the name of biblical theology by the lectionary and the way it is used than is generally recognized, for good and for ill. But my chief aim will be to propose a different sort of lectionary, one that capitalizes on the present widespread acceptance of the notion of prescribed readings, but is more sensitive to the way every selection is itself an act of biblical theology, and therefore ought to be made with great care and attention.

Biblical Theology and the Lectionary

One of the first tasks of biblical theology is to describe appropriate ways for the two testaments of the Christian canon to be related. Every pairing — and tripling — of readings makes a statement about the relationship between the testaments, which is in turn a statement about biblical theology. To take an example from Jewish liturgical practice: When a *lectio continua* reading from the first five books of the Bible (Torah) is followed by a selected reading from the prophets or writings (Haftorah), a statement is being made about the relationship between these two sections, their relative authority, and the identity of the God who inspired them both, whose identity governs the destiny and life of Israel. Lectionary is inevitably theological construction. In this simple example, law has taken priority over prophecy, since the first reading is *lectio continua* over the course of the year, and selections from the other sections of the Hebrew canon are keyed toward this central cycle of texts.

The theological construction imposed by any lectionary strategy points to the set of concerns that will preoccupy me throughout this essay. First, one of the underlying problems with the modern lectionary system involves a series of tacit assumptions about the character of biblical narrative, reinforced every time the Bible is read and heard

174

through the lens of the lectionary. One assumption is that there is some sort of obvious independent integrity to individual passages read as such, detached from original literary contexts, or supplied with a new context due to the juxtaposition of one discrete reading with several other discrete readings (and in some cases, with a psalm and collect). The final effect of the present lectionary implies that individual passages have no inherent relatedness to the literary contexts out of which they have been taken. As individual passages they are to find their true context either from some historical reconstruction, supplied by the seminary-trained preacher, or from the mode of consciousness of the hearer, commentator, or preacher. The very logic of the increasingly popular "illuminations" (brief statements read aloud to introduce the lessons) is precisely to jump into this breach and supply a "context" for listening — again, usually personalistic, psychological, or historical-critical (not surprisingly, the latter move is most often used with the Old Testament lesson, which, because it is "old," requires proper historical contextualization). I've frequently wondered if a different sort of "illumination" might be generated that would address the matter of literary or theological context, but this would be to concede the logic of the lectionary to begin with, a logic that may in fact be responsible for the sorts of problems "illuminations" seek to resolve.

Second, and of more direct theological concern, is whether the Bible has already considered the issue of context on its own terms, within its own canonical presentation. To say that the Bible might wish to be heard in a certain way is to make a very bold claim over against the training of most preachers (and the lectionary framers themselves) in historical-critical logic. The decision to read biblical passages without attention to larger literary context conforms nicely to much of the theory of form-critical method, whose starting and ending point is the individual pericope. It may be pure fortuity that an earlier, precritical decision to read biblical passages as individual units based on liturgical and calendric considerations, not in *lectio continua* formats, has coincided with the pericope mentality of form-criticism. It is also clear that other ways of hearing the Bible read aloud and preached on in public worship also existed (see Calvin's commentaries). What we may well have is an accidental convergence of precritical concern for "hearability" and liturgical appropriateness and the modern critical instinct to isolate "original units" out of the larger context of the final canonical form of a biblical book.

In fairness, the lectionary I am referring to was probably never intended to function in this way, at least as I understand it. A second, more comprehensive daily lectionary would have supplied the necessary *lectio continua* context from which the Sunday lections would take their bearings. This daily lectionary was to be a part of the central discipline of the prayer life of the clergy and dedicated layperson (several popular day-by-day devotional helps are keyed to this lectionary). Yet even here the positive contribution of a "continuous reading" approach for setting in context the Sunday lessons is very indirect, and can of course succeed only if such a daily discipline is followed.

But we are only touching the outskirts of the problem. At this juncture I am not interested in pleading for a continuous reading approach for its own sake as much as I am interested in pointing out that our present lectionary makes too great a demand on the preacher and the congregation. When one considers the larger cultural problem of the loss of biblical literacy — especially among those churches which use the lectionary! — the possibility that the congregation might be in a position to supply the needed literary framework for individual lections is practically nil. In a situation where the content of the Bible is increasingly unknown, the lectionary bears the special and maybe even unwanted burden of being the chief means by which the Bible is communicated to the church at large. Therefore it would seem expedient to reconsider its logic and to ask whether the lectionary, as it is now conceived, is a symptom or a contributing cause of problems besetting the church's competent use of the Scriptures.

My own instinct is to argue that three lessons are simply too many to try to listen to or preach on with any real success. I also believe that from the standpoint of biblical theology the wrong sort of message is sent by the order of the readings (Old Testament, Epistle, Gospel), by the linkages that are urged on us, and by the threefold character of the biblical presentation (the psalm reading further complicates this). Further, I am suggesting that a "continuous reading" approach has always done a better job emphasizing, implicitly if not explicitly, the key role literary context plays in understanding individual passages of Scripture. And finally I believe that a key challenge facing the church is lack of familiarity with the larger biblical narrative. On the one hand, then, I am arguing for a smaller set of readings for the Sunday lectionary (two rather than three), while at the same time I am concerned about remedying, with the help of the lectionary, widespread biblical illiteracy and reader incompetence. In this regard, then, how could less be better?

Here one quickly recognizes that no lectionary sets out to do everything, but at the heart of every lectionary is a system of priority, with one set of considerations given more weight than others. What I will do here is examime the system of priority of the present lectionary. An alternative proposal will not set out to do everything (improve on lectionary pairings, do better biblical theology, increase biblical literacy but also attend to "hearability," attend to liturgical year considerations, cover the whole Bible in three years, etc.), but will set priorities for what it seeks to do, given the various constraints under which it must operate, mindful of its larger goals.

The Present Lectionary

We need to consider the four questions that deal with various aspects of the lectionary. First, how many lessons should be be read? Second, in what order should we read them? Though the order we now follow may seem self-evident, it is instructive to recall the example from Jewish liturgy where the first, not the last, lesson is intended to have priority; here too the actual number of lessons read will play a role. Third, what sort of selections are made? Here we need to consider the proper length of the passages; should there be elisions and of what sort; should efforts be made to give a sense of continuous reading through the selections made? Obviously if the answer to the last question is yes, the significance of literary context for the interpretation of individual passages would be underscored. Apart from the literary aspect of selections to be made is the question of the nature of the selections themselves. On what basis are these to be made? And finally, what principles should govern the pairing or tripling of lessons?

At this last point especially the implications for biblical theology are clearest. Here I touch again on what seems to me to be the real issue at stake. The lectionary we have inherited — and modified denominationally — does biblical theology. It operates with a system of priority, with theological consequences. One of the problems with the lectionary, again probably unintended, is that while the readings themselves have been inherited, relatively consciously, the principles by which they were selected have not been equally consciously inherited. I want to emphasize that this is not a matter of assigning blame for some sort of failure to render the principles of selection immediately evident and accessible. The original constructors of the modern lectionary were Roman Catholic, and it may well be consistent with their ecclesiology and understanding of biblical theology that such principles are better inferred, if considered at all, than set forth liturgically along with the readings themselves. To put it differently, the lectionary assumes that the Bible is the church's book, to be shaped and handled as the church sees fit. It is not necessary that within the liturgy itself principles governing the selection of passages be declared, and in fact this might be a mistake. Nor is it necessary that those who prepare sermons or use the lections for Bible study have consistently before them the logic that originally governed selections made week to week. At the same time, I do wonder if the rise of "illuminations" was fostered in part by a felt need to have context and logic addressed more explicitly than the lectionary as inherited now does.

I can modify this description of things even further. On the whole it is fairly obvious why the Gospel readings have been chosen, and perhaps no further clarification is necessary: they attend to themes that are keyed to and then reinforced by a liturgical calendar, with various familiar and distinct seasons. And with a three-year cycle, it seems clear that one synoptic Gospel should be assigned to each of the three successive years. John gets spliced in at various moments in the liturgical year for reasons that are less obvious, but not all that confusing to the general observer. The other lessons (Old Testament and sometimes Epistle) generally take their cue from the Gospel lesson, which as noted is itself keyed to liturgical year considerations (the exceptions prove the general rule). To risk simplifying matters prematurely, it could be said that the Bible's own canonical organization, however one might understand that, has deferred to a larger conceptual statement about what constitutes the essential episodes in the Christian story, primarily brokered in the Gospel lessons through the course of one year, from the promised return of Christ (this last theme noticeably more muted than the others) to the birth of Christ to the birth of the church.[1]

1. Advent readings are prepared to sound these notes, if they are not drowned out by the general anticipation of Christmas.

Now it is clear that the distinction between the "Bible's own canonical organization" and the "organizing story constituted by the concept of a Christian year" could easily be overdrawn and misleading. It may not be at all clear what the "Bible's own canonically organized statement" really is, or if such a thing even exists. But I think it is fairly clear that in the present lectionary the assumption is that no such statement is being obviously or practically made and that it is the responsibility of the church, then, to supply one, which it has. My own argument will not be in favor of rejecting the conceptual system undergirding the present lectionary, much less the notion of there being a "Christian story" external to the Bible that seeks to state for Christians what the gist of the two-testament story is. Rather, I want the principles governing the present lectionary made quite clear and then enriched from time to time by other principles of selection more attuned to what I have called the "Bible's own canonically organized" patterns and internal relationships. This will result in a slightly different formulation of biblical theology, with much of the mystery and givenness of present lectionary logic brought into fuller consciousness.

Number of Readings

Let me move from the abstract and conceptual to the concrete and practical by considering the matter of the number of lessons read. The lectionary system I have been referring to, with its roots in Vatican II liturgiology, assigns three lessons for Sunday worship. Why? We could answer this question by investigating the deliberations that went into the lectionary's construction. But I want to bracket out that sort of research project and simply ask what the effect of such a move is from the standpoint of biblical theology. In other words, I want to consider the theological effect produced by the three-lesson presentation of the Bible in a year-long liturgical sequence.

A discussion of number inevitably involves order, so let that be on the table as well. In the confession to which I belong, we sit for the first two lessons and stand for the third, the Gospel reading. Whether or not this practice is adopted elsewhere, it does capture at least one aspect of the threefold, particularly ordered lectionary: its movement, in terms of relative priority, from Old Testament to Epistle

179

to crowning moment in the reading of the Gospel. That other possibilities exist for how a particular order might differently function is made clear by reference to the Torah-Haftorah practice of Jewish synagogue worship. One might want to argue that it is logical and right (or to put it in our liturgical speech, "meet and right") for the Gospel to be the crowning moment in worship, and that this is best reinforced not by having it read first (place of priority) but last (place of priority), and in my tradition, by standing when it is read. This is all well and good and I think uncontroversial.

But if this is in fact the point of the order, why are we reading an Epistle in between the Old Testament and the Gospel? At this point I wish to return to the distinction I made earlier between the Bible's own canonical organization and that imposed by the lectionary. Surely it belongs to no recognizable biblical pattern that we read an Old Testament lesson, then an Epistle or some other portion of the non-Gospel New Testament writings, and then conclude with the Gospel itself. When one considers the difficulty of listening to or successfully (in my judgment) preaching on three distinct lessons, the problem of order and number takes on a different sort of burden. It is doubtless for this reason that many congregations make the decision to select out the first or second lesson only and then pair it with the Gospel. But if the three truly belong together in some intentionally structured marriage, with a codependency mysterious yet necessary for threefold survival, then can or should one be able to simply subtract a lesson at will? Does this not disturb some subtle balance that was the express goal and hard-won accomplishment of the framers of the lectionary to begin with?

And what is the effect from the standpoint of biblical theology? First, there is no "threefoldness" anywhere structured into the Christian canon. It has been argued that threefold structures belong to the essence of each testament taken on its own (Torah, prophets, writings; gospels, Acts, Epistles) but not with great success or lasting theological significance (especially for the New Testament).[2] And of course we are not interested in structures attested to in either testament individually, but in the larger Christian canon itself, where the basic struture is transparently twofold: Old and New Testaments. Having lived with this lectionary for some time now, it is my judg-

2. See Donn Morgan, *Between Text and Community: The "Writings" in Canonical Interpretation* (Minneapolis: Fortress Press, 1990).

ment that one subtle but long-lasting effect of the threefold model is that the Old Testament lesson has been overshadowed, literally outnumbered. More difficult to state is the effect achieved when the Old Testament lesson is not related directly to the New Testament but is more complicatedly content to sit astride a first non-Gospel New Testament reading, itself oddly situated before the actual Gospel reading. Not only is the twofold character of the Christian canon lost, the way the Old Testament is related to the New Testament has become blurred. Does it relate to the Gospel by way of the Epistle? Surely not. That would be an artificial move and one unattested to in any known literary structure of the canon. How then is the Old Testament related to the New?

My own view is that the present lectionary will inevitably reinforce an understanding of the Old Testament as a document from the past, a historical preamble, as it were, because in this sort of arrangement it has become the first in a series of three, outnumbered by two lessons whose organic connection is taken to be more obvious given their common home in the New Testament, both directly speaking of Christ. This is not simply a matter of two against one. The connection between the Old and the New cannot be grasped rightly if an Epistle intrudes in a series of three, with the final lesson being set up as the finale and crowning moment in the series. Here order and number conspire to upset the delicate way in which Old Testament and New Testament are related and together, each in its own individual way, "preach Christ."

Let me be clear. The culprit is not the Epistle itself as against "the Gospel"; rather, it is the existence of a threefold pattern that breaks the Old Testament/New Testament dialectic so essential for hearing the Old Testament as a witness to Christ. The result is that the Old Testament cannot preach Christ, but must be content to provide historical background only, literally the first in a series of three. Even when the framers of the lectionary have clearly sought out passages from the Old Testament whose relationship to one or the other of the New Testament lessons is typological or allegorical, the very fact of the three-in-a-series movement will tend to produce a developmental or generally historical effect, overriding the content of the selections themselves and their very reason for being. In my judgment, this effect would be greatly reduced — if not eliminated — if we heard only two lessons each Sunday: one from the Old

Testament, then one from the New. The actual dialectical relationship between Old and New Testaments would remain intact, with the consequence that the fullest possible range of ways of relating the Old and New in witness to Christ might be safeguarded and not preempted by a model whose very threefoldness potentially trumps the content and intention of the selections made.

Theological and Hermeneutical Implications

In the context of these remarks concerning the biblical theological construal of the Scriptures in lectionary presentation, I have drawn a distinction between the Bible's own canonical shape and intention and the churchly decision to set forth on its own terms the character of that shape and intention in a specific lectionary arrangement, involving three lessons and a liturgical year whose parameters are set according to some understanding of what is the "gist" of the Christian story. It ought to be clear by now that these two matters cannot be neatly isolated, tradition on one side, Bible on the other, even though one (lectionary) flows from the other (Christian canon), with the success of one (lectionary) dependent upon its faithfulness in comprehending the other (Christian canon). But in terms of actual practice, the two working together is an inevitability that is neither to be mourned nor resolved, but refined and rethought and reshaped for each successive generation so that the fullest range of the biblical witness might be heard in its optimal tuning. A lectionary should remind the listener that there is no such thing as reading the Bible, especially the Old Testament, without an obvious point of standing.

Old Testament selections, then, ought to capture the witness of the Old Testament in its historical particularity as the Scriptures of Israel while at the same time, due to a careful juxtaposing with New Testament proclamation, be free to witness to Christ. How this witnessing goes on will be varied, because it is varied within the biblical witness itself. My concern with the threefoldness of the present lectionary is that certain types of relatedness sought out and presented by the lectionary cannot be heard in their full force because of the stereotypical character of the sequential threefold arrangement (Old Testament, Epistle, Gospel), maintained throughout the year without change or variation (except occasionally on Easter).[3] Because of the historical and developmental preoccupation of the modern critical method, and the modern mind itself, it has been very difficult to appreciate how certain unselfconscious New Testament hearings of the Old Testament might also be recaptured in the modern pulpit, as though to do so would be to abandon a point of standing that is unbiased and concerned only to hear the Old Testament on its own terms. But how could this possibly be the only desired point of standing, especially when we are not "Israel" except by adoption and when even modern Jews must strain to hear a direct word, given the intrusion of over two thousand years of commentary and simple historical distance between themselves and "Israel."

It seems at this point that the historical-critical method has an overly romanticized view of historical reconstruction, as though by an act of sheer imagination and critical decipherment we could ourselves participate in biblical events now long past, and stand alongside Moses and Joshua without any consideration that our only true access to these figures was through the cross of Christ. The cross allows us who are far off to draw near to God's own people Israel, who might now serve as examples to God's new people in Christ and as such "witness" to him and us (see Eph. 2:11-22). Even efforts to reconstruct the mind of an author, or the actual preaching content of an Israelite prophet, or the theological additions made by a redactor, and similar sorts of critical endeavor — do these not depend upon some prior notion of universal revelation or general accessibility to truth that the biblical texts themselves insist is unavailable in the form in which the critical method seeks to extract it?[4]

Apart from the (eventual) witness of the New Testament, what we know about God, we know secondhand from Israel through the

---

3. Another way to put this is that the threefold practice tends toward a "salvation history" model for biblical theology, while a twofold allows a more dialectical relationship to emerge. The actual selections from the Old Testament seem clearly at times to be striving for this type of relationship.

4. So the Psalmist concludes (Ps. 147:20): "He has not dealt thus with any other nation; they do not know his ordinances. Praise the LORD!" In the New Testament witness, Paul says of the "Israelites": "To them belong the adoption, the glory, the covenants, the giving of the law, the worship, and the promises; to them belong the patriarchs, and from them, according to the flesh, comes the Messiah, who is over all, God be blessed forever. Amen" (Rom. 9:4f.; cf. Eph. 2:12f.).

witness of her Scriptures, in accordance with which our creeds claim that Christ died and rose again. How we are entitled to know this as God's people involves the work of Christ in incorporating us into God's plan begun with Israel, which at the level of literary witness involves the beneficial retention of what Christians now call the "Old Testament" (compare simply "the Scriptures" or "Law and Prophets"), as part one of a fuller scriptural witness. Can this particular sequence of events, involving a chain of theological cause-and-effect, be simply side-stepped by the "neutral" critical mind seeking the "truth" of the Old Testament text directly, without need of confessional overlay or point of standing?

Much more could be said about this. My concern in the context of the lectionary is not to have ruled out by the particular threefold structure typological and figural readings of the Old Testament that illustrate clearly our christological — one might better say, trinitarian — point of standing, readings that stand as a corrective to much historical-critical logic and rationale involving objectivity and critical neutrality.[5]

One of the positive characteristics of the lectionary has been its capacity to retain pairings from the Old to New (whether in the Epistle or Gospel) with deep roots in the church's history of interpretation. These served as reminders that christological, figural, or allegorical readings of the Old Testament, while not now in vogue in seminaries under the influence of strictly "objective" and historical modes of reading, were nevertheless fully a part of the church's exegetical and

---

5. For a fresh reassertion of the historical-critical method, see J. Collins, "Historical Criticism and the State of Biblical Theology," *The Christian Century* (July 28–August 4, 1993): 743-47. Collins is quick to label Brevard Childs's approach "Barthian Protestantism" and Jon Levenson's "orthodox Judaism" in a tone that suggests that they have now been fully comprehended, their "bias" exposed. Also lurking around his analysis is the sense that he has no such obvious theological point of standing, and can continue to point to some area, in the academy, where "reasoned argument" not "confessional character" rules among the "community of scholars." Does this mean that there is such a thing as a real "community of scholars" studying the Bible, where "reasoned argument" can be neatly differentiated from "confessionalism" or theological perspective per se? How is that possible, especially in the late twentieth century? It may be that Collins's milder review of Barr suggests that the key is "natural theology" of the sort James Barr defends, which would make available, presumably, some sort of universal grid of rational inquiry, biblically rooted and endorsed. Why that should make any difference in the "community of scholars" where "reasoned argument" reigns and is its own reward is not clear to me.

homiletical repertoire. To say that the Old Testament can "preach Christ" is regarded by most critical minds as a hopeless anachronism (or possible only in strict historical terms).

But I think we stand on the threshhold of a recognition that all reading of the Bible is invariably affected by one's point of standing. While historicality was brought into keen consciousness in modern biblical study, what dropped in inverse proportion was the consciousness of a certain inevitable — religious, theological, or even purely academic — lens, through which the Scriptures are always viewed. This is changing, however, due in large measure to forces secular and academic (deconstruction), with derivative and in a great many cases negative consequences for theological exegesis.

But again the sword has two edges. One consequence of this sort of change is that it renders possible self-consciously christological (or trinitarian) readings of the Old Testament, however we might define these (this was no monolith in the so-called precritical period). In respect to the lectionary, my only point has been that I believe that a twofold (Old and New) model has a better chance of showcasing this than does the present threefold system.[6]

Selecting Passages

Having made a "two's company, three's a crowd" proposal for lectionary modification, and having tried to defend it with an eye toward biblical theology and modern critical trends, let me move now beyond the question of number and order to a more specific look at the selection process itself. My general point thus far has been that three lessons inevitably set up a progression while two allow for a measure of reciprocity more true to the actual character of the relationship between Old and New Testaments in the two-part Christian canon.

6. For a sustained and sophisticated discussion of the relationship between the biblical witness and the subject matter to which, for Christian confession, it points (the triune God), and especially on the possibility of returning to that same witness, particularly the Old Testament, with the knowledge of its ultimate subject matter ("the full divine reality"), see now B. S. Childs, *Biblical Theology of Old and New Testaments: Theological Reflection on the Christian Bible* (Minneapolis: Fortress, 1992), 379-83.

For purposes of eventual illustration, let me digress for a moment into a very brief history of the lectionary in the Episcopal Church. My observations will be basic and crude, restricted to recent changes in the lectionary brought on by the adoption of a new Book of Common Prayer in 1979 (with waves of earlier "trial" worship books). The earlier (1928) Book of Common Prayer had in fact two separate lectionaries: one for Morning Prayer Sunday services (with weekday Morning Prayer lessons as well), and another for Sundays when Holy Communion was to be the service of the day (or the earlier service prior to, and unrelated to, the main Morning Prayer service). In both instances only two lessons were ever read: in the former, the first was from the Old Testament and the second was from the New Testament (Gospel/Epistle distinction playing no consistent role); in the latter, the usual practice was the first from an Epistle, the second from a Gospel (readings from the Old Testament being generally rare as first lessons). However, in the Episcopal Church, and other confessions that shortly followed suit in terms at least of the lectionary, eucharistic worship became the norm for Sunday assembly, which created a need to modify the older Eucharistic lectionary so as to include Old Testament readings. This resulted in the three-lesson model presently in place. It is not clear that simply adding an additional first lesson to the two customarily read on eucharistic Sundays has solved the problem created by the move away from Morning Prayer worship and its lectionary.

A perusal of this older lectionary, "Psalms and Lessons for the Christian Year," incidentally reveals one further matter that pertained to the Sunday Morning Prayer (and Evening Prayer) lectionary. Each Sunday, choices were given of two, and sometimes three, Old Testament/New Testament pairings. In addition, one could swap lessons from Evening and Morning Prayer listings, giving one anywhere from four to six choices of Old and New pairings ("the choice thereof is at the discretion of the Minister"). That clergy sat around deliberating which pairings they would adopt is unlikely, of course; the first set given was probably chosen. Also little effort was probably expended trying to key one set to one year, the next set to the next, and so forth. Nowhere in the rubrics is any suggestion made that this lectionary was to conform to anything more than a single year cycle.

One of the ironies of prayer book revision in the Episcopal Church is that while choices were introduced for main services at every opportunity (Morning Prayer I; Evening Prayer II; Eucharistic Prayer IV) giving the new book a sort of smorgasbord feel, the same was not true of the lectionary. In a way, for all the diversity of content over a three-year cycle, from Sunday to Sunday it maintains a rather relentless stereotype in form. The reason I stress this point is that any move from a three- to a two-lectionary system is going to have to reckon with subtractions. Until now I have been arguing that especially the Epistle reading, intruding between Old Testament and Gospel, is confusing and disruptive of essential patterns in the two-testament canon. The older prayer book lectionary may have sensed this, but in any event it kept a two-lesson system by ignoring a Gospel/Epistle distinction for noneucharistic Sundays.

In my view, three main options exist for reversion to an Old Testament–New Testament lesson model. The first would be to ignore the Gospel/Epistle distinction on all Sunday worship, whether eucharistic or otherwise. The first lesson would be taken from the Old Testament, the second from the New. Church year considerations would control the reading chosen from the New, and would in turn affect the selection from the Old. A second option would be to isolate one or more parts of the Christian year when different models would obtain. For example, as it now stands the long summer season (Pentecost; Trinity; Ordinary Time) may in fact take up over half the actual year (twenty-nine propers are provided for the Sundays from Pentecost to Advent). This would be a good time to let Epistle readings predominate over Gospel readings. Continuous reading would continue to be a very workable option, now with emphasis on Epistle as the second and only New Testament reading. A final option would be to return to something of the flavor of the older two-lesson lectionary I have been describing, by allowing the minister several choices throughout the course of the year. These choices would all involve two lessons, one from Old and one from New, but with the focus either on Epistle or Gospel or some combination of the two. Having had the experience of trying to sort out the relationship between three lessons each Sunday, a return to a two-lesson model would be like removing leg weights for the preacher and congregant.

In addition, rather than let the decisions for why certain pairings have been made remain unstated, for the preacher and congregant to puzzle out or to invent, the range of choices provided could be illustrative of different, clearly stated patterns in the two-testament

187

canon. Here the lectionary might hold the potential for becoming a teaching aid for the church, preacher and congregant alike. In this same manner, from pulpit and lectern might come readings and exposition of Scripture more exemplary of patterns already at work within the full Christian canon itself.

Using the sort of clearly stated principles of selection that I have been advocating, just what might these pairings from Old and New Testament look like? Unfortunately, I have only enough space to list several possibilities.

I have repeatedly spoken about deferring to pairings that seem to be urged by the texts themselves. This can be stated more clearly and simply. The New Testament obviously can be detached from the Old, but even Marcion realized that this was not altogether easy, because the New has a material connection to the Old within its own independent literary presentation. One index to follow when making pairings, then, would be to ask whether the New Testament reading — from the Gospels or Epistles — took form with an eye toward some specific Old Testament text. Obviously, on occasion such texts are quoted or are otherwise referred to explicitly. On other occasions, as New Testament scholars have taught us, the relationship is far more subtle. Showcasing this material relationship between Old and New would be simply achieved in the lectionary by allowing the first lesson to be the same lesson referred to in the New.

One could argue that these sorts of pairings would blur the Old's per se voice in favor of the Old as heard *in Novo receptum*. But that would not be true in every instance. Matthew uses Isaiah's Song of the Vineyard to point out that the Israel which rejected proper stewardship in Isaiah's day has done so as well in Jesus' time. The present lectionary rightly pairs Isaiah 5:1-7 with Matthew 21:33-43 and thereby illustrates the Old as heard *in Novo receptum*. But in the context of Christian worship, to hear Isaiah not just as Matthew heard it, but on its own terms as a first scriptural lesson, means a word of prophetic address to Israel of old now also falls on the church, the New Israel. In this manner, the lectionary pairing illustrates the Old as heard both *in Novo receptum* and with its persistent per se voice. And to return to my other point, to hear a lesson from Philippians — which in Year A is read roughly as *lectio continua* from week to week — in between Isaiah and Matthew interferes with the close relationship rightly seen between Old and New. Trying to combine two separate principles (continuous reading and the Old's material use in the New) does not enhance "the gospel," but in fact intrudes upon it. In this instance, hearing the Old in light of the New and the New in light of the Old illustrates their essential reciprocity in communicating the gospel.

Of course, how the Old is utilized in the New is quite varied. For example, consider the lessons from Old and New used on Epiphany (Isa. 60:1-9; Matt. 2:1-12). Isaiah speaks of a light that is to arise, ostensibly that of the resplendent Zion; Matthew speaks of the light over Bethlehem toward which the wise men are drawn. Here the relationship between Old and New would appear to be figural: What is said of Zion, God's special place of tabernacling, is seen as a type of Christ, in whose flesh God was pleased to dwell. This understanding of the relationship between Old and New, while not at odds with Matthew's own plain sense, does not require an assertion that Matthew intentionally heard Isaiah 60 in the same direction as that of the lectionary. Matthew actually quotes an Old Testament text here, but it is Micah's promise of a ruler to come from Judah. One lectionary option would be to read that Micah text as a first lesson on some general understanding of prophesy and fulfillment as the principle relating Old and New. But this might underscore the wrong sort of connection (which may be why the lectionary avoids Micah), since Micah is here quoted by the religious officials being inquired of by the wicked Herod, not so much for its own sake, but so as to determine where the child can be found and destroyed.

A close reading of the Matthew text shows what a strange set of circumstances it is in fact relating. The appearance of a star signals the birth of "the king of the Jews" (2:2) to wise men from the East. Herod, frightened, wants to know where this king should be born and learns, from Micah, in Bethlehem. Herod then sends the wise men to Bethlehem "to pay tribute" and the star they had originally seen now "stops" over just the right place. They offer tribute but instead of returning to Herod to tell him where the child is, they are warned in a dream and find their way home "by another road."

An Old Testament text that speaks of a wicked king who seeks to destroy but instead ironically effects blessing and homage; that tells of a wise man from the East who offers right worship, whose eye is properly directed by God, and who sees a "star come out of Jacob" is the story of Balaam the seer in the Book of Numbers (chaps. 22–24).

189

Linking all or part of this Old Testament story to Matthew's account of the journey of the Magi might well connect with Matthew's own scriptural frame of reference, texts that in this instance are never cited directly. The relationship between Old and New would here be figural, with less of an actual contrast between Zion and the Christ child as in the present lectionary pairing. Now the continuity would be not just between the wise and obedient Balaam and Matthew's wise men from the East, but also between the wicked Balak, a foreign king and hindrance to God's people Israel, and Herod, Israel's own king.

I mentioned in passing the avoidance of Micah by lectionary framers as a first lesson to be paired with Matthew's birth narratives, a pairing that could potentially illustrate the familiar prophecy-fulfillment conception of how the Old and New are related. Advent lessons are traditionally thought of as illustrating this same conception, by using as first readings passages from Israel's prophets that tell of a righteous king (messiah). Ironically, very rarely are such passages actually quoted to the same effect in the New Testament itself. And when one looks more closely at the majority of Advent pairings, Old Testament prophecies regarding a coming messiah frequently direct the hearer through the witness of the New not to Jesus' past birth and incarnation, but ahead in time to the Second Coming.

How this particular perspective might be better reinforced in the lectionary would be to link Old Testament passages such as these to New Testament passages that direct the hearer to Christ's promised return in glory. For the sake of economy, we can return to the text just cited from Isaiah 60, which tells of Zion's exaltation. Instead of seeking a linkage where Zion's special status has been connected through figuration to Christ, one might instead select readings from the final chapters of Revelation. There, texts from Isaiah are cited to depict the Christian's final hope, in such a way that Isaiah's per se force has not been figurally translated, but retained and interpreted anew in light of Christ's incarnation, death, and ascension. Likewise, Pauline texts that direct the reader to Christ's return, or to the nature of the relationship between Israel and the Gentiles brought near in Christ might also be linked to so-called messianic texts from the prophets. Romans 9–11 offer a rich skein of scriptural citation where Paul takes up Old Testament texts and both interprets them in some fresh way or defers to their persistent per se force. Linking such texts directly with the New Testament witness from Paul, without need of a further "Gospel" reading is not now possible given the present lectionary format. But to what extent would "the gospel" be actually compromised or shortchanged if one only heard the Old and Paul's use of the Old in the context of his epistolary proclamation? Would not the now widespread eucharistic focus of Sunday assembly be sufficient to cover reference to the work and person of Christ as such, without need of some third more explicit "gospel" lesson?

Perhaps these few examples of pairings from Old and New illustrate my larger point regarding the sufficiency and appropriateness of a two-lesson lectionary. One should not defer in every instance to the New's explicit or apparent scriptural frame of reference for determining what passage from the Old should be read. Other principles presently at work in the lectionary, some tried and true, should be retained. But in every instance, these principles should be clearly spelled out to those who use the lectionary readings, if not also forming an explicit part of something akin to the "illuminations" used at present. And even if the New Testament be taken as an appropriate guide to selecting lessons from the Old, one need not worry that some form of monolithic or stereotypical conception of the Old's relationship to the New will emerge; much less is it clear that some sort of extreme selectivity in respect of the Old's per se voice would result (as the example of Matthew's use of the Balaam narratives should make clear). The New Testament's use of the Old is quite rich and varied. And in the context of Christian liturgy, with two lessons being read, the Old will not just be heard in light of the New; the New will also be heard in light of the Old, where frequently the Old's per se voice has not been translated, transformed, or stilled, but continues to sound forth in the proclamation of "the gospel." What makes this possible is the return to a two-lesson format, with far closer attention being paid to instances when the Old already serves to proclaim the gospel through its own witness as brokered in the New.

On the Efficacy of the Gospel: Thoughts on the Gospel's Implications

KENNETH G. APPOLD

The Role of the Gospel

Difficult as the task of reconstructing the historical events surrounding Jesus' brief appearance on this earth may be, one thing remains certain: a new factor entered the world of human relations. A new reason for coming together had appeared. Whatever reasons one may have had before — whether traditions of family, means of occupation and survival, or even national and religious allegiance — they were now eclipsed by him. More accurately, one could say they were eclipsed by *word* of him, since communities did not congregate around Christ until, paradoxically, after he had physically disappeared. One left home and family, abandoned job and income, and suspended one's prior beliefs because of something one *heard*. Except in extraordinary cases, what one heard was spoken by other persons. That "something," spoken and heard, came to be known as the gospel. With its utterance, a new way of living together dawned on the world. The communities that formed from hearing the announcement of Christ's gospel came to call themselves "church."

Clearly, communities — even religious communities — had existed long before the time of Christ. The early Christian church owed its uniqueness among such social groupings to the special character of its *raison d'être:* to the news it called "gospel." Without that proclamation of gospel, and the effect it produced among hundreds and soon thousands of second-century Mediterranean people, there would have been no church. Without the continued preaching of that gospel, there would be no Christian community today — nor tomorrow.

Differing cultural circumstances of the groups that received the gospel, as well as diverse historical developments of those peoples since then, have formed a colorful palette of individual Christian communities. Many such groups owe their separation principally to historical and cultural accidents. In those cases, they may discover unity in the one source that has called them into being. With that in mind, Lutherans' Augsburg Confession describes Christian unity in the following terms: "it is sufficient for the true unity of the Christian church that the Gospel be preached in conformity with a pure understanding of it and that the sacraments be administered in accordance with the divine Word" (CA 7).

This essay represents my reflection, from a particularly Lutheran perspective, on the possibility for full communion advanced by the *Concordat of Agreement* currently before American Lutherans and Episcopalians. As a point of departure, I take the above-cited statement on unity in the *Confessio Augustana.* Just as preaching the gospel — and administering the concomitant sacraments — called together the first Christian communities, so now, and at all times, does it provide sufficient grounds for Christian communion. If the gospel is truly preached, furthermore, then secondary matters such as those pertaining to organization and polity — especially if considered *adiaphora* — should remain secondary, and not rise to form impediments to such communion. The Concordat, in that case, could provide a visible witness to the continuing primacy and power of the gospel in creating Christian community. If the gospel is not proclaimed in our churches, however, then the Concordat represents little more than joining hands on a sinking ship.

One of the first fruits to spring from the Lutheran-Episcopal Dialogue series has come in the mutual recognition of each church as a community "in which the gospel is preached and taught."[1] Describing theological consensus between Lutherans and Episcopalians, the document "Toward Full Communion" makes the following statement: "As a matter of historical record, the Lutheran churches and the Anglican churches have not engaged in doctrinal controversy with

---

1. Point 2 of the 1982 "Lutheran-Episcopal Agreement," reprinted in William A. Norgren and William G. Rusch, eds., *"Toward Full Communion" and "Concordat of Agreement," Lutheran-Episcopalian Dialogue, Series 3* (Minneapolis: Augsburg; Cincinnati: Forward Movement, 1991), p. 11.

each other on the nature of the gospel, nor do their doctrinal documents contain any official condemnation of each other's doctrine."[2]

Such statements, coming as they do after considerable discussion and soul searching from the participants, appear very encouraging. Because of the hopes raised by those affirmations, another document generated by the series, entitled *Implications of the Gospel*,[3] invites particular disappointment. On first reading, one might opt to ignore the document altogether, since it remains only on the periphery of the Concordat. On the other hand, *Implications*, because of a number of careless formulations, leaves room for a misunderstood notion of gospel unfortunately already common in churches of both confessions. As such, the text allows to continue an inclination that, if unabated, would in due course render the Concordat meaningless. Without a proper understanding of gospel, neither church has much to offer the society from which it has already, to a large extent, been sidelined. Consequently, and in the interests of the Concordat itself, *Implications of the Gospel* deserves closer scrutiny.

The Gospel in *Implications of the Gospel*

The document concerns itself with "Gospel" and seeks to draw out significant implications of that gospel for churches, their polity, and their role in the world. Before delineating those implications, it advances a description of "Gospel." Striking a chord that will echo throughout the text, the document describes the gospel as an "eschatological event" (p. 19).

The word "eschatology," coined, incidentally, by seventeenth-century Lutheran theologian Abraham Calov, stems from the Greek adjective *eschatos*, meaning "last." It occurs a number of times in the New Testament, often modifying the word "days," as "in these last

2. Ibid., p. 25.
3. William A. Norgren and William G. Rusch, eds., *Implications of the Gospel, Lutheran-Episcopal Dialogue, Series 3* (Minneapolis: Augsburg; Cincinnati: Forward Movement, 1988). All references to this document will hereafter appear as a page number within the text.

days" (Heb. 1:2). The *Implications* text interprets the word to connote "outcome" (p. 18). Thus, as an "eschatological event," the gospel is viewed as being invested in the world's outcome. That outcome, according to the present document, coincides with "the final victory of the reign of God" (p. 17). At the end of time, according to such a "Gospel," God will reign over all the world.

Of course, being an "eschatological event" does not mean that the gospel itself will take place at the end of time. The text merely asserts that the gospel will be fulfilled at the end of time, and thus remains "grounded" in that future event. In other words, whether the gospel is finally true depends on whether that future outcome — namely, the victorious reign of God — does indeed take place.

In the meantime, however, the gospel is made credible by pointing to Jesus Christ as its source. As a "promise" (p. 17), it has its origins in Jesus and his "history" (p. 31): "With sin overcome and death behind him, Jesus can and does make an unconditional promise to the world: the triumph of the reign of God will finally be manifested" (p. 26). Jesus, on the strength of having recently emerged from the tomb, makes a promise; he promises that the same power that raised him from the dead will, at the end of time, prevail over all the forces of death in the world. With the resurrected Jesus before their eyes, the disciples receive a "preview" of what God will do for them and the rest of the world one day: "[The disciples] experienced proleptically, that is, in preview, the outcome of history in the midst of history. They were let in on the disclosed promise of God's final salvation" (p. 18).

Inspired by this information, the disciples found themselves "renewed" in strength and spirit to face depressing realities and, repeating Jesus' promise to others, began to gather "believers" around them. Thus, the document points to the church as the "principal implication of the Gospel in human history" (p. 34). Following the disciples' example, subsequent generations of those who believed Jesus' promise of a good "outcome" were similarly "renewed" and informed others of their news, in an effort to "include all peoples" in this "end-time messianic community" (p. 34).

Having said this, the document continues by stressing, not surprisingly, that church polity, far from being an *adiaphoron,* constitutes a further important "implication of the Gospel." The members of the church, all of whom have been inspired and renewed by Christ's promise of good times ahead, begin relating to one another in a different manner. Their life together reflects the conviction that Jesus indeed will be right, and that the powers of evil in this world no longer merit obeisance:

> [Polity] is the way the church as the body of Christ under historical conditions is freed by the gospel so to live together so that the patterns and powers of its life reflect and witness to the reign of God rather than to the patterns and powers of the "old age." Polity in the church thus testifies to the fact that the gospel gives life to a visible, historical community. (Pp. 44f.)

In sum, *Implications* describes the gospel as a promise of the world's salvific final outcome, a promise whose fulfillment is already foreshadowed by the "proleptic" disclosure of that final outcome in Christ's death and resurrection, thus making it easier to believe. Its principal implication lies in the church, since the promise is heard and believed by more than one person, and communicated to other persons, thereby constituting a community. A further implication comes with the fact that people who join that community of antici-pation modify their behavior — presumably by reorienting their pri-orities to accord with the values indicated by the promise — thereby making the polity of this "Christian" community different from others.

Thus viewed, the argument does not appear particularly ambi-tious; the implications drawn remain rather modest. It does not make a very strong case for the uniqueness of the Christian community, except to suggest that such a community exhibits "renewed" behavior patterns. It does not show, furthermore, why Christ's promise would necessarily lead to the formation of a "Church." Even in parsimony, however, the argument contains a number of critical errors, most significantly in its description of "Gospel."

Implications begins by offering a definition of "Gospel" that, if not directly misleading, certainly leaves much room for misunder-standing. That definition, once again, describes the gospel as Christ's promise of a salvific outcome for the world's history, "proleptically" disclosed by his resurrection from the dead. Before asking whether such a definition does justice to the scriptural account of "Gospel," one might direct a few questions to the definition itself, and ask

196

whether it can indeed sustain the implications desired by the document.

Promises litter human discourse and one may begin by asking how the particular "Gospel" promise differs from other promises, such as the meteorologist's promise of sunshine next week. According to *Implications,* the distinguishing characteristic of gospel promise lies in its connection to Jesus. Christ's resurrection provided the necessary support to launch a belief in the promise that God would, at the end of time, emerge victorious in the battle against evil. Christ's postresurrection appearances give the disciples a preview of what would happen in the end time. One might ask whether this preview remains restricted to those first witnesses, however, on the grounds that they alone were privy to that vision. If so, the "grounds" of the gospel promise — namely, its experiential connection to Christ Jesus — disappear with that first generation of believers. The demise of those eyewitnesses changes the so-called proleptic disclosure from an event of immediate experience to the status of secondhand account. It becomes a piece of news, like any other. Hence, the distinguishing characteristic of the gospel promise ceases to operate, and that particular promise becomes like any other, and no more worthy of our attention than any other. It differs from the meteorologist's promise of sunshine only in value, since a forecast of God's victory represents something considerably more desirable — even if less imminent — than sunshine next week.

Promises, furthermore, can either pledge the truth of an already existing fact, such as "I promise you are healthy," or they may predict a reality of the future, such as the meteorologist's promise of sunshine. Describing the gospel as the promise of a salvific outcome emphasizes the latter function. The gospel remains oriented toward something future, claiming that something *will* happen, rather than the fact that something *has* happened. The "proleptic" character that *Implications* ascribes to the gospel places the overwhelming emphasis on the predictive nature of its promise. God's full disclosure will come at some as yet unspecified end-point in the as yet unspecified future. Human history, in the meantime, remains a time of "anticipation" (p. 73).

One might ask whether such a future-oriented interpretation of God's most decisive activity does not strip the Christian message altogether of its specific power. As an anticipation of a better future, Christ's promise stands among any number of similar statements of hope that spring eternal in the human breast ("Man never Is, but

197

always To be blest"). By deferring God's victory into the *eschaton,* the authors of *Implications* diminish its significance for the present. God's victory becomes little more than a goal, no doubt an attractive one, toward which we are to direct our hope in times of present adversity. As such, it carries two rather darker implications.

First, such an interpretation of the gospel fails to guard Christ's promise from the ever-present Christian temptation of escapism. Rather than address the realities at hand, such a "promise" serves simply to inject a dose of "hope" into the human situation. In cases of genuine hopelessness, where no "positive outcome" of any kind seems possible, such preaching is simply arrogant. It is also impotent. One could hardly imagine walking into an inner-city church and proclaiming, with a look of affected "empathy," "Oh, rejoice! There *will be* a final victory, oh yes, there *will,* one day, later, at the end of time." If the Christian faith has no more to offer our societies than the vision of a final, triumphant descent from the clouds of a white-clad Messiah, then there seems little reason to continue in it.

The second temptation comes as a reaction to the first. Unsatisfied with the impotence of their message, Christians begin to fidget for "action." With God's victory identified as the end, one seeks means by which to reach that end, or to implement it prematurely. Imagined "final solutions" begin to appear; ideologies of every political persuasion arrogate to themselves the status of being "divinely ordained." As such, the gospel, interpreted as eschatological promise, provides a "blank check" with which to underwrite any human activity deemed appropriate to the eschatological end, and to fill its protagonists with an impression of righteous fervor. In the absence of a real absolute, relative human views and statements cloak themselves with an aura of the false absolute. In the absence of a real God, human beings elevate themselves to little gods.

Such undesirable implications of the misunderstood gospel cloud the implications that the document wishes to develop. Groups tending toward millennialism on the one hand, or a knee-jerk activism on the other, might well find fuel in such a gospel. Such communities could, indeed, form around that "Gospel." Whether either Episcopalians or Lutherans wish to identify themselves with such groups appears unlikely. Furthermore, what form of "polity" such groups would construct remains difficult to envision. One wonders if either otherworldly fanaticism or a puritanical hyperactivism could yield more than collections of quixotic fanatics. One hesitates to speculate about the inner-group relations conjured up by "renewal" in such a spirit. One hopes, in any case, that polities of such a kind remain distant from Christian churches. The *Implications* document, however, provides no reasoning by which to exclude them, and fails, with its weak definition of gospel, to provide grounds for a positive alternative. If the only consequences of such vagueness lay in spawning fringe groups like those caricatured above, the dangers might be minimal. In more mundane guises, however, the temptations of escapism and ideological idolatry remain a constant threat to the life of both confessions, ready at all times to step into the vacuum left by a neglected gospel.

Toward a Fuller Gospel

The definition of "Gospel" advanced by the *Implications* document does not adequately support the implications it wishes to suggest. In fact, the definition opens the door to a number of implications altogether different in character from those intended. Three points remain central to the document's definition: (1) its assertion that the gospel's content points to a future event, (2) its characterization of the gospel promise as a predictive promise, and (3) its identification of the gospel's effects as renewal and liberation. Even a brief look at the New Testament reveals crucial differences with those three elements of the definition and calls for a revised definition — one which may well serve to correct a few of the more problematic "implications."

The conviction that Christ will come again, and that that Second Coming will constitute a culmination of human experience, does have roots in the New Testament and belongs to the doctrinal *corpus* of both Episcopalians and Lutherans. In that sense, the document correctly identifies an aspect of the Christian witness. Taken as the definitive content of "Gospel," however, that message obscures a much more central component of the scriptural witness.

As the use of the word *eschatos* in the New Testament indicates, the authors of the Gospels and Epistles thought the "end time" to be imminent — if not already present. Thus, the letter to the Hebrews begins by speaking "in these last days," describing a time when a great cosmic reordering has taken place. Acts 2, more famous, finds the prophecy of Joel, which describes events of "the last days," fulfilled at Pentecost. Second Timothy (3:1), 2 Peter (3:3), and Jude (18) all speak of "the last days" as close at hand, a time for which the early churches should stand prepared.

Such language reflects a conviction that something pivotal, something of eternal significance, had happened. It does not mean that time had come to an end, only that the end time had come to the present. History itself was perceived as having reached a turning point; the very forces whose dynamic interaction make the passing of "history" a fact for our perception had reached their goal. Just as a groom awaits an absent bride and marks the days of his solitude by their proximity to her coming, so too humans had waited for the arrival of their God. And just as, on the day that distant loved one comes, time itself may seem to cease its forward motion, so too those first witnesses had seen the "end" of time. Their union forever alters the lives of both, and so for Christians also, the end has begun to happen.

The "event" that brought all of this to pass, of course, had been the entrance of Jesus Christ into the midst of those first disciples. His coming, his presence, arrived as the answer to the world's anticipations. With him, heaven's kingdom came to earth. He himself can say: "The time is fulfilled, and the kingdom of God has come near" (Mark 1:14-15). He himself proclaims: "Repent, for the kingdom of heaven has come near" (Matt. 4:17).

The evangelist John finds himself moved to write that "the true light, which enlightens everyone, was coming into the world" (John 1:9). He wrote further that

All things came into being through him, and without him not one thing came into being. What has come into being in him was life, and the life was the light of all people. . . . And the Word became flesh and lived among us, and we have seen his glory, the glory as of a father's only son, full of grace and truth. (John 1:3-4, 14)

Luke describes Satan falling "from heaven like a flash of lightning" (Luke 10:18), and all the world's demons at God's fingertips. Clearly something decisive for history and the very perception of history had taken place. The time of anticipation had ended; the end time had dawned.

The fact that we today do not perceive the course of history in quite that way, that we may feel ourselves to be merely *anticipating,* testifies to our failure to perceive that end time reign already present in our midst. It is, perhaps, quite human to view the gospel as simply pointing to the future; it is Christian, however, to see it also here and now.

How, one might ask, is God's reign present here and now? Again, the New Testament provides some helpful guidance. The term "gospel" *(euangelion)* almost invariably occurs in association with the act of preaching. Jesus himself goes about "preaching the gospel of the kingdom" (Matt. 4:23; 9:35, RSV) and commissions others to preach the gospel (Mark 13:10; 16:15); Peter speaks of the "word of the gospel" (Acts 15:7, RSV), and Paul travels the world to "preach the gospel" (1 Cor. 15:1; 2 Cor. 2:12; 11:7; Gal. 1:8, 11; 2:2, etc.). The gospel is so closely identified with preaching that the two can at times mean the same thing: Paul describes his work of ministry as labor in the gospel (Phil. 4:3), his apostolic call as being "set apart for the gospel of God" (Rom. 1:1), and his mission to Thessalonica as "gospel" (1 Thess. 2:4). "Gospel," therefore, remains inextricably linked with the activity of preaching. Rather than denote simply a set of "contents," the term "gospel" refers to an event, a "happening" involved in the act of preaching.

Preaching the gospel creates an effect. Indeed, most spoken words create an effect of one kind or another, whether they be imperatives such as "pick up your socks!" or indicatives uttered into a particularly receptive situation, such as the word "Fire!" in a crowded theater; even more mundane examples, like, "I really do like your perfume," have their effect. Similarly, the gospel, when preached, has an impact. Quite often, the New Testament describes it as a "power" (Rom. 1:16; 1 Thess. 1:8). That power remains closely connected with judgment. In the Revelation to John, an angel flies "in midheaven, with an eternal gospel to proclaim to those who live on the earth . . . He said with a loud voice: 'Fear God and give him glory, for the hour of his judgment has come'" (Rev. 14:6).

When that which one has long anticipated finally does arrive, the experience inevitably differs from one's expectations. The fulfillment rarely corresponds to what those waiting have imagined. One imagines many things. Yet, almost miraculously, to those who can suspend their expectations — their own imagined demands — for a moment and

201

look with an opened mind, the arrival of that culminating event may more than fill one's cup of longing. Not only does one receive much more than one could have imagined, but those very previous expectations seem misplaced and mistaken. One tries to forget them.

All the more is such a reaction apposite when applied analogously to the coming of Christ. Christ, as fulfilling not only personal wishes and desires, comes as the culmination of all creation and its history. Needless to say, much in creation remains that resists him, that bristles at the thought that this is all there is, a mere carpenter, crucified as a criminal, no less. These elements of resistance, who refuse to abandon their anticipations — who close their minds even more firmly — are those who experience the ultimate, and permanent, frustration. They deny themselves their fulfillment; they, and their wants, are judged.

The proclamation of Christ's arrival, and the commensurate news that "the kingdom is here," ushers in such a "day of reckoning." All who witness the event find themselves caught off guard. A great disparity manifests itself between the enormous magnitude of what has been revealed and the trifling insignificance of those who expected. The scene before the tomb on Easter morning gives expression to the overwhelming nature of that experience: "The women were terrified and bowed their faces to the ground" (Luke 24:5).

Upon hearing the proclamation, however, "they went out and fled from the tomb, for terror and amazement had seized them" (Mark 16:8). Such a reaction would appear perfectly natural of anyone who had begun to grasp the depth of what had taken place. A disparity of such magnitude could provoke only profound humility on the part of the recipient — who had been offered so much in exchange for so little. One begs to be forgiven. One cries out that the giver may overlook one's unworth and the unjustified nature of his gift. Such feelings would only intensify as one thought back and took stock of what had gone before and how one had led one's life. The apostle Paul epitomizes those feelings — and he, having led the life he did, should understand them as well as any — and gives them perhaps their most profound articulation: "all have sinned and fall short of the glory of God" (Rom. 3:23). But Paul has experienced another dimension to this gospel vision; mysteriously, Christ comes to forgive. Despite all that had gone before and all that had gone wrong, Christ calls his offer good. The effect of that proclamation on the humble sinner can be nothing short of salvific. Those who accept are redeemed. "They are now justified by his grace as a gift, through the redemption that is in Christ Jesus" (Rom. 3:24).

When one compares the image of gospel that emerges from the New Testament witness with those three facets of the *Implications* definition identified above, one immediately notices marked differences. First, rather than a simple "future" event, "gospel" denotes a *fait accompli*. Christ *has* come, our sins *have been* forgiven. To lose sight of the already accomplished nature of the gospel-news is to lose sight of the gospel itself. One cannot overemphasize that fact.

Second, one would better describe the gospel as announcement than prediction. "Gospel" and "preaching" remain entwined, and are no more separable than "medicine" and "healing." Since such preaching announces something present rather than something yet to come, one can only misleadingly describe it as a predictive promise, or a merely "proleptic" presence. (The notion of "promise" itself does, of course, remain useful — the Augsburg Confession itself uses the term — but only to specify further the nature of the announcement: Jesus *promises* that the kingdom has come; Christ *promises* that our sins are forgiven. But such promises do not serve to predict future realities — they *create* realities here and now.)

Finally, as the announcement of an accomplished fact, the gospel creates an *effect*. Many kinds of statement have a *performative* function; their utterance makes something happen. *Implications* overlooks that dimension of language. Keeping it in mind would have allowed greater clarity in its delineation of the gospel's consequences for polity. Even if the document had devoted more attention to the gospel's performative dimension, however, it would still have had to contend with the lack of specificity — and even misconception — that burdens its description of the gospel promise. Different statements, obviously, create different effects. When one places the gospel's emphasis on prediction, no matter what portion of the predicted future may be "proleptically" present, one suggests a deferral, rather than presence, of God's word to humanity. Such a view stresses historical continuity before and after Christ, with Jesus acting as a mere signpost along the way. Human beings remain defined by anticipation rather than by redemption.

As the announcement of the kingdom's presence, however, the gospel creates a different effect. Just as human words of forgiveness can alter the fundamental structure of personal relationships, redeeming lost situations and inspiring new hearts, so proclaiming God's offer of reconciliation into a fragmented and contrary world opens altogether new ways of being for those who accept that gift.

The gospel's efficacy depends upon its proper proclamation, however. One cannot view it as depending on future deeds or events for its truth; the offer stands now. No longer must humankind live in perpetual anticipation, yearning for better times, longing for the day its Lord will arrive. No longer must men and women remain enslaved to worldly unctions offered as narcotics for a seeking soul. No longer must we wonder who we are. We *are* saved! The kingdom *has* come!

The Efficacy of Communion

When we draw out the gospel's implications for the church communities, two points become clear. First, the church, as the community of those who have been born anew by the kingdom's presence in their midst, owes both its existence and its character to the gospel proclamation. The gospel's immediate effects of judgment and reconciliation make possible a "new way of being." While the external characteristics of such renewal elude precise and programmatic specification, Scripture does indicate a number of its tangible manifestations. Those fruits of the Spirit include "love, joy, peace, patience, kindness, generosity, faithfulness, gentleness, and self-control" (Gal. 5:22f.). As the gospel community, then, the church manifests the "life in the Spirit" occasioned by the gospel announcement.

The second point comes as a consequence of the first. Having accepted the news of Christ's present kingdom and reaped the spiritual benefits that accompany such acceptance, the community of believers must begin to reckon with the vast disparity between the glory of that kingdom and the empirical realities of the world. If it is by proclaiming the gospel that the kingdom's benefits become tangible, then the responsibility for an absence of such fruits of the Spirit in the world — and within the church itself, of course — rests nowhere other than with that community. Just as it has been called into existence by the gospel, the church community must continue preaching the gospel. That remains its foremost task and responsibility.

Communion between historically distinct churches must arise

above all from the joint commission of preaching the kingdom's presence. When that mandate is shared, one has sufficient cause for communion. Moreover, in light of the enormity of the churches' responsibility, it would seem counterproductive to the gospel and an impediment to its efficacy, if every opportunity for such coming together in the joint task were not seized. In the interest of the gospel, the churches must unite behind their common mission.

If that mission is not currently recognized by the majority of Lutherans and Episcopalians, then the Concordat before both confessions appears rather feckless. If, on the other hand, Episcopalians and Lutherans do acknowledge and preach the gospel — properly understood — then the Concordat could greatly enhance the effectiveness of that ministry.

The *Implications* document, while employing a number of formulations that fall short of inspiring confidence, nonetheless should not detract from the value of the Concordat itself. *Implications,* after all, is a joint project, not the product of one or the other confession. The misunderstanding it allows occurs among Episcopalians and Lutherans alike. Indeed, that document, as well as the larger challenge of the Concordat, could well serve congregations of both communities in coming to terms with their perennial mandate and the nature of their common ministry. If such discussions take place and bear fruit, then sufficient grounds for communion would appear to exist, and most secondary matters, such as questions of episcopal oversight, create no further barrier.

Theological Renewal in Communion: What Anglicans and Lutherans Can Learn from One Another

DAVID S. YEAGO

Full Communion and Theological Encounter

The Lutheran-Episcopal Concordat provides that ordinands of each church will study the authoritative documents of the other church — thus Lutherans will study the Book of Common Prayer and Episcopalians will study the Lutheran Confessions.[1] Such study, if it is to be meaningful, must take place in a larger context; it must involve in each case an encounter with the theological tradition of the other partner and with what we may call the distinctive *theological ethos* that characterizes that tradition.

The notion of the "ethos" of a theological tradition is perhaps somewhat elusive but not therefore unhelpful. It is a commonplace of ecumenical theology that theological differences between Christian communities may in many cases be traced to the differing interests, the distinctive fears and concerns, that are, so to speak, embodied in their respective traditions.[2] As Christian communities live and ponder the mystery of Christ, they become, in the course of their diverse

---

1. "Each church also promises to require its ordination candidates to study each other's basic documents." Concordat of Agreement, par. 2, in William A. Norgren and William G. Rusch, eds., *"Towards Full Communion" and "Concordat of Agreement," Lutheran-Episcopal Dialogue, Series 3* (Minneapolis: Augsburg; Cincinnati: Forward Movement, 1991), p. 98.

2. See the discussion of these points in Karl Lehmann and Wolfhart Pannenberg, eds., *The Condemnations of the Reformation Era — Do They Still Divide?* (Minneapolis: Fortress, 1990), pp. 15-20.

histories, and for all sorts of reasons, especially attuned to certain issues: dangers to be avoided, insights to be claimed, questions to be wrestled with.

Christian communities may thus be quite different from one another theologically, not because they give incompatible answers to the same questions, but rather because they have thought it important to ask very different questions. These differences, moreover, affect not only the content but also the form of theological discourse: a Christian tradition such as Roman Catholicism in which a precise statement of trinitarian doctrine is a historic priority will engage in a very different sort of theological discourse from free-church traditions that historically regard conceptual issues as, on the whole, a distraction from the real business of practical discipleship.

Thus we might define the "theological ethos" of a particular Christian tradition as the typical set of dispositions and attitudes, priorities and worries, enthusiasms and concerns, that shape the theological reflection of those formed in that tradition. Our traditions dispose us to approach the one unfathomable mystery by which Christians live from different angles, to be especially sensitive to particular patterns of insight and implication, to be deeply concerned about certain questions and find it hard to see the point of others. Of course, all of us are shaped and limited in this way by all sorts of factors, theological and nontheological, but traditional ethos retains a remarkable formative power, even in a time when traditional identities seem to be eroding. Even the most decadent Lutheran tends to be decadent in a different way from a decadent Anglican or Roman Catholic or Calvinist.

The realization that differences of this sort do not not necessarily entail disagreement is what makes it possible to regard Christian diversity as, in principle, an opportunity for mutual instruction rather than an excuse for perpetuating division. One of the dangers to theological reflection in a divided church is that our partial traditions of vision become insulated, even fortified, against one another, to the point that we make virtues of unwillingness to concede that we have anything in common with others and of imperviousness to learning from those outside the denominational circle. On the other hand, much of the theological and spiritual profit of ecumenical involvement comes precisely as one learns to appreciate the distinctive fears and concerns of Christians who are very different from oneself, thus

207

gaining access to the insights into the Christian mystery of which their traditions are the bearers.

"Full communion" between Lutheran and Episcopal churches must surely imply mutual instruction and correction in a common enterprise of theological reflection — not only in the teaching and writing of seminary professors, but also in that more basic theological reflection which necessarily accompanies Christian ministry and Christian living among the clergy and laity of both churches. The stipulation that the ordinands of each church study the authoritative documents of the other is a starting-point, but only that, toward this end. Here as elsewhere, the effect of the adoption of the Concordat by our churches will depend on the energy, devotion, and clarity of mind with which we take it as a heaven-sent opportunity for conversion, renewal, and a deeper faithfulness in our common witness to Christ.

This essay is a preliminary attempt at imagining what such a mutual engagement might be like, and how it might issue in a common Anglican-Lutheran theological ethos, suppressing neither tradition but fusing the strengths of both. I shall begin with a somewhat impressionistic, but I hope not uninformed, characterization of the theological ethos of the Anglican and Lutheran traditions, go on to consider the different ways in which these traditions typically become decadent, and conclude with some reflections on the theological renewal that might issue from a thoughtful melding of their strengths.

The Anglican Ethos: Concrete Pneumatology[3]

What strikes a Lutheran, at any rate, about the Anglican theological ethos is its focus on the contingencies and particularities of ecclesial and believing life — liturgy, order, practice, and the textures of everyday life as infused by grace. It is important to realize how different this is from the ethos of the Lutheran tradition. A Lutheran, on first

3. This discussion of the Anglican ethos will necessarily have the awkwardness, but I hope also the virtues, of an outsider's view. I hope that it may also be read as an exercise in appreciation of a Christian tradition to which I owe a great deal both spiritually and theologically.

opening Hooker's *Laws,* is likely to find it difficult to grasp the sense in which it is a theological book at all; Hooker's apparent mishmash of political theory, church history, and the *minutiae* of Church of England canon law hardly seems the sort of matter about which theology could be written. Even in Book V, where he gets down to recognizable theological *loci,* a Lutheran may well be bemused to find discussions "Of the fashion of our Churches" (chap. XIV), "Attire belonging to the service of God" (chap. XXIX), "The manner of celebrating festival days" (chap. LXX), and "Of the Learning that should be in ministers, their Residence, and the number of their Livings" (chap. LXXXI) framing a profound account of the incarnation and the sacraments.

The Lutheran tradition has few analogies to such an attempt at thinking through the *concreta* of a particular Christian community's life in a theological context. For the Anglican tradition, by contrast, Hooker is in this respect, as in others, paradigmatic. Thus one can discern the same pattern of theological discourse in two other classics of Anglican theology, F. D. Maurice's *Kingdom of Christ* and Michael Ramsey's *The Gospel and the Catholic Church:* both move easily between the deep mysteries of the faith and the concrete practices and institutions of the historic church (and of the Anglican community in particular), attempting to show how the latter have a kind of contingent sense and fitness in the context of the former.

I would like to identify the Anglican theological ethos in this respect as an ethos of *concrete pneumatology* — an attentive focus on the contingent and particular ways in which the Spirit makes us partakers of the mystery of Christ in the church.[4] Anglicans have traditionally

---

4. The fact that Anglicans have often misleadingly spoken of this feature of their tradition as "incarnationalism" only shows that Anglicans are no more adept than other Western Christians at theoretical, as distinct from concrete, pneumatology. The Orthodox are teaching us that we cannot proceed directly from the uniqueness of the incarnation to the life of the church, but that we must consider the latter in terms of the distinctive logic of the mission of the Spirit. The notion of "incarnationalism" is misleading in that it tends to make the unique event of the coming of the Logos as the particular man Jesus into a mere exemplification of a general principle. The witness of the Spirit universalizes the singular particularity of Christ without compromising that particularity. On this, see the illuminating remarks of Brother Pierre-Yves Emery of Taizé, *Le Saint-Esprit: présence de communion* (Taizé: Presses de Taizé, 1980), pp. 42-44.

been distinctively attuned, I would suggest, to the concreteness of the church, to the fact that we encounter salvation in an actual community whose reality we cannot properly envision apart from a whole complex of social practices, institutions, and even artifacts.[5] And this sense of the concreteness of the church has gone hand in hand with a matching sense of the concreteness of believing life — we come to share in the holiness of Christ as persons situated in the world in specific, contingent ways, our lives intricately bound up in commonplace obligations, ties, and circumstances that may be transfigured by grace into spiritual opportunity.

One can see this most immediately, of course, in the role played by liturgy for Anglicans in defining and sustaining Christian faith and identity; one of the hurdles that the Anglican-Lutheran dialogue must surmount is Lutheran incomprehension that anyone could seriously propose to lodge doctrinal authority in a *prayer-book*. But it would be a mistake to stop short with this well-known point, for to the extent that this description of the concretely pneumatological focus of the Anglican ethos hits the mark, its implications go much further.

It may help to explain, for example, the peculiar quality of the Anglican commitment to the historic episcopate. While one sort of Anglo-Catholic argument, prominent in the nineteenth and early twentieth centuries, made its own the juridicism of post-Reformation Roman Catholic ecclesiology, for which the details of catholic order were directly and unalterably instituted by Christ and the apostles, this line of defense was never the most characteristic. Hooker himself viewed with equinamity the prospect that the episcopate might ultimately come to be viewed as a postapostolic development;[6] his own case rests more upon a convergence of arguments

---

5. On the presence of this sensibility already in the English Reformation and its liturgy, see Bishop Rowan Williams, "Imagining the Kingdom: Some Questions for Anglican Worship Today," in *The Identity of Anglican Worship,* ed. Kenneth Stevenson and Bryan Spinks (London: Mowbray, 1991), pp. 1-13.

6. In his words:

> Now although we should leave the general received persuasion held from the first beginning, that the Apostles themselves left bishops invested with power above other pastors; although, I say, we should give over this opinion, and embrace that other conjecture which so many have thought good to follow, and which myself did sometimes judge a great deal more probable than now I do, merely that after the Apostles were deceased, churches did agree among

from antiquity, the practical experience of the church, and contingent fitness than it does upon appeals to intrinsic necessity or dominical and apostolic institution.

At work here seems to be a sense that insofar as the church is a real society in history, the contingency of a practice is no argument against its authority — an insight of crucial ecumenical importance that Roman Catholics and the heirs of the Continental Reformation have equal difficulty in grasping.[7] One has not disposed of bishops simply by showing that the episcopate is neither logically necessary to the faith nor explicitly instituted by Christ and/or his apostles; nor is it necessary to absolutize the episcopate (and so unchurch the Continental Protestants, which Hooker was not willing to do) in order to regard it as a divine gift to be gratefully received.

This perspective, I would suggest, is implicitly pneumatological: The church is the work of the Spirit, who bears faithful witness to Christ, yet does so in underiveable freedom, calling into being an actual historical community and adorning it with all manner of concrete and particular gifts to sustain its worship and common life. These gifts cannot be deduced by any a priori theoretical reasoning, but must be discerned within the untidy narrative of the church's history by a believing mind formed and schooled in the ways of the Spirit by close and deep familiarity with Scripture and the witness of tradition.

In a very different sphere, one can see the same focus in the characteristic attentiveness of the Anglican spiritual tradition to the textures of everyday life and to the immense significance of the small ways in which we do or do not respond to the grace of the Spirit in the commonplace encounters and situations that befall us in our little corners of the world. From Jeremy Taylor's *Holy Living,* through the

---

themselves for preservation of peace and order, to make one presbyter in each city chief over the rest, and to translate into him that power by force and virtue of which the Apostles, while they were alive, did preserve and uphold order in the Church, exercising spiritual jurisdiction partly by themselves and partly by evangelists, because they could not always every where themselves be present: this order taken by the Church itself (for so let us suppose that the Apostles did neither by word nor deed appoint it) were not withstanding more warrantable than that it should give place and be abrogated. (Hooker, *Laws of Ecclesiastical Polity,* 7.9.8 [citing the Keble ed.])

7. It is, of course, the taking of this point on both sides that has made possible the proposed Anglican-Lutheran consensus on the historic episcopate.

remarkable character studies in Law's *Serious Call,* to the work of Evelyn Underhill and C. S. Lewis, Anglican spiritual writing has displayed an unparalleled awareness of the contingent fabric of everyday human existence, down to its apparently insignificant detail, as the setting for the Spirit's work of sanctification.[8]

An outsider may perhaps be permitted even to say a kind word in this connection about an Anglican trait that present-day Episcopalians often view with self-mocking embarrassment: the peculiarly Anglican love of the artifacts of the church — its buildings and their appointments and liturgical paraphernalia, as well as for the antiquarianism that often accompanies it. This too, I would suggest, can be an innocent and not unserious expression of a sense that we do not encounter the Spirit's grace in a historical and communal void. The figure of John Mason Neale, for example, is witness that an antiquarian love for old Christian things may be part and parcel of a sense of the church as a distinctive community whose ways are not the ways of the world — for Neale also outraged Victorian propriety by his sponsorship of a community of women committed to nursing among the poor.[9]

Finally, viewing the Anglican ethos in these terms may shed light on the characteristic styles of theological discourse in the Anglican tradition. It is significant, for example, that so much of the substance of Anglican theology is to be found in sermons, from Donne and Andrewes through the Anglican Newman and Maurice to Scott Holland and Austin Farrer. Moreover, one cannot study Anglican theology seriously without reading pastoral guides, devotional books, and even poets (Donne and Herbert, at least). And much of the remaining Anglican theological writing (including Hooker's *Laws*) takes the form of *theologiés d'occasion,* responses to particular controversies and circumstances.

---

8. There is, to be sure, also something peculiarly *English* about this; consider only the unique feel for the interaction of character and circumstance that runs through English literature from Chaucer through Shakespeare to Dickens. But this trait of English culture was undoubtedly shaped by English Christianity, as well as the other way around; one can already see this sense of the spiritual significance of the contingent and ordinary in Julian of Norwich, for example, and even earlier in Aelred of Rievaux's interest in the spiritual and theological significance of friendship.

9. This was no joke; on one occasion the lives of Neale and the Sisters of Charity were threatened by a mob. See Eleanor A. Towle, *John Mason Neale, D.D.: A Memoir* (London: Loongmans, Green, 1906).

That these modes of theological discourse have dominated in the Anglican tradition rather than the high academic styles of scholasticism and modern systematics does not necessarily indicate a lack of theological rigor.[10] There is, surely, no intrinsic reason why a sermon, or even a guide to prayer, cannot be as conceptually disciplined as any systematic monograph, and a little experience with twentieth-century Lutheran systematic theology of the more-or-less "existentialist" variety is enough to demonstrate that an obsession with methodology is no guarantee of clarity of mind.

I would suggest rather that the form of Anglican theology has followed the interests inscribed in its traditional ethos. It has favored those more rhetorical genres of theological writing which are indeed, at their best, conceptually disciplined, but for which conceptual clarity is instrumental to the practical goal of engagement in the life of grace in the church. The Anglican theological style has been not so much *theoria* as *paraklesis* and *diakrisis,* a discourse of exhortation and discernment within the public life of the ecclesial community.[11] In this, of course, Anglicans have reflected the Patristic model, although they also show themselves the heirs of what Jean Leclercq has identified as the tradition of "monastic theology" in the medieval West.[12]

The Lutheran Ethos: Radical Christology

The Anglican sense of the concrete and contingent work of the Spirit in the life of the church has been largely lacking in Lutheranism. The Lutheran theological ethos is instead marked at its best by a sense of the strangeness of the unexpected generosity of God in Christ, the

10. I make a point of this not only to counter stereotypes of Anglicanism among my fellow Lutherans, but because I find that theologically concerned Anglicans today are perhaps all too willing to accept this characterization of their tradition.

11. There are exceptions to every typology, and of course Church of England theologians in particular took up the more systematic genres, especially in the period between the publication of *Lux Mundi* in 1880 and World War II. This period coincides with the theological careers of those educated during the dominance of contintental idealism in British philosophy.

12. See Jean Leclercq, *The Love of Learning and the Desire for God: A Study in Monastic Culture* (New York: Fordham University Press, 1961), pp. 189-231.

jolting and liberating discontinuity between all worldly imaginings and expectations of the divine and the actual way in which God has come to us in the mortal flesh of his Son. The classic model here, of course, is Luther's savage glee at the gospel's flouting of harlot reason's calculations; Lutheran theological sensibilities are shaped by his constantly reiterated, almost formulaic, insistence that the Christian faith turns this world's common sense upside-down: "This is a peculiar righteousness. . . . Reason, of course, cannot comprehend this way of speaking."[13] "And again it sounds so absurd and so false to the world . . . when Paul declares here . . ."[14] "Thus when God proposes the doctrines of faith, He always proposes things which are simply impossible and absurd — if, that is, you follow the judgement of reason."[15]

The Lutheran theological ethos might therefore best be described as an ethos of *radical Christology* — a watchful insistence on the newness of Christ. This is what is at stake in the typical Lutheran belief that all Christian discourse must submit to a "critical principle," variously articulated as "justification by faith alone" or "the proper distinction of law and gospel." Such a critical principle is essentially the cutting edge of a set of christological fears and concerns, a deep conviction that ordinary, unexamined modes of thought and discourse are likely to prove disastrously inadequate to the mystery of Christ, and that we are consequently always in danger of trimming the radical *novum* proclaimed in the gospel to the measure of this world's distorted normalcy.

Thus the Lutheran theological tradition has been intoxicated and obsessed with language and concept. Luther's own academic career began with a search for the authentic "theological mode of discourse" through close reading of the biblical texts.[16] Lutherans have been fascinated ever since, in one way or another, with questions about the possibilities and limitations of human speech and the metalinguistic

13. Luther, *Sermons on the Gospel of St. John, Chapters 14–16,* American ed., vol. 24 (St. Louis: Concordia, 1961), p. 347.

14. Luther, *Commentary on First Corinthians 15,* American ed., vol. 28 (St. Louis: Concordia, 1973), p. 116.

15. Luther, *Commentary on Galatians (1535), Chapters 1–4* (St. Louis: Concordia, 1963), p. 227.

16. See Leif Grane, *Modus loquendi theologicus: Luthers Kampf um die Erneuerung der Theologie (1515-1518)* (Leiden: Brill, 1975).

rules of gospel utterance; the most characteristic categories of Lutheran theology have been categories of discourse: law, gospel, word, promise, and so forth. The most diverse Lutheran theological projects have shared this orientation: Melanchthon's humanist synthesis of theology and rhetoric;[17] the seventeenth-century scholastic concern to locate theological discourse in relation to a general ontology;[18] the otherwise unclassifiable but unmistakeably Lutheran theological philology of Hamann; the Lutheran tradition of interpretive theory, from Flacius through Bengel and Ernesti and beyond; the deep hold of philosophical hermeneutics on the twentieth-century Lutheran theological mind.

This focus on the radical newness of Christ is also behind what Anglicans have often regarded as the "speculative" bent of Lutheran theology. Luther himself embraced vigorously the most conceptually daring form of Cyrillian theopaschite Christology, with its affirmations of a crucified God and the life-giving, deified flesh of Christ; his followers, from Johannes Brenz through the seventeenth-century Tübingen school to the nineteenth-century kenoticists, have involved themselves in even stranger paradoxes. More generally, it has often seemed obvious to Lutheran theologians that simply in the act of articulating the gospel of Christ one necessarily redescribes the whole metaphysical structure of reality. This sense that the strangeness of the gospel implies that everything is very different than we thought helps to make clear why Jakob Boehme is in his own way a thoroughly Lutheran figure, as well as the seductive attractiveness of his theosophy for many eighteenth- and nineteenth-century Lutherans. And of

17. For Melanchthon, biblical authority is based on the principle

of the native power of language as the source of semantic, logical, and existential truth. The power of reality was unleashed quite directly through *terms* properly designated and logically developed. . . . Authoritative truth was always embodied in literature that conveyed deeply human truths with a pristine *proprietas sermonis,* and these *words* of truth possessed an authoritative power to help human beings become more human. In the case of biblical letters, Scripture made a person one with Jesus Christ. (John R. Schneider, *Melanchthon's Rhetorical Construal of Biblical Authority: Oratio Sacra* [Lewiston: E. Mellen Press, 1990], p. 58)

18. On this little-known chapter of theological history, see Walter Sparn, *Wiederkehr der Metaphysik: die ontologische Frage in der lutherischen Theologie des frühen 17. Jahrhunderts* (Stüttgart: Calwer Verlag, 1976).

course Hegel could present himself as doing nothing more than work-ing out the wider implications of the Reformation gospel.

At the root of all this is a sometimes haunted sense of the opacity of our habits of speech and thought in their very structure to the mystery of Christ, and of its unbearable contradiction of all our wis-dom, which renders it almost unspeakable without pressing human language beyond its accepted limits. The utterance of the gospel demands a new language, Lutherans have believed, and theology is the attempt to spell out its grammar.[19]

This may explain why Lutheran theology, although ordered to the practical goal of gospel proclamation, has, after Luther, consistently favored theoretical and "second-order" forms of theological dis-course.[20] Where Anglicans are the heirs of medieval monastic theology, Lutherans have stood (despite a certain rhetoric to the contrary) in succession to the scholastics: In the seventeenth century we created a scholastic tradition of our own, and since the Enlightenment we have been deeply committed to methodologically self-conscious systemat-ics. Theology, Lutherans like to say, is a *critical* enterprise, the necessary yoke of discipline to which the first-order discourse of the church must submit itself, in sober acknowledgment that left to itself, it will invariably distort the gospel. The Lutheran tradition has, of course, produced a rich homiletic and devotional literature, but this, Luther-ans are likely to think, is not theological discourse but that discourse which theology criticizes and regulates.[21]

---

19. Lutherans thus tend to define their ecclesial identity in terms of a distinctive style of discourse. When Lutheran synodical examining committees worry about ordinands having a weak "Lutheran identity," they are not typically concerned about their practices of devotion or their leadership of worship. They are worried about the way they *talk* — that they have not learned to handle skillfully the idiom of law and gospel, justification and unconditional promise, and so on.

20. Therefore, although the Lutheran Church has celebrated itself as a "church of the word," there are no collections of sermons or devotional writings, apart from Luther's own, in the recognized canon of Lutheran theological classics (except, per-haps, for Kierkegaard's "edifying discourses"). This is not to say that no Lutheran writings would qualify if Lutheran perceptions of theology changed enough to permit a redefinition of the canon; I would vote for Johann Gerhard's *Meditationes Sacrae* and Christian Scriver's *Seelen-Schatz* from the seventeenth century, and the sermons and pastoral writings of the great Bavarian pastor Wilhelm Loehe from the nineteenth.

21. For this reason I do not consider the Lutheran spiritual tradition in this discussion of the Lutheran theological ethos. Indeed, Lutheran spirituality, since the

Lutherans have thus tended to conceive of theological training as a rigorous discipline of language: most recently, by the inculcation of propositional orthodoxy among conservative Lutherans, and by the vigorous application of a hermeneutic of law and gospel among mainline Lutherans.[22] This can slide into a kind of verbal fetishism,[23] but at its best, it reflects Luther's sense that the articulation of the mystery of Christ and his gospel is a high and difficult art, which ultimately only God can teach, but which nonetheless calls for our utmost devotion, our vigilant attentiveness, and our most painstaking scholarship.

Two Paths to One Decadence

Every Christian tradition has the vices of its virtues, and in a divided church, especially, these vices can all too easily go unchallenged and pave the way to theological and communal decadence. I want briefly in this section to look at the different ways in which Anglicans and Lutherans are betrayed by the limitations of their distinctive traditions into a common theological helplessness. I will speak at more length about the Lutheran situation, as seems fitting, especially since the Episcopal contributors to this volume may be expected to provide an abundance of Anglican self-criticism.

To an outsider, at least, the danger of the Anglican ethos is that its pneumatological concreteness devolves into mere ecclesial empiricism, into an unreflective taking-for-granted of things as they are. This can, of course, take more than one form. It is possible for Anglican affirmation of the church's concreteness to be uncritically accepting of its entanglements with national, state, or class interests;

---

second half of the seventeenth century, has often been in protest against the verbal-conceptual preoccupations of the theological tradition.

22. I have not seen what might be called the sociological side of this phenomenon discussed elsewhere, but it is really quite a remarkable feature of the culture of Lutheran seminaries. Students are soon made aware, in all sorts of explicit and informal ways, that certain patterns of discourse, and even certain words, are identified as "legalistic" or "works-righteous" and therefore are unacceptable.

23. I have, for example, known Lutheran seminarians to be so traumatized by the appearance of the word "merit" on a page of pre-Reformation theology that they simply cannot see anything else there.

it is possible for Anglican sensitivity to the contingent social locations of Christian life to become thoughtless compliance with cultural and ideological definitions of those locations ("doing the duties of one's station").

But it is also possible for this ecclesial empiricism to take the form of an equally thoughtless progressivism, the loss of the critical distance from which it is possible to distinguish the work of the Spirit from whatever is happening now. Speaking somewhat hesitantly, as an outsider, I would nonetheless venture to say that the contemporary public discourse of the Episcopal Church at least presents the appearance of being locked into a theologically sterile stand-off between merely conservative and merely progressive forms of ecclesial empiricism. Personal experience and anecdotal evidence suggest that perhaps the majority of Episcopal priests and laity know better than this and are frustrated by it; the difficulty seems to be precisely that the *sensus fidelium* is not finding expression in the public discourse of the church.

The Lutheran path to decadence is rather different: Where Anglicans become absorbed in the empirical, Lutherans become alienated from it. Most simply, this has taken the form of a long-standing Lutheran indifference to the whole more-than-verbal and more-than-conceptual dimension of practice and order in the church's life.[24]

For example, American Lutherans have often prided themselves on being a "liturgical church," but they have typically been quite oblivious to liturgical practice.[25] I have known Lutheran theologians of stature to whom it was simply inconceivable that it could matter theologically under any circumstances how one performed the liturgy,

24. There have been exceptions also to this characterization. For example, a lively and continuous subtradition of concrete ecclesial-liturgical consciousness has existed among Lutherans since the early nineteenth century, for which Wilhelm Loehe and the late Arthur Carl Piepkorn are something like patron saints. See Michael Plekon and William S. Wiecher, eds., *The Church: Selected Writings of Arthur Carl Piepkorn* (Delhi, N.Y.: American Lutheran Publicity Bureau, 1993). At present one should point to the enormous (and largely unappreciated) labors of professor Philip Pfatteicher to give American Lutherans the fullest possible access to their own liturgy. But this concern has never become typical or dominant, and it is perhaps revealing that its representatives are often derided as "more Episcopalian than Lutheran."

25. This has changed in the interim, but I believe that when I was in seminary a decade ago, a Methodist seminary was more likely to have a qualified liturgical scholar on staff than was a Lutheran seminary.

so long as one did not utter any sentences such as "God is not triune" or "We are justified by works." Thus too, Lutherans have persistently misread their own confessions to conclude that all matters of church order are "things indifferent," which we could arrange in any way that came to mind.[26]

Moreover, the focus of their ethos on speech and language can betray Lutherans into ecclesial and pastoral ineffectiveness. Lutherans tend to believe that one can reform the church simply by nailing manifestos to church doors.[27] They are not very good at paying attention to the concreteness of practice and institution in a theologically informed fashion; they like to imagine that bold and faithful speech will somehow magically set things right.[28] Likewise, present-day Lutherans are often suspicious of spiritual discipline and direction, preferring to think that lives are renewed as it were automatically by the incantatory power of gospel utterance. The Pietists knew better, but since the nineteenth century, both conservative and mainline Lutherans have regarded Pietism as an embarrassing deviation rather than a source of insight.

Finally, for some twentieth-century forms of Lutheran theology, alienation from the concrete becomes a matter of theological principle. The Lutheran concern for the radical newness of Christ hardens into a radicalism for which anything that takes up social and historical space in the world can be related only by a negative dialectic to the eschatological salvation of God. The empirical church can be no more than an institution of this world like any other, differing only in the modesty with which it submits to the eschatological sentence of death on everything worldly. The Christian life is a purely secular life, distinguished only by its renunciation of any pretension of holiness. The mystery of Christ touches the world only at the dimensionless point of proclamation, which saves us precisely as the limit set to all that we are and can be.

26. For a critique of this understanding of *adiaphora,* see Eric W. Gritsch and Robert W. Jenson, *Lutheranism: The Theological Movement and Its Confessional Writings* (Philadelphia: Fortress, 1976), pp. 191-206.

27. Luther learned better during the Saxon Church Visitation of 1527, but that sobering event has not been part of the Lutheran image of "reformation." See Luther's preface to "Instructions for Visitors of Parish Pastors in Electoral Saxony," American ed., vol. 40 (Philadelphia: Fortress, 1958), pp. 269-73.

28. I owe this point to observations made on various occasions by Dr. Christa R. Klein.

This dialectical radicalism of course makes impossible any positive theological shaping of the church's institutions and practices; indeed, it forbids the attempt. The pretensions of the empirical church may be rebuked, but the formation of its life is essentially a matter of secular politics; for the church to have a distinctively theological public life of its own, it must be possible to regard the church as in some way the socially concrete presence of the kingdom of God.

When this principled alienation from the empirical leavens the usual simple Lutheran inability to focus on practice and institution, the result is the helplessness that afflicts the contemporary ELCA: a public life that is indeed becoming a mere extension of secular political struggles, a minor front in the culture wars, and a communal discourse that is frustratingly unable to bring theological conviction effectively to bear on questions of common purpose and order. Here again, many, perhaps most, Lutheran clergy and laity know better, but the *sensus fidelium* cannot seem to find a voice.

Toward Renewal in Communion

In ecumenical essays it is permissible to dream, and in this concluding section I would like to dream a bit about what might result if Episcopalians and Lutherans took the Concordat as an occasion for the renewal of the mind and life of their churches. To hope for great things from our denominations may, given their present disarray, seem wildly implausible; but it is even more likely that if we expect little, our prophecy will be self-fulfilling.

Episcopalians are floundering for want of a critical point of reference to prevent their attunement to the concrete from sliding into mere drift; Lutherans are floundering because they do not know how to bring their radical discourse of christological newness to bear on their life together. Anglican and Lutheran strengths and weaknesses thus complement one another in a remarkable way; the two traditions need one another, or rather, the two churches need the coherent synthesis of their differing theological sensibilities.

Such an Anglican-Lutheran synthesis might yield a distinctive and promising approach to what is perhaps the most pressing question now facing the universal church: the question of the mode of Christian presence in the world, of the way in which the eschatological newness of Christ relates to the present age and the role of the church in that relationship. An enormous burden of history makes this an extraordinarily difficult problem for contemporary Christians to address: the painful and continuing history of the church's involvement with political and social power-holders;[29] the pervasive influence of modernity's definition of "public" with "secular" and its consequent relegation of religion to the sphere of private motivation;[30] the eclipse of the sense of the church's catholicity by denominationalism in the wake of the Western schism, and the far-reaching and debilitating changes this has worked in the very ideas of ecclesial identity and authority.[31]

This will be, I am convinced, the crucial item of unfinished theological business that this millenium of church history will bequeath to the next century. The future of Christianity in the northern hemisphere and probably also in Latin America will depend upon the way in which it is addressed. What issues will be determinative for emergent African and Asian Christianity is not yet clear, but they are unlikely to be wholly unrelated to this question of the mode of Christian presence in the world. Despite all of the fashionable talk of local theologies and global diversity, it seems quite probable that twenty-first-century Christians will be bound together more closely than we now realize by a common and threatening problematic.

Finding our way in this situation will require not only new theology but a renewed sensibility, a new shared perception of what it means to be the church. The understanding toward which the most promising departures are groping is that of the church as the present public assembly of the eschatological city, a real community in the midst of the historical world, with its own way of life shaped not by the projects and power struggles of the nations, but rather by the Spirit

29. This is not as easy to renounce as it is sometimes thought; the distance from "throne and altar" to "*Zeitgeist* and altar" is really very short.

30. See John Milbank's now-classic analysis in *Theology and Social Theory: Beyond Secular Reason* (Oxford: Blackwell, 1990).

31. The terms of the disappointing Vatican response to the *Final Report* of the Anglican–Roman Catholic International Commission show this problem at work; but so do the bulk of the responses of Lutheran churches around the world to the Faith and Order document *Baptism, Eucharist and Ministry* (Geneva: World Council of Churches, 1983).

of the crucified and risen Jesus Christ.[32] Enormous labor lies before us, a labor of reflection to delineate clearly the conceptual contours of such a sense of ecclesial identity, and a labor of *paraklesis* and persuasion to give it life in the practice of the churches.

I do not suppose, of course, that Anglicans and Lutherans can carry out this work by themselves; and nothing in this essay should be taken to suggest that the Episcopal-Lutheran Concordat will be fruitful in the absence of continuing ecumenical initiatives by each church (or perhaps, in time, by the two churches together). But it is surely the case that a renewed sense of the church's identity will require something like the Lutheran sensitivity to the radical newness of the mystery of Christ and something like the Anglican sensitivity to the concreteness of the work of the Spirit. The church of Christ will survive even if our denominations sink into irreversible decay; but our renewal in communion could be significant for the whole people of God.

There is much, to be sure, that militates against this prospect. It is very difficult for theological discourse to penetrate the poisoned atmosphere of the public life of either church. Our leaders are increasingly preoccupied with the maintenance and indeed the survival of the institutions that they manage, and are correspondingly short-tempered with paracletic reminders of the church's vocation; to suggest that the Gospels define our situation in a more practical way than does the current proliferation of religious market research seems to many of them mere self-indulgent fantasy. Clergy and laity in both churches are at once dissatisfied with the present situation and suspicious of those who protest; they have had enough of manipulation by divisive special interests.

But there are also reasons for hope. The erosion of our traditional identities, shaped by the Western schism, creates confusion but also opens the way to new insight. A growing body of Anglican theology is as sensitive to the implications of the radical newness of Christ as anything in the Lutheran tradition,[33] while Lutheran theologians are turning their attention to pneumatology and its concrete ecclesiologi-

32. As the Augustinian flavor of this description suggests, a reclaiming of the catholic tradition must be central to the new thinking to which we are called.

33. In this context I must mention the challenging work of Donald M. MacKinnon; see his collection *Themes in Theology: The Three-Fold Cord* (Edinburgh: 1987).

cal implications.[34] Pastors and people share a genuine if not very articulate desire for clarity about Christian identity, for some alternative to the battle of false alternatives that is exhausting both churches; the surge of interest in spirituality, muddled as it often is, in part expresses this desire. The growing alienation of local churches from the denominations, while fraught with destructive implications for the future, is at least pressing them to ask hard questions about their own mission as Christian assemblies.

But there is no way forward for either church, I suspect, from within the set of dispositions and attitudes that each currently takes for granted. The Concordat will not, to be sure, solve any of the problems of either church in any obvious or easy way; there is probably something to the cynical view that it will only saddle each church with the problems of the other. But it may well be that in the long run, running the risks of communion holds out the only realistic possibility for the renewal of both churches; it may be that, in the mercy of God, the encounter of our two very different traditions may generate the light by which we may see our way forward. That would only mean that, as we might expect, our future lies in doing that to which we know we are called: "Bear one another's burdens, and in this way you will fulfill the law of Christ" (Gal. 6:2).

---

34. Robert W. Jenson's *Visible Words: The Interpretation and Practice of Christian Sacraments* (Philadelphia: Fortress, 1978), was something of a breakthrough for American Lutheran theology in this respect; cf. Wolfhart Pannenberg, *Systematische Theologie,* vol. 3 (Göttingen: Vandenhoeck & Ruprecht, 1993). See also Bruce D. Marshall, "The Church in the Gospel," *Pro Ecclesia* 1 (Fall 1992): 27-41, and Reinhard Hütter, "Ecclesial Ethics, the Church's Vocation and Paraclesis," *Pro Ecclesia* 2 (Fall 1993): 433-50.

Appendix:
Concordat of Agreement between the Episcopal Church and the Evangelical Lutheran Church in America

Preface

The Lutheran-Episcopal Dialogue, Series III, proposes this Concordat of Agreement to its sponsoring bodies for consideration and action by The General Convention of the Episcopal Church and the Church-wide Assembly of the Evangelical Lutheran Church in America in implementation of the goal mandated by The Lutheran-Episcopal Agreement of 1982. That agreement identified the goal as "full communion (*communio in sacris*/altar and pulpit fellowship)."[1] As the meaning of "full communion" for purposes of this Concordat of Agreement both churches endorse in principle the definitions agreed to by the (international) Anglican-Lutheran Joint Working Group at Cold Ash, Berkshire, England, in 1983,[2] which they deem to be in full accord with their own definitions given in the Evangelical Lutheran Church in America's working document, "Ecumenism: The Vision of the ELCA" (1989), and given in the "Declaration on Unity" of the Episcopal Church, General Convention of 1979. During the process of consideration of this Concordat of Agreement it is expected that our churches will consult with sister churches in our respective communions (through, for example, the Anglican Consultative Council and the Lutheran World Federation) as well as those with whom we are currently engaged in dialogue.

Concordat of Agreement

1. The Episcopal Church hereby agrees that in its General Convention, and the Evangelical Lutheran Church in America hereby agrees that in its Churchwide Assembly, there shall be one vote to accept or reject, as a matter of verbal content as well as in principle, and without separate amendment, the full set of agreements to follow. If they are adopted by both churches, each church agrees to make those legislative, canonical, constitutional, and liturgical changes that are necessary and appropriate for the full communion between the churches which these agreements are designed to implement without further vote on the Concordat of Agreement by either the General Convention or the Churchwide Assembly.

A. Actions of Both Churches

Agreement in the Doctrine of the Faith

2. The Evangelical Lutheran Church in America and the Episcopal Church hereby recognize in each other the essentials of the one catholic and apostolic faith as it is witnessed in the unaltered Augsburg Confession (CA), the Small Catechism, and The Book of Common Prayer of 1979 (including the "Episcopal Services" and "An Outline of the Faith"), and as it is summarized in part in *Implications of the Gospel* and *Toward Full Communion between the Episcopal Church and the Evangelical*

225

Lutheran Church in America, the reports of Lutheran-Episcopal Dialogue III,[3] and as it has been examined in both the papers and fourteen official conversations of Series III.[4] Each church also promises to require its ordination candidates to study each other's basic documents.

Joint Participation in the Consecration of Bishops

3. In the course of history many and various terms have been used to describe the rite by which a person becomes a bishop. In the English language these terms include: ordaining, consecrating, ordering, making, confecting, constituting, installing.

What is involved is a setting apart with prayer and the laying-on-of-hands by other bishops of a person for the distinct ministry of bishop within the one ministry of Word and Sacrament. As a result of their agreement in faith, both churches hereby pledge themselves, beginning at the time that this agreement is accepted by the General Convention of the Episcopal Church and the Churchwide Assembly of the Evangelical Lutheran Church in America, to the common joint ordinations of all future bishops as apostolic missionaries in the historic episcopate for the sake of common mission.[5]

Each church hereby promises to invite and include on an invariable basis at least three bishops of the other church, as well as three of its own, to participate in the laying-on-of-hands at the ordination of its own bishops.[6] Such a participation is the liturgical form by which the church recognizes that the bishop serves the local or regional church through ties of collegiality and consultation whose purpose is to provide links with the universal church.[7] Inasmuch as both churches agree that a ministry of *episkope* is necessary to witness to, promote, and safeguard the unity and apostolicity of the church and its continuity in doctrine and mission across time and space,[8] this participation is understood as a call for mutual planning, consultation, and interaction in *episkope,* mission, teaching, and pastoral care as well as a liturgical expression of the full communion that is being initiated by this Concordat of Agreement. Each church understands that the bishops in this action are representatives of their own churches in fidelity to the teaching and mission of the apostles. Their participation in this way embodies the historical continuity of each bishop and the diocese or synod with the apostolic church and ministry through the ages.[9]

B. Actions of the Episcopal Church

4. In light of the agreement that the threefold ministry of bishops, presbyters, and deacons in historic succession will be the future pattern of the one ordained ministry of Word and Sacrament in both churches as they begin to live in full communion,[10] the Episcopal Church hereby recognizes now the full authenticity of the ordained ministries presently existing within the Evangelical Lutheran Church in America. The Episcopal Church acknowledges the pastors and bishops of the Lutheran Church in America as priests within the Evangelical Lutheran Church in America and the bishops of the Evangelical Lutheran Church in America as chief pastors exercising a ministry of *episkope* over the jurisdictional areas of the Evangelical Lutheran Church in America in which they preside.[11]

5. To enable the full communion that is coming into being by means of this Concordat of Agreement, the Episcopal Church hereby pledges, at the same time that this Concordat of Agreement is accepted by its General Convention and by the Churchwide Assembly of the Evangelical Lutheran Church in America, to begin the process for enacting a temporary suspension, in this case only, of the 17th century restriction that "no persons are allowed to exercise the offices of bishop, priest, or deacon in this Church unless they are so ordained, or have already received such ordination with the laying on of hands by bishops who are themselves duly qualified to confer Holy Orders."[12] The purpose of this action will be to permit the full interchangeability and reciprocity of all Evangelical Lutheran Church in America pastors as priests or presbyters and all Evangelical Lutheran Church in America deacons as deacons in the Episcopal Church without any further ordination or re-ordination or supplemental ordination whatsoever, subject always to canonically or constitutionally approved invitation (see pars. 14, 15, and 16 below). The purpose of temporarily suspending this restriction, which has been a constant requirement in Anglican polity since the Ordinal of 1662,[13] is precisely in order to secure the future implementation of the ordinals' same principle within the eventually fully integrated ministries. It is for this reason that the Episcopal Church can feel confident in taking this unprecedented step with regard to the Evangelical Lutheran Church in America.

6. The Episcopal Church hereby endorses the Lutheran affirmation that the historic catholic episcopate under the Word of God must

always serve the gospel,[14] and that the ultimate authority under which bishops preach and teach is the gospel itself.[15] In testimony and implementation thereof, the Episcopal Church agrees to establish and welcome, either by itself or jointly with the Evangelical Lutheran Church in America, structures for collegial and periodic review of its episcopal ministry as well as that of the Evangelical Lutheran Church in America, with a view to evaluation, adaptation, improvement, and continual reform in the service of the gospel.[16]

C. Actions of the Evangelical Lutheran Church in America

7. The Evangelical Lutheran Church in America agrees that all its bishops will be understood as ordained, like other pastors, for life service of the gospel in the pastoral ministry of the historic episcopate,[17] even though tenure in office of the churchwide bishop and synodical bishops may be terminated by retirement, resignation, or conclusion of term however constitutionally ordered. The Evangelical Lutheran Church in America further agrees to revise its rite for the "Installation of a Bishop"[18] to reflect this understanding. In keeping with these principles the Evangelical Lutheran Church in America also agrees to revise its constitution (e.g., 16.51.41.) so that all bishops, including those no longer active, shall be members of the Conference of Bishops.[19]

8. As regards ordained ministry, the Evangelical Lutheran Church in America affirms, in the context of its confessional heritage, the teaching of the Augsburg Confession that Lutherans do not intend to depart from the historic faith and practice of catholic Christianity.[20] The Evangelical Lutheran Church in America therefore agrees to make constitutional and liturgical provision that only bishops shall ordain all clergy. Presbyters shall continue to participate in the laying-on-of-hands at all ordinations of presbyters. It is further understood that episcopal and presbyteral office in the church is to be understood and exercised as servant ministry, and not for domination or arbitrary control.[21] Appropriate liturgical expression of these understandings will be made.[22] Both churches acknowledge that the diaconate, including its place within the threefold ministerial office, is in need of

continued study and reform, which they pledge themselves to undertake in consultation with one another.[23]

9. In light of the above agreements and of the actions of the Episcopal Church, the Evangelical Lutheran Church in America hereby recognizes now the full authenticity of the ordained ministries presently existing within the Episcopal Church, acknowledging the bishops, priests, and deacons of the Episcopal Church all as pastors in their respective orders within the Episcopal Church and the bishops of the Episcopal Church as chief pastors in the historic succession exercising a ministry of *episkope* over the jurisdictional areas of the Episcopal Church in which they preside. In preparation for the full communion that is coming into being by means of this Concordat of Agreement, the Evangelical Lutheran Church in America also pledges, at the time that this Concordat of Agreement is accepted by the Churchwide Assembly of the Evangelical Lutheran Church in America and the General Convention of the Episcopal Church, to begin the process for enacting a dispensation for ordinands of the Episcopal Church from its ordination requirement of subscription to the unaltered Augsburg Confession (Constitution of the Evangelical Lutheran Church in America 10:21) in order to permit the full interchangeability and reciprocity of all Episcopal Church bishops as bishops, of all Episcopal Church priests as pastors, and of all Episcopal Church deacons as my be determined (see Par. 8 above), within the Evangelical Lutheran Church in America without any supplemental oath or subscription, subject always to canonically or constitutionally approved invitation (see Pars. 14, 15, and 16 below). The purpose of this dispensation, which heretofore has not been made by the Evangelical Lutheran Church in America for the clergy of any other church, is precisely in order to serve the future implementation, in the full communion that will follow, of the agreement in the doctrine of the faith identified in Paragraph 2 (above) of this Concordat of Agreement.

D. Actions of Both Churches

Joint Commission

10. Both churches hereby authorize the establishment of a joint ecumenical/doctrinal/liturgical commission to moderate the details of these

changes, to assist joint planning for mission, to facilitate consultation and common decision making through appropriate channels in fundamental matters that the churches may face together in the future, to enable the process of new consecrations/ordinations of bishops in both churches as they occur, and to issue guidelines as requested and as may seem appropriate. It will prepare a national service that will celebrate the inauguration of this Concordat of Agreement as a common obedience to Christ in mission. At this service the mutual recognition of faith will be celebrated and, if possible, new bishops from each church will be consecrated/ordained for the synods or dioceses that have elected them, initiating the provisions hereby agreed upon.

Wider Context

11. In thus moving to establish one ordained ministry in geographically overlapping episcopates, open to women as well as to men, to married persons as well as to single persons, both churches agree that the historic catholic episcopate, which they embrace, can be locally adapted and reformed in the service of the gospel. In this spirit they offer this Concordat of Agreement and growth toward full communion for serious consideration among the churches of the Reformation as well as among the Orthodox and Roman Catholic churches. They pledge widespread consultation during the process at all stages. Each church promises to issue no official commentary on this text that has not been approved by the joint commission as a legitimate interpretation thereof.

Existing Relationships

12. Each church agrees that the other church will continue to live in communion with all the churches with whom the latter is now in communion. Each church also pledges prior consultation about this Concordat of Agreement with those churches. The Evangelical Lutheran Church in America continues to be in full communion (pulpit and altar fellowship) with all member churches of the Lutheran World Federation. This Concordat of Agreement with the Episcopal Church does not imply or inaugurate any automatic communion between the Episcopal Church and the other member churches of the

Lutheran World Federation. The Episcopal Church continues to be in full communion with all of the provinces of the Anglican Communion, and with Old Catholic Churches of Europe, with the united churches of the Indian sub-continent, with the Mar Thoma Church, and with the Philippine Independent Church. This Concordat of Agreement with the Evangelical Lutheran Church in America does not imply or inaugurate any automatic communion between the Evangelical Lutheran Church in America and the other provinces of the Anglican Communion or any other churches with whom the Episcopal Church is in full communion.

Other Dialogues

13. Both churches agree that each will continue to engage in dialogue with other churches and traditions. Both churches agree to take each other and this Concordat of Agreement into account at every stage in their dialogues with other churches and traditions. Where appropriate, both churches will seek to engage in joint dialogues. On the basis of this Concordat of Agreement, both churches pledge that they will not enter into formal agreements with other churches and traditions without prior consultation with each other. At the same time both churches pledge that they will not impede the development of relationships and agreements with other churches and traditions with whom they have been in dialogue.

E. Full Communion

14. Of all the historical processes involved in realizing full communion between the Episcopal Church and the Evangelical Lutheran Church in America, the achieving of full interchangeability of ordained ministries will probably take longest. While the two churches will fully acknowledge the authenticity of each other's ordained ministries from the beginning of the process, the creation of a common, and therefore fully interchangeable, ministry will occur with the full incorporation of all active bishops in the historic episcopate by common joint ordinations and the continuing process of collegial consul-

231

tation in matters of Christian faith and life. Full communion will also include the activities of the joint commission (Par. 10 above), as well as the establishment of "recognized organs of regular consultation and communication, including episcopal collegiality, to express and strengthen the fellowship and enable common witness, life and service."[24] Thereby the churches are permanently committed to common mission and ministry on the basis of agreement in faith, recognizing each other fully as churches in which the gospel is preached and the holy Sacraments administered. All provisions specified above will continue in effect.

15. On the basis of this Concordat of Agreement, at a given date recommended by the joint commission, the Evangelical Lutheran Church in America and the Episcopal Church will announce the completion of the process by which they enjoy full communion with each other. They will share one ordained ministry in two churches that are in full communion, still autonomous in structure yet interdependent in doctrine, mission, and ministry.

16. Consequent to the acknowledgment of full communion and respecting always the internal discipline of each church, both churches now accept in principle the full interchangeability and reciprocity of their ordained ministries, recognizing bishops as bishops, pastors as priests and presbyters and *vice versa,* and deacons as deacons. In consequence of our mutual pledge to a future already anticipated in Christ and the church of the early centuries,[25] each church will make such necessary revisions of canons and constitution so that ordained clergy can, upon canonically or constitutionally approved invitation, function as clergy in corresponding situations within either church. The churches will authorize such celebrations of the Eucharist as will accord full recognition to each other's episcopal ministries and sacramental services. All further necessary legislative, canonical, constitutional, and liturgical changes will be coordinated by the joint ecumenical/doctrinal/liturgical commission hereby established.

Conclusion

We receive with thanksgiving the gift of unity which is already given in Christ.

He is the image of the invisible God, the first-born of all creation; for in him all things were created, in heaven and on earth, visible and invisible, whether thrones or dominions or principalities or authorities — all things were created through him and for him. He is before all things, and in him all things hold together. He is the head of the body, the church; he is the beginning, the first-born from the dead, that in everything he might be pre-eminent. For in him all the fulness of God was pleased to dwell, and through him to reconcile to himself all things, whether on earth or in heaven, making peace by the blood of his cross. Col. 1:15-20

Repeatedly Christians have confessed that the unity of the church is given, not achieved. The church can only be one because it is constituted by the gospel in word and sacrament, and there is but one gospel. What Christians are seeking when they engage in the tasks and efforts associated with ecumenism is to discover how the unity they have already been given by the gospel can be manifested faithfully in terms of the church's mission.[26]

We do not know to what new, recovered, or continuing tasks of mission this proposed Concordat of Agreement will lead our churches, but we give thanks to God for leading us to this point. We entrust ourselves to that leading in the future, confident that our full communion will be a witness to the gift and goal already present in Christ, "that God may be everything to every one" (I Cor. 15:28). It is the gift of Christ that we are sent as he has been sent (John 17:17-26), that our unity will be received and perceived as we participate in the mission of the Son in obedience to the Father through the power and presence of the Holy Spirit.[27]

Now to the one who by the power at work within us is able to do far more abundantly than all that we ask or think, to God be glory in the church and in Christ Jesus to all generations, for ever and ever. Amen. (Eph. 3:20-21)

The Epiphany of Our Lord
January 6, 1991

APPENDIX

Notes to the Concordat of Agreement

1. Cf. the complete text of the 1982 Agreement in paragraph 1 of the report *Toward Full Communion* which accompanies this proposed Concordat of Agreement.

2. *Anglican-Lutheran Relations: Report of the Anglican-Lutheran Joint Working Group, Cold Ash, Berkshire, England — 1983,* in William A. Norgren, *What Can We Share?* (Cincinnati, Forward Movement Publications, 1985), pp. 90-92. The relevant portion of the report reads as follows:

> By full communion we here understand a relationship between two distinct churches or communions. Each maintains its own autonomy and recognizes the catholicity and apostolicity of the other, and each believes the other to hold the essentials of the Christian faith:
>
> > a) subject to such safeguards as ecclesial discipline may properly require, members of one body may receive the sacraments of the other;
> >
> > b) subject to local invitation, bishops of one church may take part in the consecration of the bishops of the other, thus acknowledging the duty of mutual care and concern;
> >
> > c) subject to church regulation, a bishop, pastor/priest or deacon of one ecclesial body may exercise liturgical functions in a congregation of the other body if invited to do so and also, when requested, pastoral care of the other's members;
> >
> > d) it is also a necessary addition and complement that there should be recognized organs of regular consultation and communication, including episcopal collegiality, to express and strengthen the fellowship and enable common witness, life and service.
>
> To be in full communion means that churches become interdependent while remaining autonomous. One is not elevated to be the judge of the other nor can it remain insensitive to the other; neither is each body committed to every secondary feature of the tradition of the other. Thus the corporate strength of the churches is enhanced in love, and an isolated independence is restrained.
>
> Full communion should not imply the suppressing of ethnic, cultural or ecclesial characteristics of traditions which may in fact be maintained and developed by diverse institutions within one communion.

3. Cf. the working document, "Ecumenism: The Vision of the Evangelical Lutheran Church in America," D,1 and 2, adopted by the Evangelical Lutheran Church in America on August 25, 1989, "to offer provisional and interim guidance for this church during the 1990-1991 biennium"; and the "Declaration on Unity" adopted by the 1979 General Convention of the Episcopal Church.

4. Lutheran-Episcopal Dialogue III has held the following meetings, with the papers presented and discussed listed under each meeting:

1) December 4-7, 1983, Techny, Illinois
   Walter R. Bouman, "Lutheran Analysis and Critique of *The Final Report* of

234

the Anglican–Roman Catholic International Commission (ARCIC)"
J. Robert Wright, "Anglican Analysis and Critique of *The Ministry in the Church* (report of the international Roman Catholic/Lutheran joint Commission), as well as of the concept of 'bishop' in the *Book Of Concord*"

2) June 10-13, 1984, New York, New York
William H. Petersen, "Implications of the Gospel"
Walter R. Bouman, "The Gospel and Its Implications"
L. William Countryman, "The Gospel and the Institutions of the Church with Particular Reference to the Historic Episcopate"
Robert J. Goeser, "Augustana 28 and Lambeth 4: Episcopacy as Adiaphoron or Necessity"
Joseph A. Burgess, "Teaching Authority in the Lutheran Tradition"
John H. Rodgers, Jr., "Teaching Authority in the Church: The Gospel, the Church, and the Role of Bishops — Some Anglican Reflections"
William A. Norgren, "The Way to Full Communion"
J. Robert Wright, "Lutherans and Episcopalians: The Way Forward"
William G. Rusch, "Mutual Recognition of Ministries"

3) January 27-30, 1985, Techny, Illinois
Marianne H. Micks, "Mission and Prayer"
Paul Berge, "A Response to Bill Countryman's paper, 'The Gospel and the Institutions of the Church' "
Wayne Weissenbuehler, "Critical Questions and a Few Reflections on the paper *Implications of the Gospel* by the Rev. Dr. William H. Petersen"
Marianne H. Micks, "Questions Arising from Walter Bouman's Paper, 'The Gospel and Its Implications' "
Mark Dyer, "Some Questions for Dr. Goeser Concerning Augustana 28 and Lambeth 4: Episcopacy as Adiaphoron or Necessity"

4) June 2-5, 1985, Erlanger, Kentucky
Jerald C. Brauer, "Bishops and the Lutherans in the United States"

5) January 26-29, 1986, Techny, Illinois
William G. Rusch, "Towards Full Communion"
J. Robert Wright, "Some Initial Reactions to the Paper of William Rusch"
Roland Foster, "The Development of Episcopacy in the American Episcopal Church"
Jerald C. Joersz, "Altar and Pulpit Fellowship: LCMS' Model for External Unity in the Church"
L. William Countryman, "Discussion Questions on 'Teaching Authority in the Lutheran Tradition,' by Joseph A. Burgess"
Walter R. Bouman, "Questions on John Rodgers' 'Teaching Authority in the Church' "

6) June 8-11, 1986, Cincinnati, Ohio
J. Robert Wright, "Anglican/Episcopal Recognition of the Augsburg Con-

fession — An Actual Possibility"
John H. Rodgers, Jr., "A Comparison of the Catechisms of Lutheran and Episcopal Churches"
Walter R. Bouman, "Lutheran Recognition of the Book of Common Prayer"
Robert Goeser, "The Word of God According to Luther and the Confessions"
Marianne H. Micks, "The Doctrine of the Church in Anglican Thought"

7) January 11-14, 1987, Techny, Illinois
Discussion of "The Gospel and Its Implications"

8) June 7-11, 1987, Techny, Illinois
Paul Berge, "The Gospel and Its Implications in Galatians, The Augsburg Confession, and the Thirty-Nine Articles"
Discussion of *Implications of the Gospel*

9) January 3-6, 1988, Techny, Illinois
Walter R. Bouman, "Report on the Niagara Falls Consultation on *Episkope* and the Proposed *Niagara Report*"
William G. Rusch, "Recognition and Reception as Ecumenical Concepts"
William A. Norgren, "Relations Between the Churches of England and Sweden, with Special Emphasis on Recognition of Faith"
Discussion and Final Adoption of *Implications of the Gospel*

10) January 5-8, 1989, Delray Beach, Florida
Samuel Nafzger, "Hopes and Expectations of the Lutheran Church–Missouri Synod in Ecumenical Dialogue"
Robert Goeser, "The Augsburg Confession in the Life of the Lutheran Church"
William A. Norgren, "Ecclesial Recognition"
William G. Rusch, "Some Comments on Recognition by Lutheran Churches"

11) June 4-7, 1989, Burlingame, California
L. William Countryman, "The Historic Episcopate: Further Reflections"
John Booty, "The Place of the Book of Common Prayer in Anglicanism"
Paul Erickson, "The Place of Luther's Small Catechism in Lutheranism"
Paul Berge, "Niagara Recommendations from a Lutheran Point of View"
James Griffiss, "Niagara Recommendations from an Anglican Point of View"

12) January 4-7, 1990, Delray Beach, Florida
Richard Norris, "Bishops and the Mutual Recognition and Reconciliation of Ministries"
Discussion of the LED III Report, *Toward Full Communion Between the Episcopal Church and Evangelical Lutheran Church in America,* and the proposed Agreement

13) June 17-20, 1990, New Orleans, Louisiana

Michael Root, "Full Communion Between Episcopalians and Lutherans: What Would it Look Like?"

J. Robert Wright, "Response to the Paper by Michael Root"

Eric W. Gritsch, "Episcopacy: The Legacy of the Lutheran Confessions"

Sir Henry Chadwick, "Response to the Paper by Eric Gritsch"

John H. P. Reumann, "Report on the Work of the Evangelical Lutheran Church in America's Task Force on the Study of Ministry with Special Reference to the work of Lutheran-Episcopal Dialogue III"

Discussion of the LED III Report, *Toward Full Communion Between the Episcopal Church and the Evangelical Lutheran Church in America,* and the proposed Agreement

14) January 3-6, 1991, Delray Beach, Florida

Robert Jenson, "The Episcopate as 'Sign' in Ecumenical Dialogue"

Discussion of and final action on the LED III Report, *Toward Full Communion Between the Episcopal Church and the Evangelical Lutheran Church in America,* and the proposed "Concordat of Agreement"

5. Cf. Richard Grein, "The Bishop as Chief Missionary," in Charles R. Henery, editor, *Beyond the Horizon: Frontiers for Mission* (Cincinnati: Forward Movement Publications, 1986), pp. 64-80.

6. *The Niagara Report* (London: Church House Publishing, 1988), Pars. 91 and 96; The Council of Nicaea, Canon 4.

7. Michael Root, "Full Communion Between Episcopalians and Lutherans in North America: What Would It Look Like?" (Unpublished Paper, LED III, June 1990), pp. 10-16. Cf. Michael Root, "Bishops as Points of Unity and Continuity" (Unpublished Paper, Lutheran-United Methodist Dialogue, May 1986).

8. *The Niagara Report,* Par. 69; The Pullach Report, Par. 79; The Lutheran–United Methodist Common Statement on Episcopacy, Par. 28.

9. Cf. Resolutions of the 1979 and 1985 General Conventions of the Episcopal Church, The Canterbury Statement, Par. 16, of the Anglican–Roman Catholic International Commission, and the Evangelical Lutheran Church in America's provisional statement, "Ecumenism: The Vision of the Evangelical Lutheran Church in America," D,3.

10. Chicago-Lambeth Quadrilateral 4.

11. *The Niagara Report,* Par. 94. Cf. Raymond E. Brown, *Priest and Bishop: Biblical Reflections* (New York: Paulist Press, 1970), pp. 83-85.

12. Preface to the Ordinal, The Book of Common Prayer, p. 510.

13. Cf. *The Study of Anglicanism,* ed. Stephen Sykes and John Booty (London/Philadelphia: SPCK/Fortress, 1988), pp. 149, 151, 238, 290, 304-305; Paul F. Bradshaw, *The Anglican Ordinal* (London: SPCK, 1971), Chapter 6.

14. *The Niagara Report,* Par. 91, Augsburg Confession Article 7, Article 28.

15. Cf. Joseph A. Burgess, "An Evangelical Episcopate," in Todd Nichol and Marc Kolden, editors, *Called and Ordained* (Minneapolis: Fortress Press, 1990), p. 147.

16. Cf. *The Niagara Report,* Pars. 90, 95, and especially 100-110 as examples of

the questions and concerns involved in such evaluation. Cf. also *Baptism, Eucharist and Ministry*, Ministry Par. 38.

17. Cf. *The Niagara Report*, Par. 90.

18. *Occasional Services* (Minneapolis: Augsburg Publishing House, 1982), pp. 218-223.

19. We understand the term "regular" to mean "according to constitutionally regulated provisions." A revised constitution of the Evangelical Lutheran Church in America may, for example, give voice but not vote in the Conference of Bishops to bishops who are no longer actively functioning in the office of bishop by reason of retirement, resignation to accept another call, or conclusion of term.

20. Augsburg Confession, Article 21 (Tappert, page 47); cf. Treatise on the Power and Primacy of the Pope, Par. 66 (Tappert, p. 331).

21. Cf. II Cor. 10:8; also *Anglican-Orthodox Dialogue: The Dublin Agreed Statement 1984* (St. Vladimir's Seminary Press, 1985), pp. 13-14, and *ARCIC, The Final Report* (London: SPCK and Catholic Truth Society, 1982), pp. 83 and 89.

22. Cf. *The Niagara Report*, Par. 92.

23. *Baptism, Eucharist and Ministry*, Ministry Par. 24. Cf. James M. Barnett, *The Diaconate: A Full and Equal Order* (New York: The Seabury Press, 1981), pp. 133-197; John E. Booty, *The Servant Church: Diaconal Ministry and the Episcopal Church* (Wilton, CT, Morehouse-Barlow, 1982); and J. Robert Wright, "The Emergence of the Diaconate: Biblical and Patristic Sources," *Liturgy*, Vol. 2, No. 4 (Fall 1982), pp. 17-23, 67-71.

24. The Cold Ash report, par. d. See footnote 2, above.

25. Cf. John D. Zizioulas, *Being as Communion* (New York: St. Vladimir's Seminary Press, 1985), pp. 171-208.

26. *Implications of the Gospel*, Par. 98.

27. *The Niagara Report*, Pars. 25-26.

The Dissenting Report of
Lutheran-Episcopal Dialogue, Series III

The undersigned have voted against the report "Toward Full Communion Between the Episcopal Church and the Evangelical Lutheran Church in America" and the proposed "Concordat of Agreement."

We believe that Scripture and the Augsburg Confession clearly teach that the Word of God rightly preached and rightly administered in the sacraments of Baptism and the Lord's Supper constitutes the sole and sufficient basis for the true unity of the Christian church. This unity Lutherans and Episcopalians already share in Christ. In this "Concordat," however, the historic episcopate is made to be a necessity for church fellowship and thus essential to the unity of the church. Under the terms of this "Concordat," the process toward "full communion" will thus not be realized until there is complete interchangeability of ordained ministries on the basis of the joint ordination of all active bishops of the ELCA — ordained as bishops after the acceptance of this "Concordat" — into the historic episcopacy through the Anglican succession. We believe such provisions for the ministry of the church belong to the realm of the *adiaphora* (things often important but never essential to the unity of the church). To introduce the historic episcopate into the ELCA under the terms of this "Concordat" is to make an *adiaphoron* into a matter of necessity.

We believe that the present context calls for a clear witness to the central insights of the Reformation and a commitment to unassuming servanthood on behalf of Christ's mission in the world. We believe that Christian ecumenism best serves the apostolic mission of the church when it provides for the speaking of God's Word and the administration of the Sacraments in a multitude of ways appropriate to a variety of times and places.

We cherish the fellowship now existing between the Episcopal Church and the ELCA. We look forward to the maturation of this friendship and the engagement of both churches in broader ecumenical ventures as well. We believe that to introduce the historic episcopate into the ELCA under the terms of the "Concordat" could needlessly jeopardize a treasured friendship as well as endanger the collaboration in the gospel and table fellowship we now enjoy. We believe that it could also provoke controversy and division among the congregations and ministers of the ELCA.

Robert J. Goeser
Professor of Church History
Pacific Lutheran
  Theological Seminary

Paul S. Berge
Professor of New Testament
Luther Northwestern
  Theological Seminary

The Assenting Report of Lutheran-Episcopal Dialogue, Series III

(At the concluding session of the dialogue, the participants authorized
the co-chairpersons of the dialogue to release a response to the
Dissenting, or Minority Report if they deemed this appropriate.)

We, the undersigned ELCA members of Lutheran-Episcopal Dialogue
III, respect the right of our dissenting colleagues to *interpret* the report
and the agreement for full communion as they choose. However, we
cannot recognize their interpretation as correct. The initiative of the
Episcopal members of the dialogue has been to recognize the existing
pastoral ministry of the Evangelical Lutheran Church in America as
authentic and to propose a temporary suspension of the preface to the
ordinal so that pastors of the ELCA can be invited to function in place
of priests of the Episcopal Church. That initiative has made it *possible,*
not necessary, for us to propose simultaneously and in concert with
our Episcopal colleagues the joint consecration of future bishops resulting in the future participation of ELCA bishops in the historic
episcopal succession. In this we have simply been free to propose the
restoration of the traditional polity which the Lutheran *Book of Concord*
espouses (Pars. 42-47 of the Report). To be given this freedom is in
no way "to make an *adiaphoron* into a matter of necessity."

We regret the fact that our colleagues could not endorse the
mandate of our churches in which we were directed to move beyond
present level of fellowship toward full communion. We regret the fact
that they could not endorse the definition of full communion approved
by the Anglican and Lutheran world communions, which calls for the
bishops of one church to "take part in the consecration of the bishops
of the other, thus acknowledging the duty of mutual care and concern."

We regret the fact that they no longer endorse the conclusion of
the Lutheran Council in the U.S.A. report on "The Historic Episco-

pate," which both of them helped to formulate in 1984, and in which they stated:

> When the "historic episcopate" faithfully proclaims the gospel and administers the sacraments, it may be accepted as a symbol of the church's unity and continuity throughout the centuries provided that it is not viewed as a necessity for the *validity* (our emphasis) of the church's ministry.

We regret the fact that our colleagues cannot endorse the full position of the Lutheran "Formula of Concord" on *adiaphora,* namely, that the church has the "liberty to avail itself" of elements of the tradition which it might have to resist if required of it under persecution or duress (Epitome, Article X, p. 494). Our churches are able to invite bishops to participate in each other's future episcopal consecrations (Concordat of Agreement, Par. 3) *because* both churches do *now* recognize the full authenticity of each other's ministries without the imposition of any demands or further conditions (Concordat of Agreement, Pars. 4 and 9).

We fully agree with our colleagues

> that Christian ecumenism best serves the apostolic mission of the church when it provides for the speaking of God's Word and the administration of the Sacraments in a multitude of ways appropriate to a variety of times and places

because we support the provision of the Lambeth Quadrilateral that the historic episcopate can be "locally adapted in the methods of its administration to the varying needs of the nations and peoples called of God into the Unity of His Church" (Report, Par. 33).

We pray that the controversy and division which our colleagues fear not be incited by those who are determined in advance to resist full communion between our churches and to oppose full collegiality among our bishops.

The Rev. Dr. Paul Erickson
The Rev. Dr. Walter R. Bouman
The Rev. Dr. William G. Rusch
The Rev. Wayne E. Weissenbuehler, Bishop
The Rev. Cyril Wismar, Sr.

Statement of Lutheran Church–Missouri Synod Participants

Representatives of the Lutheran Church–Missouri Synod have been full participants in all three rounds of the Lutheran-Episcopal Dialogue. The LCMS representatives to these discussions have welcomed with appreciation this opportunity to engage in interconfessional dialogue with brothers and sisters in Christ. The Synod's participation in such discussions reflects its longstanding commitment to the biblical mandate that Christians seek to manifest externally the unity already given to them in the body of Christ and to do so on the basis of agreement in the confession of the gospel "In all its articles (FC SD X, 31)."

The Representatives of the LCMS have recognized that due to agreements reached among the other representatives of the dialogue, and in particular, the Lutheran/Episcopal Interim Sharing of the Eucharist Agreement adopted by the non-LCMS participant churches in 1982, the aim of the third round of dialogue has shifted to focus on the achieving of full communion (altar and pulpit fellowship) between the Episcopal Church and the Evangelical Lutheran Church in America. In response to a specific invitation, the LCMS has continued to send representatives as full participants in LED III, even while it has not been a part of the 1982 Agreement, nor the efforts to reach full communion. Although Missouri Synod participation has been limited by these circumstances the LCMS representatives wish to express their gratitude to all the members of the dialogue for welcoming LCMS participation in this phase of dialogue. The LCMS participants remain committed to the value of the discussions themselves as vehicles to achieve greater understanding of and agreement in "the truth as it is taught in the Scriptures and confessed in the Lutheran symbols" ("Guidelines for Participation in Ecumenical Dialogs," prepared by the Commission on Theology and Church Relations, 1975).

We, the LCMS representatives of LED III, ask our gracious God to bless the efforts of our friends and colleagues on the dialogue to achieve a common witness to the gospel of Jesus Christ. We express our best wishes to all present and past members of the dialogue and thank God for the friendships we have come to enjoy and the commonalities we share. And, we look forward to future opportunities to address together differences in doctrine and practice which continue to divide the church.

The Rev. Carl Bornmann
The Rev. Dr. Norman E. Nagel
The Rev. Jerald C. Joersz

List of Participants

Episcopal Church, U.S.A.

The Rev. Dr. L. William Countryman   Voted: YES
The Church Divinity School of the Pacific
Berkeley, California

The Rt. Rev. Mark Dyer   Voted: YES
Bishop of Bethlehem
Bethlehem, Pennsylvania

The Rt. Rev. Richard F. Grein   Voted: YES
Bishop of New York
New York, New York

The Rev. John R. Kevern, *secretary*   Voted: YES
Assistant, St. James Cathedral
Chicago, Illinois

The Very Rev. William Petersen   Voted: YES
Dean, Bexley Hall
Colgate-Rochester Divinity School
Rochester, New York

The Very Rev. John H. Rodgers, Jr.   Voted: YES
Director, Stanway Institute for World Mission and Evangelism
Trinity Episcopal School for Ministry
Ambridge, Pennsylvania

The Rt. Rev. William G. Weinhauer, *co-chair*   Voted: YES
Bishop of Western North Carolina (retired)
Asheville, North Carolina

Staff
The Rev. Dr. William Norgren
The Ecumenical Officer
The Executive Council of the Episcopal Church
New York, New York

Consultant
The Rev. Dr. J. Robert Wright
The General Theological Seminary
New York, New York

The Evangelical Lutheran Church in America

The Rev. Dr. Paul S. Berge   Voted: NO
Luther Northwestern Theological Seminary
St. Paul, Minnesota

The Rev. Dr. Walter R. Bouman   Voted: YES
Trinity Lutheran Seminary
Columbus, Ohio

The Rev. Dr. Paul E. Erickson, *co-chair*   Voted: YES
Bishop (Retired), Illinois Synod of the L.C.A.
Wheaton, Illinois

The Rev. Dr. Robert J. Goeser   Voted: NO
Pacific Lutheran Theological Seminary
Berkeley, California

The Rev. Dr. William G. Rusch   Voted: YES
Executive Director, Office for Ecumenical Affairs
Evangelical Lutheran Church in America
Chicago, Illinois

The Rev. Dr. Edward D. Schneider   Voted: NO
Good Shepherd Lutheran Church
Champaign, Illinois

The Rev. Wayne E. Weissenbuehler   Voted: YES
Bishop, Rocky Mountain Synod
Denver, Colorado

The Rev. Cyril M. Wismar, Sr.   Voted: YES
Auxiliary Bishop (Retired)
East Coast Svnod/A.E.L.C.
Falls Village, Connecticut

Staff
The Rev. Dr. Daniel F. Martensen
Associate Director, Office for Ecumenical Affairs
The Evangelical Lutheran Church in America
Chicago, Illinois

The Lutheran Church–Missouri Synod

The Rev. Carl Bornmann   Voted: ABSTAIN
St. John's Lutheran Church
Luxemburg, Wisconsin

The Rev. Dr. Norman E. Nagel   Voted: ABSTAIN
Concordia Theological Seminary
St. Louis, Missouri

The Rev. Jerald Joersz   Voted: ABSTAIN
Assistant Executive Director,
Commission on Theology and Church Relations
The Lutheran Church–Missouri Synod
St. Louis, Missouri

Staff
The Rev. Dr. Samuel Nafzger
Executive Director,
Commission on Theology and Church Relations
The Lutheran Church–Missouri Synod
St. Louis, Missouri